WASHINGTON IRVING
A BIBLIOGRAPHY

WASHINGTON IRVING

From a line engraving (1831) by M. I. Danforth, after the painting (1820) by C. R. Leslie in the collection of The New York Public Library

WASHINGTON IRVING

A Bibliography Compiled by

WILLIAM R. LANGFELD

With the Bibliographic Assistance of

PHILIP C. BLACKBURN

NEW YORK
The New York Public Library
1933

TABLE OF CONTENTS

POSTHUMOUS WORKS

LIST OF ILLUSTRATIONS

WASHINGTON IRVING—A BIBLIOGRAPHY

Compiled by WILLIAM R. LANGFELD

With the bibliographic assistance of PHILIP C. BLACKBURN

INTRODUCTION

IRVING AND THE COLLECTOR

RECENT years have witnessed a vast expansion of interest in book collecting. The reading public has multiplied in numbers and advanced in knowledge and discrimination. It is inevitable that a certain proportion of this growing body of readers should be lured by the beguilement of first editions.

The most logical field for an American collector is that of American literature. The worthies of his own land are nearest his heart, their works are more accessible, and most items may be obtained at moderate prices. Many of these authors have been the subject of exhaustive bibliographies. In the case of Washington Irving there appears to be none that is extensive and thoroughgoing in its scope.

Irving is particularly deserving of study. Historically, he is practically the Father of American literature. No American writer has been longer in vogue or more highly regarded over a period of years both in this country and abroad. The constant republication of his works here and in England is evidence of the high esteem in which he has long been held. His personality has an engaging charm; he possesses undeniable literary merits; his wit, his urbanity, his touches of quaint eighteenth-century style, his scholarship, the plots of his tales — all have a distinct appeal. To the bibliographer, the variations in the editions of his books, the occasional "points," the existence of little known items offer an absorbing study.

ASSOCIATION WITH THE NEW YORK PUBLIC LIBRARY

The name of Washington Irving is closely associated with The New York Public Library — both historically and by the notable collection of Irvingiana that has been brought together in its Reference Department. Named by John Jacob Astor, in the third codicil (1839) of his will, as a trustee of the library to be created under his bequest, Irving consulted in 1840 with Astor and Joseph Green Cogswell (also designated in the will as a trustee, and in 1849 chosen as the first superintendent of the Astor Library), as to plans for the organization and book collection of the proposed library. On February 18, 1849, he was chosen by the trustees as the first president of the Astor Library — an office he held until his death ten years later. The Astor Library, later to be combined with the Lenox Library and the Tilden Trust to make The New York Public Library, owed much during this formative period to Irving's knowledge of men and affairs, as well as of books.

The New York Public Library had long owned some important Irving manuscripts. In 1925, the collection of Irvingiana assembled by the late Isaac N. Seligman was presented to the Library, in his memory, by Mrs. Seligman. At the same time, Mrs. Seligman's nephew, Mr. George S. Hellman, presented certain Irving manuscripts and portraits, which were placed on exhibition with the Seligman collection. Mr. Hellman, in 1929, added the remaining portion of his collection to that already given — this gift being made in honor of his mother, Mrs. Frances Hellman. The Seligman-Hellman collections, with other Irving material from the Library's collection, are kept on permanent exhibition in the Fifth Avenue entrance hall of the Library's Central Building. Catalogues of the Seligman and Hellman collections were printed in the *Bulletin* in February, 1926, and April, 1929, respectively, and were later reprinted in separate form.

THE BIBLIOGRAPHY — ITS MECHANISM

The data of this list have been obtained from many sources. The collations of all first editions have been made from copies in the collection of the compiler, with few exceptions. Information as to the first English editions has been secured in some cases from English book-dealers, or other persons in England, and where such is the case it has been mentioned; catalogues of the Bibliothèque Nationale, British Museum, Library of Congress, and The New York Public Library have been searched.

Capitals and italics have been indicated, but not black letter. Where pages are irregular in size, being untrimmed, the largest size is given. Title-pages and collations of the first American edition of each book are given immediately under the book title; those of first English editions follow all matter concerning American editions.

FLYLEAVES

The problem of flyleaves has always vexed bibliographers, who looked at them; dealers, who sold them; and collectors, who bought them. The present is no exception; the extreme proponents of both viewpoints have represented to us that, (a) *any* blank leaf before or after the printed matter should be counted; and, (b) *none at all* should be reckoned with. Agreeably to the tradition, neither school of practice has been followed; the result may be satisfactory to none. For the purposes of this bibliography, we have counted as flyleaves, any unprinted leaves, other than the free half of the end- (or lining-) paper, either before or after the printed matter of the book itself. The exception to this is that if an extra sheet is pasted to the free half of the end-paper, it is not counted. Thus there may be two blank leaves, but no flyleaves, as was frequently the case; the first American edition of *Columbus* is an example. Advertisements cannot generally be regarded as part of the book itself, but are rather something extraneous or foreign, associated with the casing process. This is true even of printed wrappers bearing advertisements. It is therefore possible to have several pages of advertisements before a front flyleaf or after a back one. (A notable exception is the first American edition of *Abbotsford and Newstead Abbey,* q. v.) It is realized that this allows room for the vagaries of the binders, but we call your attention to the fact that, since at times the status of a blank leaf cannot be determined without ripping the book apart, in no instance is the number of flyleaves considered a necessary 'point' in identifying an edition or issue.

If it seems to some that the allowance of flyleaves for a given title is somewhat parsimonious, we say that we have preferred to err on the side of strictness than to require an unobtainable quantity of blank paper. Responsible dealers and careful collectors will naturally concern themselves with sound copies of books. A collector obviously does not rejoice in a copy which bears the scars of mutilation and removed sheets. Flyleaves should indicate a sound copy, but bibliographically they tell nothing more than the fact that either the binder or printer was a generous man.

Similarly, the matter of advertisements at times threatens to become a fetish. When three copies of a first issue of a book vary only in the number of advertisements, an earlier date on them is likely to prove attractive, but it is not reliable. Publishers' advertisements were inserted so wholly willy-nilly that their importance hovers around the vanishing-point. Where we have found advertisements, we have noted them, but here again, as with flyleaves, they are more ornamental than useful.

Any such standard as the one arbitrarily laid down here, will be confounded with exceptions. We cannot formulate any rule which would cover the cases of freak ways of binding. In the second volume of the first American edition of *The Alhambra,* for instance, the blank half of page 235–236 (which would be called p. 237–238) is used as the end-paper for the back cover, and two blank sheets from the first signature are sewn between this end-paper and the last page of text. Such cases are, we are grateful to say, rare.

No effort has been made to dissect the body of the text. That is, in a number of cases there are sub-titles following blank pages through the text. These unnumbered pages have not been listed, since they are not, as a rule, of bibliographic interest.

There has been no attempt to include all works of critical, biographical, or reminiscent interest, except full biographies and a few volumes of particular concern, since such books are constantly appearing. If a list were to be fully inclusive it would necessarily embrace every history of American literature and every literary and historical work on the period 1800 to 1860 in America. A list of such critical books or essays is given in the *Cambridge History of American Literature.* It is full, but not, however, complete.

It is apparent that Irving is an author whose works are particularly adapted to illustration and tempting to illustrators. His popularity, his availability as a classic for gift-book purposes, the romance and whimsicality of his characters — have made a strong appeal to many artists. Irving's tremendous and lasting popularity is perhaps in no way better demonstrated than by the great number of illustrated editions of his books which have appeared and are still appearing frequently. Most of the prominent artists of the last century in this field have illustrated one or more of Irving's books. It is worthy of note also that perhaps more of these illustrated editions have been published in England than in America. Where it is reasonably certain that the book noted is the first publication with the particular illustrations mentioned, it is listed as a first edition; otherwise the date given is merely that of the volume to which reference was found. The list of illustrated editions has been compiled from the author's collection, from other private libraries, and from catalogues of libraries and book dealers. Whenever possible, publisher, page size and number of pages have been given. Additional publications are, of course, constantly being issued.

The bibliography of the plays on which Irving collaborated with Payne has been derived from published letters of Irving and Payne, biographies of both authors, and standard literary histories. In several cases the fact or extent of Irving's participation could not be definitely established.

It did not prove practicable to compare all manuscripts viewed with each of Irving's published works. It is therefore possible that some errors may appear in the manuscript lists. A few pages described as unpublished may prove to be merely unidentified portions of a published work. In stating the number of pages, particularly of long manuscripts, there may be variances from computations by others, as in several instances portions of two pages were mounted as one, extra unnumbered pages inserted, some leaves written on both sides while the body of the manuscript was written on one side only, etc. Different methods of counting would give different results. The principal object in mentioning these manuscripts is to locate, identify, and describe complete manuscripts, as well as important (and some unimportant) portions. When the pagination of the printed page is given, it is that of the first edition.

Copies have been located sufficiently to indicate where they are to be found. This is not a census of first editions; no effort has been made to list all holdings. In the case of manuscripts, all such material that has come to our attention has been included; likewise copies of unusual interest have been cited.

All editions have been mentioned which contain new material or offer any variations from the text of the first edition, and certain others, such as Paris editions of the same year. The collection of the compiler contains many additional volumes, including copies of all the revised 1848 [etc.] set, most of the Paris editions, and others.

ACKNOWLEDGMENTS

The preparation of this list has been a pleasure, because of a lifelong interest in the works of Irving in the one case, and a great interest in whichever Muse rules Bibliography in the other. Not the least of the pleasure has been the courteous and helpful assistance received from many sources and the agreeable contacts with others of like interests. Among the many persons who have generously given of their time and information, special thanks are due to Mr. Whitman Bennett; Mr. Barnet J. Beyer; Mr. Albert A. Bieber; Dr. William G. Braislin;

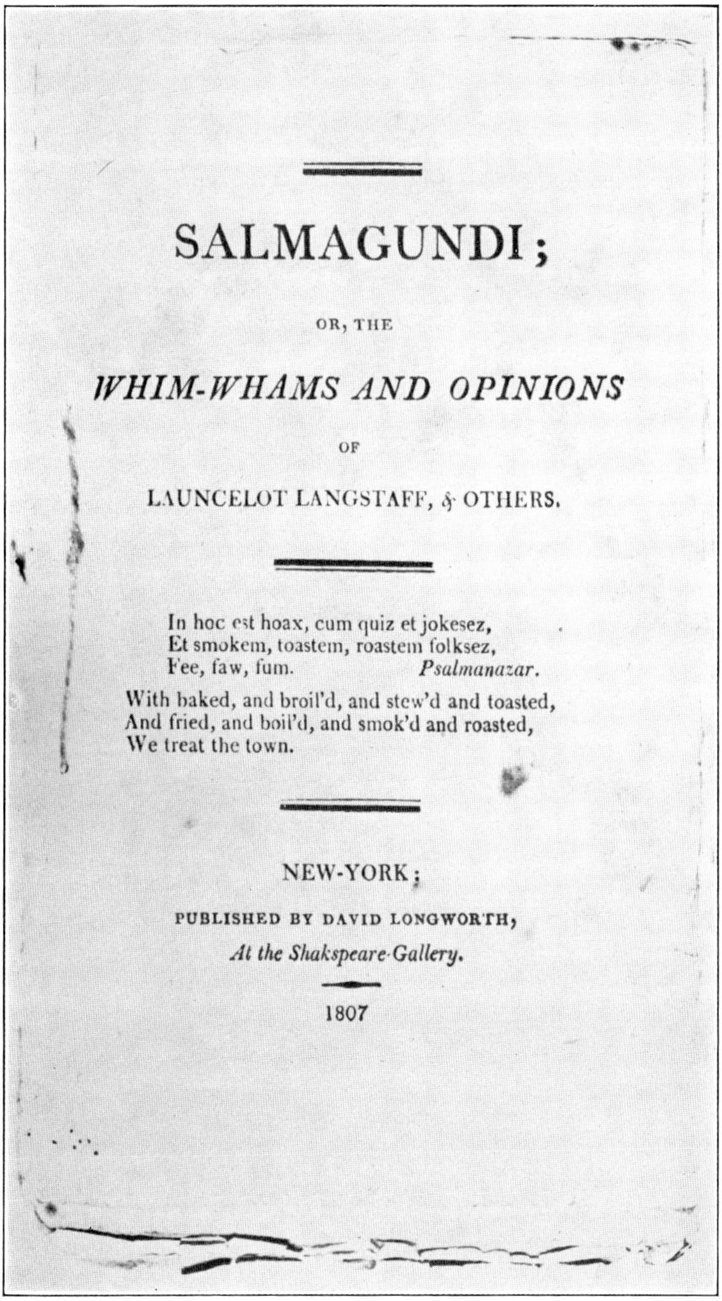

SALMAGUNDI;

OR, THE

WHIM-WHAMS AND OPINIONS

OF

LAUNCELOT LANGSTAFF, & OTHERS.

In hoc est hoax, cum quiz et jokesez,
Et smokem, toastem, roastem folksez,
Fee, faw, fum. *Psalmanazar.*

With baked, and broil'd, and stew'd and toasted,
And fried, and boil'd, and smok'd and roasted,
We treat the town.

NEW-YORK:

PUBLISHED BY DAVID LONGWORTH,

At the Shakspeare-Gallery.

1807

PLATE II

Salmagundi, No. 2. The first edition wrapper. From the collection of Alfred L. Rose, Esq.

Dr. Maurice Chazin; Mr. James H. Drake; Mr. George S. Hellman; Mr. Kennard McClees; Mr. Boies Penrose, 2nd; Mr. Carl H. Pforzheimer; Mr. Alfred L. Rose; Dr. A. S. W. Rosenbach; Mr. Alwin J. Scheuer; Mr. Charles Sessler (Miss Mabel Zahn); Dr. Robert E. Spiller; Mr. Leon C. Sunstein; Mr. Arthur Swann; the Rev. Dr. Roderick Terry; Dr. Stanley T. Williams; Mr. Carroll A. Wilson; Mr. Owen D. Young.

We are grateful also for assistance from England: from Mr. Reginald Atkinson; the British Museum; Mr. Stephen Hunt of Southborough; Maggs Brothers; and Mr. F. D. Webster of Tunbridge Wells, who supplied many useful facts about English editions.

American institutions have been kind, and our indebtedness includes certain of their officials: The American Antiquarian Society (Mr. R. W. G. Vail); Columbia University Library; The Free Library of Philadelphia; The Henry E. Huntington Library and Art Gallery; The Library Company of Philadelphia, including its Ridgway Branch; The Library of Congress; The Mercantile Library of Philadelphia; The New York Historical Society; The Pierpont Morgan Library; Yale University Library; University of Pennsylvania Library.

CHRONOLOGICAL LIST OF WORKS

SALMAGUNDI

1807–08

(See Plate II)

First Edition Wrappers

(double rule) / SALMAGUNDI; / OR, THE / *WHIM-WHAMS AND OPINIONS* / OF / LAUNCELOT LANGSTAFF, & OTHERS. / (double rule) / In hoc est hoax, cum quiz et jokesez, / Et smokem, toastem, roastem folksez, / Fee, faw, fum. *Psalmanazar.* / With baked, and broiled, and stew'd and toasted, / And fried, and boil'd, and smok'd and roasted, / We treat the town. / (double rule) / NEW-YORK: / PUBLISHED BY DAVID LONGWORTH, / *At the Shakspeare-Gallery.* / (French rule) / 1807

Second Edition Wrappers

District of }
New-York } *ss.* BE IT REMEMBERED, that on the sixth day of March, in the thirty-first year of the Independence of the United / States of America, *David Longworth,* of the said Dis- / trict, hath deposited in this office, the title of a Book, / the right whereof he claims as proprietor, in the words / and figures following, to wit: / SALMAGUNDI; / OR, THE / *WHIM-WHAMS AND OPINIONS* / OF / LAUNCELOT LANGSTAFF, & OTHERS. / (double rule) / In hoc est hoax, cum quiz et jokesez, / Et smokem, toastem, roastem folksez, / Fee, faw, fum. *Psalmanazar.* / With baked, and broil'd, and stew'd and toasted, / And fried, and boil'd, and smok'd and roasted, / We treat the town. / (French rule) / In conformity

SALMAGUNDI, continued

to the Act of the Congress of the United / States, entitled "An Act for the encouragement of / "Learning, by securing the Copies of Maps, Charts, / "and Books, to the Authors and Proprietors of such / "Copies, during the times herein mentioned;" and al- / "so to an act entitled "An Act supplementary to an / "act entitled, An Act for the encouragement of Learn- / "ing, by securing the copies of Maps, Charts, and / "Books, to the Authors and Proprietors of such Copies, / "during the times therein mentioned, and extending / "the benefits thereof, to the Arts of Designing, Engrav- / "ing and Etching historical and other prints." / EDWARD DUNSCOMB. / Clerk of the District of New-York / (rule) / NEW-YORK: PUBLISHED BY DAVID LONGWORTH.

Above is given a collation of both the first and the second edition of the wrappers of "Salmagundi." Those listed above as second edition are the ones usually found; to date four copies of the first edition wrappers have been seen.

Since the point may be regarded as somewhat controversial, and since it will be a disappointment to many collectors to discover that their wrappers are of the second edition, some account of the reasoning is only fair.

On the first edition wrapper:

1. The Davis advertisement is omitted on the back wrapper.
2. This wrapper is dated.
3. The elaborate copyright notice is omitted; (no copyright notice appears anywhere in the volume).
4. This wrapper appears on Parts 2 and 3 — early Parts only.

On the second edition wrapper:

1. The advertisement for the Davis volume appears on the back wrapper.
2. The wrapper is not dated.
3. The copyright notice appears. The Copyright Law of April 29, 1802, required a complete notice of copyright to be printed in every copy of each book.
4. These wrappers are those used for the remainder of the entire series, and have appeared on every number. The first change came in Parts 5 and 6, when a hyphen was inserted in "thirty-first." This is the only change in the front of the second edition wrappers for the entire 20 numbers. The advertisements on the back were changed frequently after Part 10.

The first edition wrapper may have been only a trial issue. If Longworth wished to protect his copyright he would have had to print a copyright notice, which he at once did, and printed the second edition which is entirely different. The number of first edition wrappers seems to have been very small.

The hyphen in line 2 of the second edition wrappers begins to appear with Part 5, though not until Part 7 came out were those wrappers without the hyphen exhausted.

Reconstruction of the history of these wrappers would show that Longworth printed up a large quantity, without dating or numbering, so that they could be used for each new Part as it appeared. The first edition, being evidently a very small one, was soon used up; or it may have been discarded, to be used on Parts 2 and 3 by accident. The entirely new set-up constituting the second edition began to run low somewhere about the time Part 5 was being released, and a new lot was made, with the hyphen appearing; this supply was exhausted with Part 9, and Part 10 appears with new advertisements on the back. From this point forward the wrappers were reprinted frequently, each time with new advertisements on the back, and with no change on the front.

Salmagundi was published in twenty numbers, the first dated Saturday, January 24, 1807; the last, Monday, January 25, 1808. The pamphlets had tan paper covers. The covers and page sizes run approximately from 5¾ x 3¾ to 6⅝ x 4¼ inches, as the covers and sheets were uncut and varied. The parts were numbered consecutively 1 to 20; beginning with No. 11, they were numbered, in addition, as No. 1 of Vol. 2, etc. A title-page for Vol. 2 and a complete index were included, at the end of the last number. These were not counted in the pagination. The text of the entire twenty numbers is paged consecutively (3) to 430. Many copies bear at the top of the first page the words "second edition," "third edition," etc. It has been claimed that there was only one edition and that this notation was printed on some copies merely to create the impression of popularity. A comparison of the different editions, however, proves this opinion to be incorrect, since such comparison reveals variations in text, in the typesetting, number of words to the line, etc.

We have seen bound copies of the first edition containing indexes to Vol. 2 only, indexes to both volumes, with and without title-pages to Vol. 1, and with a portrait of Launcelot Langstaff both as frontispiece and inserted before No. 8. We believe the latter proper. All the title-pages which we have seen, both to Vol. 1 and to Vol. 2, bear the date 1808. The plate of Launcelot Langstaff is found in at least six states; 1: without a title; 2: with the title "Launcelot Langstaff"; 3: with the title "LAUNCELOT LANGSTAFF, ESQ."; 4: with the title "Launcelot Langstaff, esq. (black letter) / FROM THE ORIGINAL DRAWING." 5: with the title "Launcelot Langstaff, esq." in black letter; 6: with the title "LAUNCELOT LANGSTAFF." We have seen the fourth state only in copies of the second edition (1814), though we have seen the first state in the first three American editions (1807–08, 1814, 1820), and the second, third, fifth and sixth states in the first edition. The first three states seem to have been inserted more or less at random and were possibly supplied indiscriminately to subscribers after all or several of the numbers had been issued.

We have been able to discover no data as to which of these items properly belong in a first issue. As the book was issued in twenty parts it is probable that, with the increasing popularity of the work, the publishers found that copies were being preserved and bound, and therefore added the features of title-pages and indexes. The 1808 date on the title-page supports the view that it was an afterthought of the publishers.

There were two issues of the first edition of several Parts of *Salmagundi.* In certain Parts, notably Part 8, the changes were so frequent that there is little evidence for priority. For details of such Parts, see the list of the distinctions between first and second issues of the first edition, which follows. (*It should be noted that this distinguishes the first and second issues of the first edition, not the first and second editions themselves, as in the case of the table accompanying the "Sketch Book."*)

PART I

Page	Line	First Issue	Second Issue
20	2	dress he! then	dress! he then
	—	*line above and below imprint*	*line below imprint only*

PARTS II-III

no differences

PART IV

Page	Line	First Issue	Second Issue
74	27	(ro Lousy anee)	(or Lousy anee)
75	31	whim-wham	whim wham
76	4	steal,	steal
	21	nigglety nag	nigglety-nag
77	27	Tony	Toney
79	7	good man,	good man
80	—	*period after* SALMAGUNDI (*top*)	*no period*
81	7	hertofore	heretofore
	18	it's	its
	23–24	"THE ECHO" "SALMAGUNDI"	*no quotation marks*
	24	*line ends* they	*line ends* re-

PART V

[The variations in this Part cannot be called first and second issue; there is no evidence of priority: the error might easily have been made when the type was adjusted or tightened in the bed.]

	Issue i		*Issue ii*
page 99, line 35	introducini-	*or*	introducing
36	unrg	*or*	unri-

PART VI

Page	Line	First Issue	Second Issue
123	36	mortal stab	mortal
124	6	suce	such
	—	[*Imprint*] printed and published	Printed and Published

[Part 6 also appears as a hybrid, with both first and second issue readings in the same copy.]

SALMAGUNDI, continued

PART VII

no differences

PART VIII

[Part 8 presents a variety of variations, the differences being in the punctuation. There is no way of determining priority. We give below a list which describes the two copies most widely differing. The copy in the right-hand column is the second *edition;* that in the left-hand column a first *edition, issue* unknown. If we proceed on the assumption that the reading most different from the known second edition is the earliest, then the copy described in the left-hand column is somewhere among the early issues. There can be no doubt, after a stylistic examination of this part, that the copies with a multitude of commas were outrageously ill pointed. But the only allowable conclusion must be that the more commas, the probable priority of appearance.]

Page	Line	First Edition	Second Edition
145	1	straws	straw's
	34	arms,	arms
146	19	publish,	publish
147	32	himself,	himself
148	3	substantial,	substantial
	4	poet,	poet
	11	lampooned,	lampooned
	29	heroics,	heroics
155	14	at one time	at one time,
	15	at another,	at another
	30	perseverence	perseverence,
	35	instance,	instance
156	7	hub-bub,	hub-bub
	17	wrong	wrong,
	18	addition,	addition
	33	money,	money
	34	memorial	memorial,
157	15	started,	started
	26	lodoiska	Lodoiska
	34	modesty,	modesty
160	27	lord mayor,	lord mayor
	33	word,	word

PARTS IX-X

no differences

PART XI

Page	Line	First Issue	Second Issue
214	31	beer barrels indeed	beer barrels, indeed

PARTS XII-XIV

no differences

PART XV

Page	Line	First Issue	Second Issue
324	—	*no imprint*	*imprint*

PART XVI

Page	Line	First Issue	Second Issue
325	4	wits	wits,
	5	correct,	correct
	6	servations;	servations,
328	22	couple	couple,
330	1	transferred, bodily,	transferred bodily
	14	lodgement	lodgment
	16	and,	and
	24	Spring;	Spring,
331	13	philosophy	philosophy,
334	18	around;	around,
336	35	far from	Far From

[One copy has been seen with *philosophy,* and *Far From* as in second issue, with all other readings as in the first issue.]

PART XVII

Page	Line	First Issue	Second Issue
350	22	ancsetors	ancestors

PART XVIII

There are two readings for each of the two lines in this Part. They cannot be called issues, but are rather variants. A copy may have any arrangement of the readings:

Page	Line	*Issue i*		*Issue ii*
373	33	art to our	*or*	ar to our
374	4	and, so far	*or*	and so far

PART XIX

no differences

PART XX

Page	Line	First Issue	Second Issue
417	34	who exhibit herself	who exhibits herself

The second edition of Part 10 is imprinted "second edition, revised and corrected," although other numbers are imprinted "second edition," "third edition," only. The revision in Part 10 is more extensive than the variations from the first issues in the other numbers.

Copies of Parts 10–20 have been found which show internal evidence that, although they have retained the Part designations, they were not issued nor printed in Parts, but were rather printed as a book, and issued as such. The title-page is dated 1808. The key to the situation lies in the fact that this edition bears signature letters running through the letter S. As the individual Parts of *Salmagundi* were issued, the signature was always A and, if needed B, so that in bound copies of the separate Parts, only those signature letters appear. In making up a book some other means was needed to ensure proper binding, and so the customary method of consecutive signature letters was adopted.

This edition bears the page numbers of the second edition of the Parts in wrappers, and much of the type used in the Parts is used here. There is no note at the top of the Parts however, (Part 12 excepted) to show that it is a later reprint; the only key is in the aforementioned signature letters.

Part 12 of this book reprint of the second edition in wrappers is to be found in two issues. The distinction is on the first page of Part 12 [p. (229)]. In the first issue *Whim Whams* is correctly spelled; in the second it appears as Whim Wmams; the first issue has (*second edition*) at the top. The second issue is very badly set and shows evidence of a hastily produced printing; it was probably needed to fill out the series when the supply of this Part ran low.

The tremendous popularity of this work, which popularity mounted as more and more of it appeared, would account for the frenzied haste to get it before the public; likewise the original issue seemed to have been soon exhausted, and the succeeding edition in one volume (Parts 10–20) rushed to print to supply the public demand for the second half of this singular series.

The second edition in book form appeared in two volumes in 1814, published by David Longworth. This edition has many variations from the text of the first, and also includes an index

SALMAGUNDI, continued

and two tables of contents, the second being an amplified summary, and several plates by A. Anderson. The third edition, published in two volumes by Thomas Longworth and Co. in 1820, contains numerous engravings by A. Anderson, but omits the index and amplified table of contents. It apparently follows the text of the second edition. Another edition was published in 1835 by Harper as part of Paulding's Collected Works. This differs from all preceding editions.

An edition in English was published in Paris in 1834. We have not seen this, but we assume that it differs in text from all of the early American and English editions herein mentioned, since the introduction to *Salmagundi* in the collected edition of Irving's works published by Putnam in 1860 states that the text is that of the original (i. e. first) edition with a few "verbal corrections following the Paris edition of 1834, which had more or less of the author's supervision." This 1860 edition varies from all of the other editions and one may take it that the Paris 1834 edition does likewise.

The contents were written by Washington Irving, James Kirk Paulding and William Irving. The following articles may be definitely assigned:

No. 1. First article to Washington Irving and Paulding jointly; second article, "From the Elbow Chair of Launcelot Langstaff, Esq.," to Paulding; third and fourth articles, "On Theatrics," and "N. Y. Assembly," to Washington Irving.

No. 2. First article, "From the Elbow Chair of Launcelot Langstaff, Esq.," to Washington Irving; second article, "Mr. Wilson's Concert," to Paulding; third article, to Paulding; fourth article, "To Launcelot Langstaff, Esq.," to William Irving; concluding article, to Washington Irving.

No. 8. First article, signed "Anthony Evergreen," to Washington Irving.

No. 10. "Stranger in Philadelphia," omitted after the first American and English editions, to Washington Irving.

No. 11. "Mine Uncle John," to Paulding.

All of the Letters from "Mustapha Rub-a-dub Keli Khan" are by Washington Irving, except the one in no. 3 (by Paulding, one paragraph only by Washington Irving), the one in no. 18 (by Paulding), and those in nos. 5 and 14 (by William Irving).

All of the poetry is by William Irving.

SALMAGUNDI; / OR, THE / WHIM-WHAMS AND OPINIONS / OF / LAUNCELOT LANGSTAFF, ESQ. / AND OTHERS. / (double rule) / In hoc est hoax, cum quiz et jokesez, / Et smokem, toastem, roastem, folksez, / Fee, faw, fum. *Psalmanazar.* / With baked, and broiled, and stewed, and toasted, / And fried, and boiled, and smoaked, and roasted, / We treat the town. / (double rule) / REPRINTED FROM THE AMERICAN EDITION, / WITH / AN INTRODUCTORY ESSAY / *And Explanatory Notes,* / BY JOHN LAMBERT. / (French rule) / VOL. I. [II.] / (French rule) / LONDON: / PRINTED FOR J. M. RICHARDSON, 23, CORNHILL, / OPPOSITE THE ROYAL EXCHANGE. / (wavy rule) / 1811.

Collation: Vol. I: [i], title-page; [ii], printer's imprint; [iii–iv], contents; (i) – iv, preface; (v) – liv, introductory essay; (1) – 211, text; 211, printer's imprint; (212), blank.

Vol. II: [i], title-page; [ii], printer's imprint; [iii – iv], contents; (1) – 230, text; 230, printer's imprint.

Binding: An examination of several copies has failed to disclose the original binding.

Page Size: The copies were of different page sizes, evidently cut, but the largest was 6 7/16 x 4 13/16 inches. Apparently there were, originally, yellow end papers.

A few extracts from *Salmagundi* had been published in England in 1810 in the first edition of *Travels through Lower Canada and the United States of North America, in the years 1806, 1807, and 1808,* by John Lambert, p. 234–292. These extracts are "From My Elbow Chair," "Letter from Mustapha Rubadub Keli Khan" (omitting two paragraphs), and "Fashions," all from the third number, and are in all probability the first publication in England of any of Irving's work. The second edition of Lambert's *Travels* was published in 1814, and since it appeared after the English *Salmagundi,* it did not contain the extracts listed above. It had, however, a reference to them. The edition collated above is, however, the first English edition and follows in the main the text of the first American edition although there are a few slight changes. Another edition, probably the second English edition, was published in London in 1824, printed by T. Davison for Thomas Tegg, Rodwell and Martin, and R. Griffin and Co., Glasgow. It bears no edition note on the title-page, has a PREFATORY NOTICE on p. (iii) – iv dated November, 1823, and apparently follows the text of the second American edition. Another edition in the same year, by the same printer for the same publishers, bears on the title-page: NEW EDITION / CORRECTED AND REVISED BY THE AUTHOR. In this edition the prefatory notice becomes a publisher's notice, is considerably expanded, occupying p. (iii) – vi, and is undated; the text differs from that of all preceding editions.

A Paris edition, published by Baudry in 1824, also varies from all of these American and English editions. Except as noted no two of the editions mentioned are exactly alike in text.

Copies: Apparently there exists no perfect set of first editions, first issues, of all Parts in wrappers. The first edition wrappers described above, have not been seen on any Part later than the third; a perfect set could, presumably, have second edition wrappers beginning with Part 4.

In the following list of holdings, there is no attempt to list the condition of separate Parts, as to which issue of the first edition they may be. The library of Mr. Alfred L. Rose contains a set of Parts in wrappers (except Parts 1, 4, 11, 20) of which all Parts are first edition. The library of the Rev. Dr. Roderick Terry contains a bound copy of the first edition of all numbers; the library of Mr. Carroll A. Wilson contains a set of all Parts in wrappers (except Part 13) of which Parts 2, 12, 17, 18 and 19 are second edition and the remainder first. The collection of the compiler contains several bound copies, with the Parts in various editions; a first edition of Lambert's *Travels;* and sundry subsequent editions. The Henry E. Huntington Library and Art Gallery contains a copy with all the wrappers bound in except the front cover of no. 1 and the back cover of no. 3; Parts 1 and 2 are second edition; the remainder first. The New York Public Library contains a copy of Part 6 in wrappers, and a bound volume of the parts. Yale University Library contains a set in wrappers, of which Part 1 is the third edition, and the remainder first.

Where wrappers are referred to in the paragraph preceding, second edition wrappers are meant. Four copies with the first edition wrappers have been seen to date: Parts 2 and 3 in the possession of Mr. Alfred L. Rose, Part 2 in the collection of Dr. William G. Braislin, and also in the Yale University Library.

KNICKERBOCKER'S HISTORY OF NEW YORK
1809

A HISTORY / OF / NEW YORK, / FROM THE BEGINNING OF THE WORLD TO THE / END OF THE DUTCH DYNASTY. / CONTAINING / Among many Surprising and Curious Matters, the Unutterable / Ponderings of WALTER THE DOUBTER, the Disastrous / Projects of WILLIAM THE TESTY, and the Chivalric / Achievements of PETER THE HEADSTRONG, the three / Dutch Governors of NEW AMSTERDAM; being the only / Authentic History of the Times that ever hath been, or ever / will be Published. / (double rule) / BY DIEDRICH KNICKERBOCKER. / (double rule) / De waarheid die in duister lag, / Die komt met klaarheid aan den dag. / (French rule) / IN TWO VOLUMES. / (French rule) / Vol. I [II.] / (double rule) / PUBLISHED BY INSKEEP & BRADFORD, NEW YORK; / BRADFORD & INSKEEP, PHILADELPHIA; WM. M'IL- / HENNEY, BOSTON; COALE & THOMAS, BALTIMORE; / AND MORFORD, WILLINGTON, & CO. CHARLESTON. / (dotted rule) / 1809.

Collation: Vol. I: three flyleaves; folding view of New Amsterdam about 1640; (iii), title-page; (iv), copyright notice; (v), [dedication] TO THE / NEW YORK / HISTORICAL SOCIETY / *This Work is respectfully / Dedicated, as a humble and unworthy Tes- / timony of the profound veneration and ex- / alted esteem of the Society's / Sincere Well wisher / and / Devoted Servant /* DIEDRICH KNICKERBOCKER. / ; (vi), blank; (vii) – xiv, ACCOUNT OF THE AUTHOR; (xv) – xxiii, [preface] TO THE PUBLIC; (xxiv), blank; (1) – 268, text; flyleaf.

Vol. II: flyleaf; (i), title-page; (ii), copyright notice; (1) – 258, text; flyleaf.

Page size: 7⅜ x 4⅝ inches (in boards); 7 1/16 x 4¼ (in leather).

Binding: Issued in two bindings: one, brown mottled sheepskin, with a red leather label on the spine stamped in gilt: / KNICKERBOCKER'S / NEW YORK / and below this 1 and 2 on the respective volumes; the other, slate-blue boards with tan paper backs.

Published December 6, 1809.

The largest size in which the view in Vol. I. has been found is 15½ x 5 9/16 inches.

The second edition, in two volumes, was published on June 3, 1812. It contained as frontispiece in Vol. I a chart and in Vol. II a picture of Knickerbocker. The text frequently varies from that of the first edition. The publishers were Inskeep & Bradford, New York, and Bradford & Inskeep, Philadelphia. To the "account of the author" considerable material was added.

The third edition, in two volumes, was published by M. Thomas, Philadelphia, in 1819. The dedication to the New York Historical Society was omitted. This fact and the enlarged "account of the author" in this and the second edition are significant in view of the elaborate literary hoax

KNICKERBOCKER'S HISTORY OF NEW YORK, continued

which accompanied the first appearance of the book. This third edition has a frontispiece to Vol. I, "Dutch Courtship," by C. R. Leslie, and to Vol. II, "A Schepen Laughing at a Burgomaster's Joke," by Washington Allston. These were procured by Irving from the artists while he was in London. There is no change in the text from the second edition.

An edition in two volumes was issued in 1836 by Carey, Lea & Blanchard, Philadelphia. It is called "a new edition" on the title-page.

A revised edition appeared in 1848, published by George P. Putnam as Vol. I of Irving's collected works. An author's apology, narrating the "jeu d'esprit" of the first publication, and copies of the original advertisements in the newspapers are inserted. There are also numerous changes in text. Another revision, with additional corrections, was published in a limited edition by the Grolier Club in 1886.

The first Paris edition was by Baudry, 1824.

A / HISTORY / OF / NEW YORK, / FROM THE / BEGINNING OF THE WORLD / TO THE / END OF THE DUTCH DYNASTY. / CONTAINING, / AMONG MANY SURPRISING AND CURIOUS MATTERS, / THE UNUTTERABLE PONDERINGS OF WALTER THE DOUBTER, / *THE DISASTROUS PROJECTS OF WILLIAM THE TESTY,* / AND THE CHIVALRIC ACHIEVEMENTS OF PETER THE HEADSTRONG, / THE THREE DUTCH GOVERNORS OF NEW AMSTERDAM : / *Being the only authentic History of the Times that ever hath been published.* / (rule) ; / BY DIEDRICH KNICKERBOCKER, / (AUTHOR OF THE SKETCH BOOK.) / (French rule) / A NEW EDITION. / (rule) / De waarheid die in duister lag, / Die komt met klaarheid aan den dag. / (rule) / LONDON : / JOHN MURRAY, ALBEMARLE-STREET. / (rule) / 1820.

Collation: (1) – 4, advertisements; flyleaf, on which the double leaf of advertisements was pasted; (i), pre-title; (ii), printer's imprint and advertisement of the "Sketch Book"; (iii), title-page; (iv), blank; (v) – xxi, ACCOUNT OF THE AUTHOR; (xxii), blank; (xxiii) – xxxii, TO THE PUBLIC; contents, eight unnumbered pages not included in the pagination; (33) – 520, text; 520, printer's imprint.

Binding: Light blue boards, grey-brown paper spine, white paper label, printed in black: (rule) / KNICKERBOCKER'S / NEW / YORK. / (short rule) / *New Edition.* / (short rule) / *12s.* / (rule).

Some copies are bound in pink boards and do not contain the advertisements.

Page size: 9⅛ x 5¾ inches.

The above is accepted as the first English edition although it states "a new edition" on the title-page. It was published in one volume and follows the text of the second American edition.

There was an edition by Wright, in 1820. This was a pirated edition, and appeared, according to one English bookdealer, before the Murray edition. W. Wright also issued an edition in 1821, having "second edition" on the title-page. The description of the 1820 edition is as follows: A / HUMOUROUS HISTORY / OF / NEW YORK, / FROM THE BEGINNING OF THE WORLD, / TO THE END OF / The Dutch Dynasty; / CONTAINING, AMONG MANY SURPRISING AND CURIOUS MATTERS, / THE UNUTTERABLE PONDERINGS OF / WALTER THE DOUBTER, / THE DISASTROUS PROJECTS OF / WILLIAM THE TESTY, / AND THE / CHIVALRIC ACHIEVEMENTS OF / PETER THE HEADSTRONG; / THE THREE DUTCH GOVERNORS OF NEW AMSTERDAM; / BEING THE ONLY AUTHENTIC HISTORY OF THE TIMES THAT / EVER HATH BEEN PUBLISHED. / (French rule) / A NEW EDITION. / (rule) / By DIEDRICH KNICKERBOCKER, / AUTHOR OF "THE SKETCH BOOK," / (rule) / LONDON: / PRINTED FOR W. WRIGHT, 46, FLEET-STREET. / (rule) / 1820.

Collation: (i), pre-title; (ii), blank; frontispiece, portrait of Knickerbocker; (iii), title-page; (iv), printer's imprint; (i) – x, ACCOUNT OF THE AUTHOR; (xi) – xvi, TO THE PUBLIC; (1) – 495, text; 495, printer's imprint; (496), blank.

Page size: 9⅛ x 5⅝ inches, uncut.

Binding: Original binding not known; all copies examined were bound in full leather.

This book also exists with the pre-title as a half-title after the title-page, but appearances would seem to require it before the title; certainly its logical place is there. Since, however, we have not seen any copies in the original binding, the location of this leaf cannot be finally settled.

In the *second issue,* pages vii–viii in the "Account of the Author" and pages xiii–xiv in "To the Public" have been replaced with new leaves. The errors in the *first issue* were: p. vii, 1. 5, "vain-glory" instead of "vainglory"; p. xiii, 1. 1, no dot over "i" in "enriched"; p. xiv, 1. 6, a comma instead of a dash before "I might"; and l. 16, "die d o" instead of "died to."

The 1821, *second edition,* also has the cancelled leaf vii–viii, and the second issue reading.

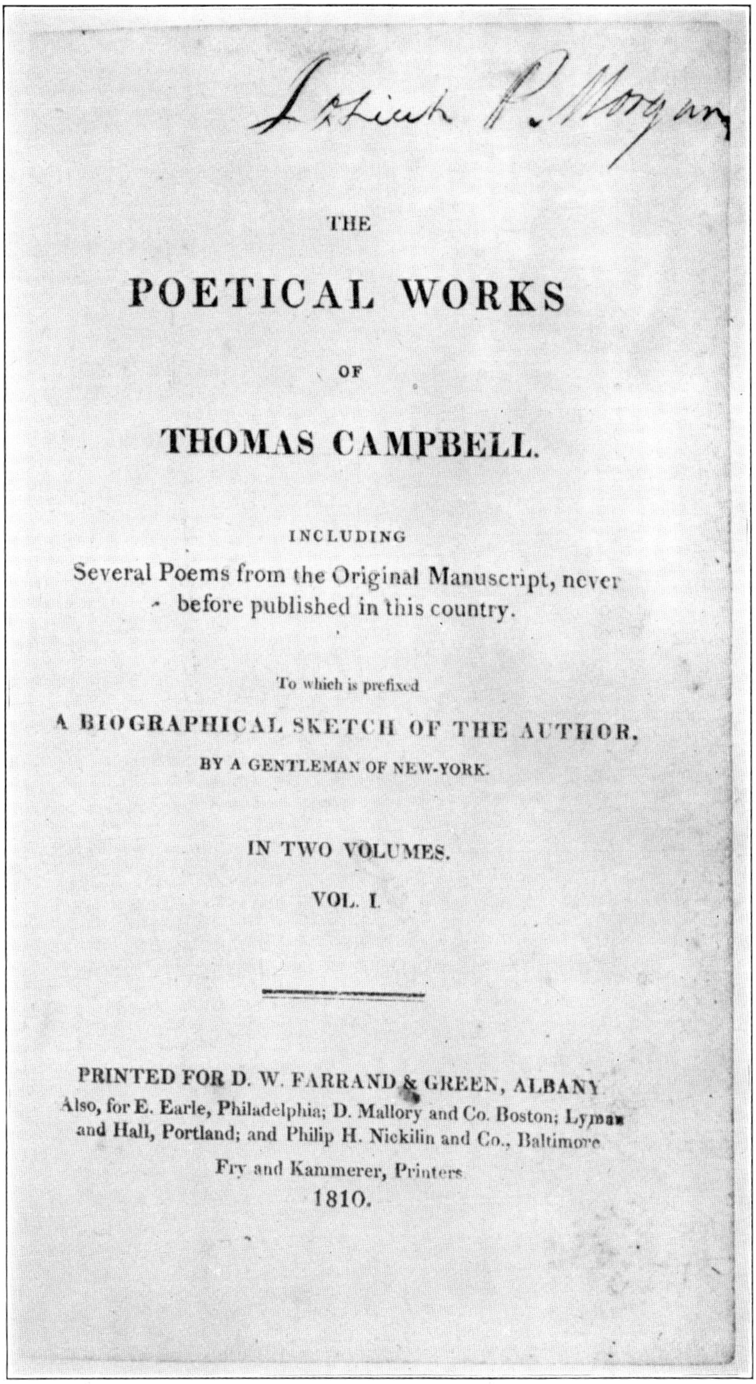

Lt. Lieut. P. Morgan

THE

POETICAL WORKS

OF

THOMAS CAMPBELL.

INCLUDING

Several Poems from the Original Manuscript, never before published in this country.

To which is prefixed

A BIOGRAPHICAL SKETCH OF THE AUTHOR.

BY A GENTLEMAN OF NEW-YORK.

IN TWO VOLUMES.

VOL. I.

PRINTED FOR D. W. FARRAND & GREEN, ALBANY

Also, for E. Earle, Philadelphia; D. Mallory and Co. Boston; Lyman and Hall, Portland; and Philip H. Nickilin and Co., Baltimore.

Fry and Kammerer, Printers

1810.

PLATE III

Title-page, showing the Albany imprint and the error in the spelling of Nicklin.
From the collection of the compiler.

Copies: The New York Public Library contains copies of the first edition, untrimmed, with original covers both in boards and leather. The collection of the compiler contains an untrimmed copy of the first edition; copies of the second and third American editions, and copies of all the London editions of 1820. The Pierpont Morgan Library contains two copies of the first edition: one, in leather binding, page size 6 13/16 x 4¼ inches, with black leather label lettered: HISTORY / OF / NEW YORK; the other, a rebound copy. The library of Rev. Dr. Roderick Terry contains a copy of the first edition bound in leather, with the title printed directly on the binding, in a slightly smaller page size than the copies in The New York Public Library and the collection of the compiler. Dr. Terry's collection also contains a copy of the Grolier Club, 1886, edition, printed on vellum. Mr. Barnet J. Beyer has in his possession a copy of the first American edition, with many annotations in Irving's hand, and with the documents relating to the court-martial of General Butler by General Wilkinson (Gen. Poffenburgh in the story).

Manuscripts: The New York Public Library contains 12 p. ms., the Author's Apology to Knickerbocker's History of New York, revised edition of 1848 (complete); 2 p. (not consecutive) of the original ms.; 1 p. ms., the first page of chapter 7, Book 3. The library of the Rev. Dr. Roderick Terry contains 1 page of the ms. of this book, as does that of Mr. Carroll A. Wilson. Dr. A. S. W. Rosenbach recently (1929) purchased some forty-four pages of the manuscript comprising 7 p., "To the Publick"; 1 p. note, Book 2, chapter 1; 3 p., last part Book 2, chapter 1; 2 p., Book 2, chapter 2; 1 p., Book 2, chapter 3; 1 p., Book 3, chapter 5; 2 p., Book 3, chapters 8 and 9; 1 p., Book 4, chapter 1; 3 p., Book 4, chapter 6; 2 p., Book 4, chapter 9; 3 p., Book 4, chapter 12; 3 p., Book 5, chapter 3; 2 p., Book 5, chapters 4 and 5; 8 p., Book 5, chapter 9; 4 p., rough notes on the character of Peter Stuyvesant; and 2 p. of unidentified fragments. The Henry E. Huntington Library and Art Gallery contains a printed copy of *A History of New York*, 2 volumes, incomplete, interleaved with author's corrections and revisions for the edition of 1854. (HM3131.)

LIFE OF THOMAS CAMPBELL
1810

(See Plate III)

(This was published in both a one-volume and a two-volume edition.)

(The two-volume edition)

THE / POETICAL WORKS / OF / THOMAS CAMPBELL. / INCLUDING / Several Poems from the Original Manuscript, never / before published in this country. / To which is prefixed / A BIOGRAPHICAL SKETCH OF THE AUTHOR, / BY A GENTLEMAN OF NEW-YORK. / IN TWO VOLUMES. / VOL. I. (II.) / (double rule) / PRINTED FOR D. W. FARRAND & GREEN, ALBANY. / Also, for E. Earle, Philadelphia; D. Mallory and Co. Boston; Lyman / and Hall, Portland; and Philip H. Nickilin and Co., Baltimore. / Fry and Kammerer, Printers. / 1810.

The imprint on the title-page varies. The book was apparently sold by all of the persons or firms named in the imprint, and each seller probably had his name as the leading imprint, with all the other names below.

Collation: Vol. I: (i), title-page; (ii), blank; (iii), contents; (iv), blank; (v), sub-title; (vi), copyright entry; (vii) –xliii, BIOGRAPHICAL SKETCH; (xliv), blank; (xlv), sub-title; (1), analysis; (2), blank; (3) – 146, text.

Vol. II: flyleaf; (i), pre-title; (ii), blank; (iii), title-page; (iv), blank; (v), contents; (vi), blank; (vii), sub-title; (viii), blank; (ix), advertisement; (x), blank; (1), sub-title; (2), blank; (3) – 170, text; flyleaf.

Page size: (boards), 7⅝ x 4 9/16; (leather), 6 13/16 x 4⅛ inches.

Binding: The book was published in both boards and leather. On the latter is a red leather label, printed in gold: (double rule) / (wavy rule) / CAMPBELL'S / POEMS / (wavy rule) / (double rule). At intervals down the spine are four double rules, between the first and second of which is 1 (2). At the top of the spine in the copies in boards was printed: (wavy rule) / CAMPBELL'S / POEMS. / (wavy rule) / (and at the bottom:) (wavy rule) / VOL. I. (II.) / (wavy rule). Mr. P. K. Foley states, in his "American Authors" that the Philadelphia imprint was the leading imprint on the cover of copies in boards. We have seen one copy in boards with no imprint on the cover.

It will be observed that in the collation above, the publisher Nicklin is misspelled Nickilin. This appears on some copies with the Albany imprint, and is corrected on others. The copies with the correct spelling of the name present a different collation for Vol. II: (1), title-page; (2), blank; (3), contents; (4), blank; (5), advertisement; (6), blank; remainder as described above.

We have seen only copies with the Albany imprint wherein the Nicklin was incorrect. Since there was a correction, it would seem that copies with the error are earlier.

LIFE OF THOMAS CAMPBELL, continued

(The one-volume edition)

THE / POETICAL WORKS / OF / THOMAS CAMPBELL. / INCLUDING / Several Pieces from the Original Manuscript, never / before published in this country. / To which is prefixed / A BIOGRAPHICAL SKETCH OF THE AUTHOR, / BY A GENTLEMAN OF NEW-YORK. / (double rule) / PRINTED FOR PHILIP H. NICKLIN & CO., BALTIMORE. / Also, for D. W. Farrand and Green, Albany; D. Mallory and Co., / Boston; Lyman and Hall, Portland; and E. Earle, / Philadelphia. / Fry and Kammerer, Printers. / 1810.

Collation: (1), title-page; (2), blank; (3) - (4), contents; (5), sub-title; (6), copyright entry; (7) - 41, biographical sketch; (42), blank; (43), sub-title; (44), blank; (45) - 296, text.
Page size: 7¾ x 4⅝.
Binding: boards.

The imprint varies in the one-volume edition as in the two-volume. This book exists also as two volumes in one with separate pagination (probably the two-volume set bound without the second title-page); as two volumes in one with consecutive pagination. The contents of the one-volume edition is that of the two-volume edition, but differently arranged.

There is no means of establishing any priority, either among the imprints, nor between the one- and two-volume editions. The work was doubtless brought out simultaneously as a joint publishing enterprise by the several publishers named on the title-page; the one-volume edition may have been merely for convenience, and done at the same time as the other. The attempt at a joint publication is an interesting note on the methods of the times. It was not often tried, and the reason for selecting this work is not evident. The venture was not continued beyond the first edition.

Further information will be found in the section Books which Irving Edited.

Copies: The library of Mr. Albert A. Bieber contains both the one- and the two-volume edition, as does that of Dr. William G. Braislin; the collection of the compiler contains a copy of the two-volume edition. The New York Public Library contains a copy of each of the two editions.

BIOGRAPHY OF JAMES LAWRENCE
1813

(See Plate IV)

BIOGRAPHY / OF / JAMES LAWRENCE, ESQ. / LATE A CAPTAIN IN THE NAVY OF THE / UNITED STATES: / together with / A COLLECTION OF THE MOST / INTERESTING PAPERS, / RELATIVE TO / The Action between the Chesapeake and Shannon, / and the Death of / *CAPTAIN LAWRENCE,* / &C. &C. / (double rule) / EMBELLISHED WITH A LIKENESS. / (double rule) / *NEW-BRUNSWICK:* / PRINTED AND PUBLISHED BY L. DEARE, / AT WASHINGTON'S HEAD. / (rule) / 1813.

Collation: Flyleaf; engraved portrait of Lawrence facing title-page; (1), title-page; (2), copyright entry; (3), contents; (4), blank; (5)–8, preface; (9)–244, text, of which pages (9)–55 contain the biography by Irving reprinted from the *Analectic Magazine* of August, 1813, and pages 56–60 contain the notes referring to this sketch reprinted from the *Analectic Magazine* of September, 1813; flyleaf.
Page size: 6 1/16 x 3 3/16 inches (uncut). In cut copies the size is 5⅜ x 3 7/16 inches.
Binding: Dark gray-green boards, the paper covering front and back covers and spine being a single piece. The title-page is reprinted on the front cover, slightly enlarged, and within an ornamental border. Printed in black on the spine: (two double rules) / BIOGRAPHY / OF / CAPT. LAWRENCE. / (double rule) / (French rule) / (double rule) / DEARE'8 / EDITION. / (double rule). All copies examined, save one, were bound in full leather.

The portrait facing the title-page is a circular stipple engraving, 2 6/16 inches in diameter (with border). Underneath: Edwin sc. / James Lawrence Esq.r / late of the United States Navy. (Fielding 112.)

For a detailed description of an uncut copy in printed boards, see the *Bulletin of The New York Public Library,* November, 1932, p. 742–743.

The Biography by Irving was reprinted in Vol. 2 of *Spanish Papers.*

SKETCH BOOK

1819–1820

(See Plates V and VI)

THE / SKETCH BOOK / OF / *GEOFFREY CRAYON, Gent.* / (French rule) / No. I. [II., etc.] / (rule) / "I have no wife nor children, good or bad, to provide for. A mere spectator of / other men's fortunes and adventures, and how they play their parts: which me- / thinks are diversely presented unto me, as from a common theatre or scene." / BURTON. / (rule) / *NEW-YORK:* / PRINTED BY C. S. VAN WINKLE, / No. 101 Greenwich-street. / (dotted rule) / 1819. [*See below as to dates of the other numbers and punctuation of publisher's address.*]

Collation: Part I: Cover; (i), title-page; (ii), copyright entry; (iii) – iv, prospectus; (5) – 93, text [(5) – 10, The author's account of himself.]; 94, note; fly-leaf; cover. Notice of Part II on outside back cover.

Part II: Cover; (95–96), blank; (97), title-page; (98), copyright entry; (99), sub-title; (100), blank; (101) – 169, text; (170), blank; cover. Notice of Part III on outside back cover. Some copies have a slip inserted facing page (97), stating that some articles have been reprinted without permission and warning against copyright infringement.

Part III: Cover; (171), title-page; (172), copyright entry; (173), sub-title; (174), blank; (175) – 242, text; cover.

Part IV: Cover; (243), title-page; (244), copyright entry; (245), sub-title; (246), blank; (247) – 335, text; (336), blank; cover.

Part V: Cover; (337), title-page; (338), copyright entry; (339), sub-title; (340), blank; (341) – 443, text; (444), blank; cover. We have seen one copy with a leaf of advertisements bound in before p. (337).

Part VI: Cover; (1), title-page; (2), copyright entry; (3), sub-title; (4), blank; (5) – 120, text; cover. Publisher's advertisement on outside back cover.

Part VII: Cover; (1), title-page; (2), copyright entry; (3), sub-title; (4), blank; (5) – 123, text; (124), blank; cover. Advertisement differing from that on Part VI on outside back cover.

Page size: 9⅛ by 5⅝ inches maximum, different pages varying materially in uncut copies.

This book was published simultaneously in New York, Boston, Philadelphia, and Baltimore, in seven numbers. The first was deposited for copyright May 15, 1819, and appeared June 23. Copyright dates of the other numbers were July 26 (appearing July 31), August 11 (appearing September 13), October 12 (appearing not later than November 30), and December 16, 1819 (appearing January 1, 1820), February 10 (appearing March 15), and August 12, 1820 (appearing September 13, 1820). The cover was a brownish tan paper bearing a double rule in which was printed: No. 1... Price 75 cents. [*first number; see below for others*] / (rule) / THE SKETCH BOOK. / (rule) / C. S. VAN WINKLE, PRINTER, [*see below as to imprint on the sixth and seventh numbers*] / 101 Greenwich-street.

Some copies have been seen wanting the slip opposite p. (97). Discussion has arisen concerning this slip, and its status is, unfortunately, unsettled. Its status is a matter of opinion rather than fact; lengthy arguments may be adduced by either side to prove — conclusively — that its contention is the only correct one. Some feel that it was undoubtedly ordered placed in every copy of Part II, and is therefore necessary for a perfect Part. Others feel as strongly that the mere fact that it was an inserted slip whose contents were not printed with the rest of the book indicates that some copies may have been issued without the slip; and in the absence of definite evidence priority cannot be assigned to copies either with or without the inserted slip. The Irving-Brevoort letters contain no reference to this slip nor to the matter of suppressing pirating; we feel that if the incident had been of the importance some suppose, mention would most certainly have been made of it in the detailed correspondence between Irving and Brevoort.

There are only two logical conclusions that may be proclaimed: (a) no valid proof of priority has been produced; (b) its necessity for a perfect Part is solely a matter of opinion, as is its general importance. We are of the opinion further that its importance has been overemphasized.

Several points should be noted regarding the first edition, including many variations from the second edition. The second edition is so printed on all wrappers. Copies of the second edition with original covers are apparently even scarcer than those of the first edition, but the following facts have been established by comparison. In the first edition the first five numbers are paged consecutively, the last two separately. In the second edition the pagination of the first two numbers is consecutive, but the last five are paged separately, having respectively 92, 93, 108, 120 and 123

SKETCH BOOK, continued

pages. In the first edition the first five numbers are dated 1819, the last two 1820. In the second edition the first number is dated 1819, the last six 1820. The first edition bore nothing as to edition on the cover; the second had "second edition" printed at the top of the outside cover. On the title-page of the first number only of the first edition the printer's address is given as "Greenwich-street"; in all other numbers of the first edition and in all numbers of the second edition it is given as "Greenwich Street," omitting the hyphen, and capitalizing the "S" in "Street." The hyphen is printed on the cover in all numbers of the first edition, and on the cover of the numbers of the second edition which we have seen. In the first edition of Part I, the dotted rule above the date, on the title-page, is made of eleven dots; in the second edition, of but ten. In the third number of the first edition there is a curious repetition in numeration of pages 203 to 210. In the first edition, Part I, the Note is on page 94 and has "Charles v." in the third line; in the second edition, the verso of page 93 is blank, the next page is numbered 94, contains the note and has "Emperor Frederick" in the third line. Beginning with the third American edition, and in all English editions, "der Rothbart" is inserted after "Frederick." In the second American edition, 1820, the page of the note is misnumbered 94; in the third edition, 1822, this is correctly numbered 95. Part II also exists with p. (98) blank. Since this was a copyright entry, it would seem that its omission was an oversight which was corrected in later copies of the book. In the first edition the imprint on the covers only of Parts VI and VII is changed to: PUBLISHED BY HALY AND THOMAS, NEW YORK, / AND M. THOMAS, PHILADELPHIA, although the imprint on the title-page remains the same. In the second edition on Parts VI (probably) and VII the imprint on the cover is C. S. Van Winkle. A curious error occurred in the dating of the copyright entry in the first edition. The first five numbers are dated 1819; in the copyright entry this is given as the 43rd year of independence, in the first three numbers. This is correctly given as 44th year in the fourth and fifth numbers. A similar apparent anomaly is found in the sixth number, dated 1820, which has 44th year in the copyright entry; this is changed to 45th year in the seventh number. In considering the copyright entries, it should be remembered that July 4th came between the issuance of Parts I and II and Parts VI and VII, changing the "year of independence." The copyright entries in the second edition are the same as in the first, except in parts II and III, in which it is stated as the 44th year of independence. In the third edition (1822–23) the copyright entries on both numbers are given as the 44th year of independence.

In the first edition, the price is stated on the cover of Part I as 75¢; on Part II as 62½¢; we have, however, seen one copy of Part II with the price printed 50¢. On Part III there is a variation: we have seen several copies with the price given as 62½¢, but this has 75¢ written over in ink; we have seen one copy with 75¢ printed on the cover. During the printing of this number, an error in price was discovered, "after a few copies had been struck off" and the error was corrected by hand in the copies already printed, and the type re-set for the remainder. Whether any uncorrected copies were sold is not stated. Those copies with the written correction in ink are therefore the earlier issue of the first edition. Parts IV and V are priced 75¢ and Parts VI and VII, 87½¢. All outside back covers of the second edition are blank, except that of Part V, which carries an advertisement of *Knickerbocker.* Prices for the second edition are: Part I, 75¢; Part II, 62½¢; Parts III – V, 75¢; Parts VI – VII, 87½¢.

There were two editions of the *Sketch Book* in parts, and a third edition of at least the first three parts. These all differ in text. While there is a general consistency in the text of these editions, some variant copies have been found, more particularly of Part I, which contain part of the text of the first edition and part of that of the second.

The book was prepared for the press by Henry Brevoort; Irving was abroad at the time. Many believe, and it is possible, that he exercised editorial functions, and made changes in phraseology. It is almost certain that the printer changed the punctuation.

A perusal of the published correspondence between Irving and Brevoort establishes several facts:

1. That Irving directed certain word for word corrections in Part I, which are therefore identifiable; these are contained in his letters of July 28, 1819, and August 12, 1819; Brevoort refers to the first in his letter of September 9, 1819; Irving's instructions were not all followed carefully, as some of the changes were not made in the second edition;

2. That Irving later sent marked corrected copies of Parts I and II to Brevoort, of which there is no record beyond the text of the various editions; Brevoort acknowledges receipt of Irving's letter of September 21, 1819, containing these corrected copies, in his letter of November 9, 1819;

3. That both (1) and (2) were received by Brevoort after the first two Parts had been printed and after all of Part I and almost certainly all of Part II had been sold; Brevoort's letter of September 9, 1819 states this to be the condition at that date, and assures Irving that the corrections "*shall* be carefully inserted" (italics ours); this refers, of course, only to those in the letter of July 28, as the other letter (2) had not yet been written; obviously the corrections could only be made in a second edition;

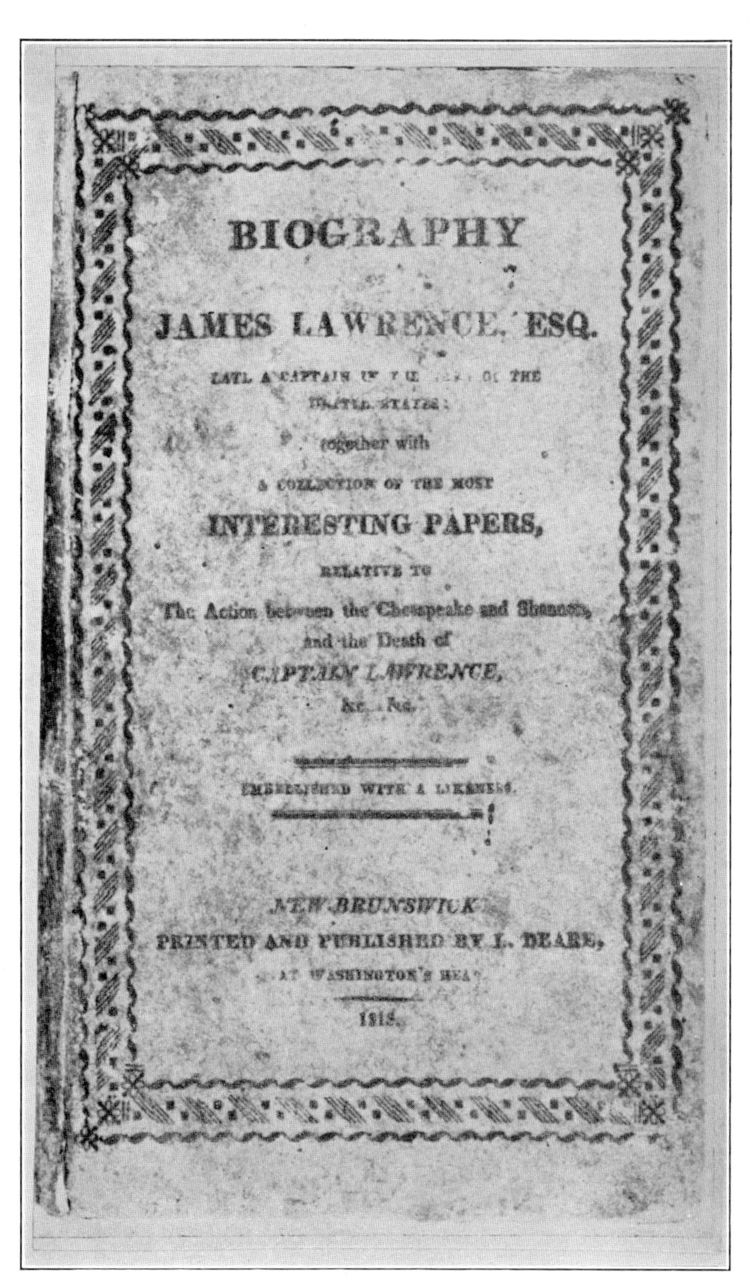

BIOGRAPHY

JAMES LAWRENCE, ESQ.

LATE A CAPTAIN IN THE [illegible] OF THE
UNITED STATES:
together with
A COLLECTION OF THE MOST
INTERESTING PAPERS,
RELATIVE TO
The Action between the Chesapeake and Shannon,
and the Death of
CAPTAIN LAWRENCE,
&c. &c.

EMBELLISHED WITH A LIKENESS.

NEW-BRUNSWICK:
PRINTED AND PUBLISHED BY L. DEARE,
AT WASHINGTON'S HEA[illegible]

181[illegible]

PLATE IV

Biography of James Lawrence. Front cover, from an uncut copy in boards, in the James Lawrence collection of Mrs. Michael Gavin.

4. That these corrections were made in the second edition (with some omissions, as a comparison of the letters and text will reveal);

5. That the correspondence makes no reference to any changes in text by Brevoort or the printer; on July 28, 1819, Irving wrote: "I have not discovered an error in the printing."

As one reads these letters, and notes the discussion of all the details of publication, it seems improbable that, had Brevoort made numerous or important revisions, either he or Irving would have failed to mention that fact.

Through the kindness of Mr. Boies Penrose, 2nd, of Devon, Pa., it was possible to consult the original manuscript of Part I (except "The Wife"), Part II (except "The Broken Heart") and Part III. This furnished rather more circumstantial proof of conclusions previously reached by conjecture; it coincided with the readings which had been taken as the first edition. Those copies bearing "Second edition" or "Third edition" on their cover show an increasing departure from the manuscript, and it is therefore assumed (where not otherwise verifiable) that those readings most nearly corresponding to the author's text are the earliest appearance.

It is thus possible to place the textual changes in Parts I and II in three classes:

(a) changes made after the printing of the first editions, identifiable by Irving's letters to Brevoort. These are indicated by a dagger (†); one of Irving's corrections, in Part I, p. 45, l. 8, was never made, as it is the same in the first four editions and in the revised edition. He may have gone back to his original form in the corrected copies which he later sent.

(b) changes where comparison has been made with the original manuscript; these were presumably made by Irving in the corrected copies of the first two numbers which he sent to Brevoort. These have been starred (*). In this category of cases there is the possibility that Brevoort and not Irving made any particular change, but it is our opinion that such cases, if they exist, are few. It must in honesty be admitted that copies exist which show some evidence of such editing, unless other explanation can be given; but it follows also that the copy most nearly corresponding with the original manuscript must have been printed before the alteration was made and be a prior variant of the first edition.

(c) variations where there was no comparison with the original manuscript — or, more properly, for which we did not find the original manuscript. In these cases it is assumed that the readings corresponding with the second edition are later variants.

The conclusions given here are based partly on facts found on examination of several copies of each edition, in the letters of Irving and Brevoort, and partly on comparison with the original manuscript, and on deductions from all these facts. If Brevoort has edited the text he would presumably have begun with the first pages. Variant copies should therefore differ throughout the earlier portions. Copies seen or described do not agree with this hypothesis. Furthermore, in the fairly large number of copies extant, there should be found a certain consistency among the variants; a number of copies should show the same differences; there should be a reasonable ratio between the variant and (for want of a better term) non-variant copies. Variants should be relatively numerous, whereas they appear to be unusual. It would not be unreasonable to expect to find a series of variants progressively departing from the first, i. e. from that agreeing most closely with the manuscript.

Many persons informed on the subject have been of the opinion that the binder assembled whatever signatures were at hand, that copies were sold of which part was the first and part the second edition. To us this seems highly doubtful as to Part I, and practically so for Part II, since the Brevoort letter of September 9, 1819, definitely states that *all copies of Part* I *had been sold,* and that of Part II only 150 copies remained unsold. The printing of the second edition of Part II was not begun until the end of 1819 or the early part of 1820; it is dated 1820.

If instances are found of such mixed signatures, they are explicable only on the assumption that at some time in the history of the particular copy at hand, some one endeavored to make a perfect copy from two or more imperfect ones, unaware that sheets of more than one edition were going into the make-up of the bound volume. We have seen or heard of a few such variants, but none was in original wrappers.

Below follow two comparative lists: the first a table of the non-textual variations (a summary of what has before been stated); and a somewhat detailed analysis of the textual changes. While the presence or absence of certain particular readings does not forever establish priority of a part, the comparisons described above would indicate that some variations (those marked with a dagger: †) may definitely be assigned to the edition indicated, while others may with reasonable certainty be accorded priority and assigned to the edition indicated. A partial list only is given; time and space prohibit any attempt at a definitive analysis.

It should be pointed out that the distinction here made is between EDITIONS and not ISSUES. If all copies of the *Sketch Book* existed with the original wrappers, there would be no need of such a list; such is not the case, and the only means of identifying an edition is by the internal evidence it presents.

SKETCH BOOK, continued

IMPORTANT NON-TEXTUAL VARIATIONS

First Edition:	Second Edition:
First five Parts paged consecutively; remainder separately.	First two Parts paged consecutively; remainder separately.
First five Parts dated 1819; remainder 1820.	First Part dated 1819; remainder 1820.
Part I: "Greenwich-street"; all others "Greenwich Street," on title-page.	All copies "Greenwich Street" on title-page.
Part I: Eleven dots in rule above date on title-page; ten in others.	Ten dots in rule above date on title-page in all copies.
Part I: p. 94, "Charles V"	Part I: verso of p. 93 blank; next page numbered 94; "Emperor Frederick." (In the *third edition* "der Rothbart" is added and this page is correctly numbered.)
Part II: French rule on title-page. Dotted rule on title-page.	Part II: Double rule on title-page. Rule on title-page.
Part III: Copyrighted in 43rd year of Independence.	Part III: Copyrighted in 44th year of Independence.
Parts VI & VII: Imprint on cover only, changed [see page 16].	No change.
Hyphen in street address on cover in all Parts.	No hyphen.

TEXTUAL VARIATIONS

PART I

Page	Line	First Edition	Page	Line	Second Edition
†iv,	3	that	iv,	3	which
†21,	6 *et seq*	I question whether Columbus, when he discovered the new world, felt a more delicious			None but those who have experienced it can imagine the delicious
†29,	11	or elysium			nor elysium
*30,	1–2	but which few men exercise, or this world would be	30,	1–2	and which, if generally exercised, would convert this world into (In the *third edition* there is a further change: "but which not many exercise, or this world")
†30,	9	or the quickening			or the quickening

Irving wrote to change this to "nor the quickening." One copy of the second edition has not this change, but shows other changes on the same page, which might indicate it was edited by Brevoort, were it not for the fact that it has all the non-textual variations of the second edition. It therefore seems probable that the change was forgotten until the third edition. It is also possible that the changes in the second edition were made only from the marked copies Irving had sent over, and that the changes in his letters were neglected. This page contains several variations and part is reset.

Page	Line	First Edition	Page	Line	Second Edition
41,	14	love	41,	14	love (In the *third edition* after the word "love" is added "at home")
†41,	--	Entire second sentence, occupying about half the page, is in the plural: "married men" etc.			Entire sentence is put in the singular: "a married man" etc.
45,	9	but feels	45,	9	but will feel (The *third edition* reads: "it feels")
	10	when even		10	if even (The *third edition* reads: "when even")
†80,	3	not one			none

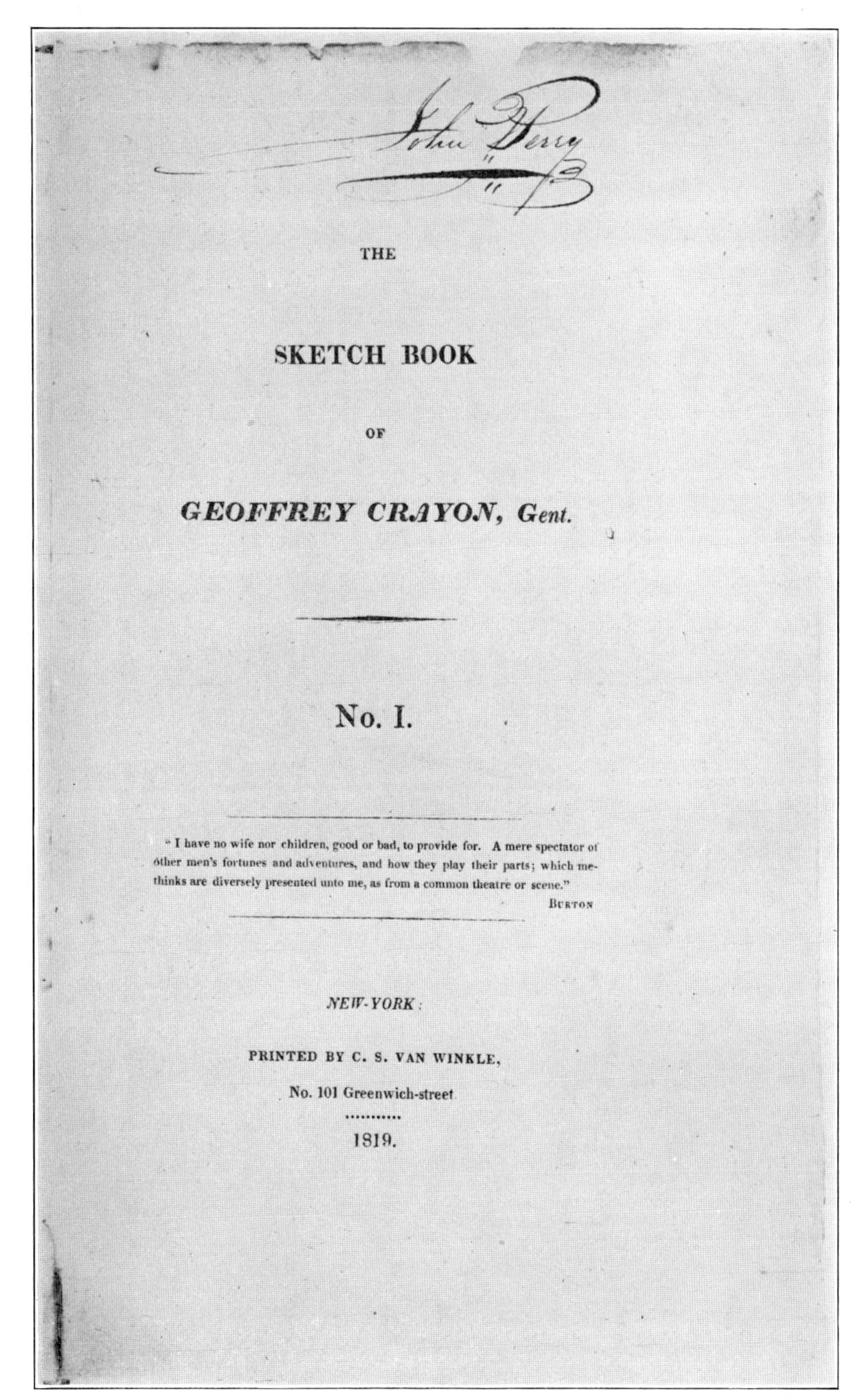

John Perry

THE

SKETCH BOOK

OF

GEOFFREY CRAYON, Gent.

No. I.

"I have no wife nor children, good or bad, to provide for. A mere spectator of other men's fortunes and adventures, and how they play their parts; which methinks are diversely presented unto me, as from a common theatre or scene."

BURTON

NEW-YORK:

PRINTED BY C. S. VAN WINKLE,

No. 101 Greenwich-street

....

1819.

PLATE V

Sketch Book, Part I. First edition title-page.

In The New York Public Library. (*Reduced*)

PART I, *continued*

First Edition Page	Line	First Edition	Second Edition Page	Line	Second Edition
†--	4	for his old			for his old (The *third edition* reads: "for an old")

Irving wrote to change this phrase to "not one of which he recognized for an old acquaintance." The second edition change from "not one" to "none" may have been done by Brevoort or through carelessness. The change to "for an old" does not appear until the third edition, for which the explanation for p. 30, 1. 9 [*q. v.*] may also hold. There are other textual changes on the page, and the last half is reset.

First Edition Page	Line	First Edition	Second Edition Page	Line	Second Edition
	12	that both he and the world around him were bewitched			he doubted whether both he and the world around him were not bewitched

PART II

(All items in Part II should be considered marked with an asterisk: *)

First Edition Page	Line	First Edition	Second Edition Page	Line	Second Edition
103,	6	But it has been	103,	6	It has been (The *third edition* reads: "It has also been")
	13	plea-		13	pleasure;
	14	it is left		14	her oracles concerning America are (The *third edition* reads "It has been left")
	17	America — to treat of a country		17	America. From such sources she draws her information respecting a country (The *third edition* reads: "From such sources she is content to receive her information respecting a country")
	19	where		19	in which
104,	18	gratifications	104,	18	personal gratifications
	--	last word on page is "servile"		--	last word on page is "painful"
105,	4	they	105,	4	which
	8	Or, perhaps, they have been		8	They may, perhaps, have been
	12	sagacity.		12	sagacity, and
	13	Where		13	where
	15	that indulges		15	which in-
	17	They		17	Such persons
	19	that (on line 20) he		19	"that he" omitted
	21	compete		21	contend
	22	and the shrewdness		22	and vie with the shrewdness
106,	1	Or, perhaps	106,	1	Perhaps
	5	and, accustomed		5	and, having been
	7	many strata below of society		7	below of good society
107,	5	test	107,	5	examine
	10	discrepancy		10	inaccuracy (The *third edition* reads: "any inaccuracy")
	17	Nay, what is worse, they		17	Nay, they
108,	6	woven	108,	6	wove
	7	wove		7	woven
	12	*second edition words omitted*		12	the combined misrepresentations of
	12	of England, united, cannot conceal		12	of England, if we could conceive of such great spirits united in so despicable an attempt, could not conceal (The *third edition* reads: "of England, united, if we could for a moment suppose their great minds stooping to so unworthy a combination, could not conceal")

SKETCH BOOK, continued

PART II, *continued*

First Edition			Second Edition		
Page	Line		Page	Line	
	16	but to		18	but also to
	21	and which		21	and
108,	--	*Paragraph ends on this page.*	108,	--	Page ends "acknowledged"
109,	12	do	109,	14	does
	21	provoked that rivalship		23	provoked rivalship
	22	that hostility		25	hostility
		page ends "present"			page ends "hos-"
123,	10	and cope with the people in all their conditions, and all their habits and humours.	123,	10	mingle with the people of all ranks and conditions, and become familiar with the habits and humours incident to each.
126,	8	a vast place	126,	8	An immense metropolis
130,	--	(last line) not even	130,	--	not even (In the *third edition* this reads: "even")
131,	1	can easily pervert	131,	1	can easily pervert, or ever entirely destroy (In the *third edition* this reads: "cannot easily pervert, and can never entirely destroy")
132,	10	as he does in the lower orders	132,	10	as he does when casually mingling with the lower orders (In the *third edition* this reads: "as he does when he casually mingles with")
		no signature number			The half-title "Rural life" has the signature number "16" at the bottom.

A variant copy of the second edition was discovered too late for inclusion in the table above. It has "Second Edition" on the wrapper; there follow some of the readings which correspond to the first edition text. (These citations refer to the reading listed above.) Page 103, lines 6, 13, 19; page 105, lines 4, 8, 17; page 106, lines 1, 5, 7 (of society); page 108, line 16; etc.

PART III

Page	Line	First Edition	Page	Line	Second Edition
175,	2	to Windsor, to visit the castle	5,	2	to Windsor castle
	3	It is a proud old pile, stretching its irregular walls and massive towers along the brow of a lofty ridge, waving its royal banner in the clouds, and looking down with a lordly air upon the surrounding world. It is a place that I love to visit, for it is full of storied and poetical associations.		3	It is a place full of storied and poetical associations. The very external aspect of the proud old pile is enough to inspire high thought; rearing its irregular walls and massive towers, like a mural crown round the brow of a lofty ridge — waving its royal banner in the clouds — and looking down with a lordly air upon the surrounding world.
	10	soft vernal kind that calls		12	voluptuous vernal kind which calls
	11	the latent		12	all the latent
176,	1	makes him quote poetry	6,	1	filling his mind with music, and causing him to quote poetry
	4	I felt myself most disposed to linger	6,	5–7	I passed with indifference by whole rows of warriors and statesmen, but lingered
	--	*Entire sentence of second issue omitted.*		10–14	and as I gazed. . . beauty.
	7	As I traversed		14	In traversing
	16–17	But the most interesting object of my visit was	7,	1–2	In this mood of mere poetical susceptibility I visited

Plate VI

Sketch Book, Part III. Top of first and second issue wrappers, showing the price change.
From the collection of the compiler.

PART III, *continued*

First Edition			Second Edition		
Page	Line		Page	Line	
177,	1	*Entire phrase of second issue omitted.*		8–9	It stands on a mound which elevates it above the other parts of the castle,
	2 *et seq*	a Gothic hall filled with weapons of various kinds, is still shown hanging against the wall, a suit of armour that once belonged to James.		11 *et seq*	which is a Gothic hall, furnished with weapons of various kinds and ages, I was shown a coat of armour hanging against the wall, which I was told had once belonged to the captive prince.
	5–6	From hence a staircase conducts		15–16	From hence I was conducted up a staircase
	7–8	with gobelin tapestry, which formed James's prison.		16–17	with storied tapestry, which formed his prison.
	--	*Entire phrase of second issue omitted.*		18–21	and the scene. . .and fiction.
202,	6	There was a supercilious	44,	5–6	but had a supercilious
203,	7	"They kept" begins a new paragraph.	45,	6	*No new paragraph.*
204,	--	Last line begins "attentive to."	47,	1	Same line is at beginning of page instead of end of preceding page.
205,	--	Second line from bottom begins "fields, chatting."	48,	--	Last two lines, page 205 in first issue, are the first two lines, page 48.
227,	9	but a picture	77,	9	but she informed me that a picture
240,	12	ont he site (In some copies this has been corrected).			

PART IV

Page	Line	First Edition	Page	Line	Second Edition
254,	15	Begins "self in old"	12,	15	Begins "like yourself in old" Remainder of page and following pages reset.
261,	--	Last line "would overwhelm the world with productions"	19,	--	Last line "would overstock the world"
285,	19–20	attachment of the brute;	43,	19–20	of mere animal attachment.
	20	for the love of the animal		20	The latter
	22	love of the human soul		22	the love that is seated in the soul
297,	4	Line ends "of."	55,	4	Line ends "of the." Rest of paragraph and the following pages reset.
319,	--	*Last line broken in one copy.*			
253,	2	harem; on page 254, line 16, the word is spelled "harams."			

PART V

Page	Line	First Edition	Page	Line	Second Edition
341,	4 *et seq*	They recal the fond picturings of an ideal state of things which I was wont to indulge	5,	12	They recal the pictures my fancy used to draw.
342,	1	those good old times.		17	those honest days of yore.
346,	17	in former days	10,	18	even in former days
430,	8	The hyphen after "esta" is omitted in several copies.			

PART VI

Page	Line	First Edition	Page	Line	Second Edition
38,	--	Last line begins "species"	38,		"order"
93,	9	"historian" on line 9.	93,	8–9	"histo-rian" hyphenated and on lines 8 and 9.
105,	9–10	"la-mentations" thus hyphenated.	105,	9-10	"lamenta-tions" thus hyphenated.

SKETCH BOOK, continued

PART VI, *continued*

First Edition			Second Edition		
Page	Line		Page	Line	
106,	16–17	"yeo-men" hyphenated and on two lines.	106,	16	"yeomen" ends line 16.
	18	"ever" is the first word.		17	"ever" is the last word of line 17; rest of paragraph reset.
114,	12	"comb" is the first word.	114,	11	"comb" is the last word of line 11; rest of paragraph reset.
115,	14	"when" is the first word.	115,	13	"when" is the last word of line 13; rest of paragraph reset.
116,	3–4	"Intelli-gence" thus hyphenated.	116,	3–4	"intelligence" ends line 3; rest of paragraph reset.
	--	"The old country wives" begins last line of page.		--	*Same words begin next to last line.*
117,	10	"schoolhouse" written as one word.	117,	9	"school-house."

PART VII

5,	2	(quotation) they resorte,	5,	2	there resorte
21,	20	notes, and piling	21,	20	notes, piling
33,	6	which lavish	33,	6	that lavish
	18	placid air		18	placid demure face (Lines 15, 16 and 17 reset for this change).
	19	some shrew		19	some pestilent shrew
34,	19	Walton	34,	19	Izaak
	--	*22 lines on page.*		--	*23 lines on page; last line is at the top of page 35 in the first issue.*
36,	10	reccollections	36,	10	recollections
41,	13–14	"thick-et" thus hyphenated.	41,	13	"thicket" at end of line is unhyphenated; next three lines reset.
	16–17	was the only		16–17	was almost the only
45,	3	*end of paragraph.*	45,	3	*no paragraph.*
	11	"lashed up" in quotation marks.		11	*Quotation marks omitted.*
	17–18	The Arethusa		17–18	*Omitted.*
46,	--	Last line *et seq:* The sentence beginning "The scene" ends the paragraph.	46,	--	*This sentence omitted; no new paragraph.*
					Pages 45–49 all partially reset.
64–65,		No paragraph ending at the end of page 64; "favour" is on page 65 and does not end the paragraph.	64,		"favour" ends both the paragraph and page 64.

There were three editions of Part I and Part II, each dated 1822; and Part III, dated 1823. We have also seen a copy dated 1824, marked "fourth American edition." It is evidently the first American appearance not in Parts. It is doubtful that there was ever any third edition of Parts IV – VII in separate form. An edition in two volumes was issued in 1836 by Carey, Lea & Blanchard, Philadelphia, and called "a new edition."

A revised edition was published in 1848, about October 1, by Putnam, as Vol. II of Irving's collected works. It has a new preface and contains minor variations in text from both the first American and the first English edition. Two articles from the *Analectic Magazine,* "Traits of Indian Character" and "Philip of Pokanoket" are included in all English editions and in all American editions beginning with the fourth, with considerable revision. An edition published in Paris in 1824 contained the preface and followed in the main the text of the English first edition. There were, however, some further revisions, most of which were kept in the revised edition of 1848. There was also an edition published in Dresden, in 1823.

THE / SKETCH BOOK / OF / GEOFFREY CRAYON, Gent. / (rule) / "I have no wife nor children, good or bad, to provide for. A mere / spectator of other men's fortunes and adventures, and how they play / their parts; which methinks are diversely presented unto me, as from / a common theatre or scene." / BURTON. / (rule) / (decorative design) / London: / JOHN MILLER, BURLINGTON ARCADE. / rule / 1820. /

Collation: Vol. I: Six pages of advertisements smaller than page size of book; (i), pre-title; (ii), printer's imprint; (iii), title; (iv), blank; (v) – vi, advertisement; (1), contents; (2), blank; (3) – 354, text [p. (3) – 8, THE AUTHOR'S ACCOUNT OF HIMSELF.]; 354, printer's imprint.

Vol. II: Flyleaf; (i), pre-title; (ii), printer's imprint; (iii), title-page. This has been entirely reset; it has no decorative design and after the quotation from Burton is as follows: (rule) / VOL. II. / (double rule) / LONDON: / JOHN MURRAY, ALBEMARLE-STREET. / (rule) / 1820.; (iv), blank; (v), dedication; (vi), blank; (vii), contents; (viii), blank; (1), sub-title; (2), blank; (3) – 419, text; 419, printer's imprint; (420), blank.

Page size: 8¾ x 5½ inches, probably trimmed.

Binding: Boards with paper labels. (We have not seen this copy.)

The first number only was reprinted in England in the *London Gazette* in 1819. The first complete English edition was published in 1820, in two volumes, the first by John Miller in February containing the first four numbers, and the second by John Murray in July, containing the last three numbers. The English edition has a different introduction from the American, contains many minor differences in text, and includes two articles reprinted, greatly revised, from the *Analectic Magazine,* "Traits of Indian Character" and "Philip of Pokanoket" not included in the first two American editions. Publication was begun by Miller, who failed after the first volume had been published. Murray continued publication of the first volume and also published the second volume.

Copies: The Library of Owen D. Young, Esq., as does that of Alfred L. Rose, Esq., contains a copy of first edition, all seven parts in the original covers uncut; the Henry E. Huntington Library contains first editions of all seven parts in original wrappers except that the front cover of No. 4 and both covers of No. 5 are missing. The Library of the American Antiquarian Society of Worcester, Mass., contains second editions of all parts in original covers. The collection of the compiler contains all Parts in original wrappers (except the first, which has the wrappers bound in), as follows: first edition: Parts I – III, V – VI; second edition: Parts II – V, VII; a copy of the seven Parts in two volumes, all first edition except Part I; various copies of second and third editions; and others.

The New York Public Library has the following: seven parts in two volumes, no covers, all first edition; Parts I–VI in one volume, no covers, of which Part VI is first edition and Parts I–V are second edition; Parts I–VI in one volume, no covers, of which Part II is first edition and Parts I, III–VI are second edition; Part I, first edition, in covers; Part I, first edition, without covers; Part II, first edition, in covers (torn); Part V, first edition, title-page and five leaves only; Part VII, second edition, without covers; Part VII, second edition, in covers.

The Yale University Library contains a set of seven Parts in wrappers, all first edition. In December, 1932, there was sold at the American Art Association-Anderson Galleries a set of seven Parts in wrappers, all first editions.

Manuscripts: The library of Mr. Boies Penrose, 2nd, of Devon, Pa., contains 232 p. of the ms. of this book, as follows:

1 p., Directions to printer; 1 p., Title-page; 2 p., Prospectus; 4 p., The Author's Account of Himself; 15 p., The Voyage; 37 p., Roscoe; 38 p., Rip Van Winkle; 1 p., Title-page to Part II; 20 p., English Writers on America; 17 p., Rural Life in England; 16 p., The Art of Book-Making; 20 p., A Royal Poet; 13 p., The Country Church; 17 p., The Widow and Her Son; 27 p., The Boar's Head Tavern, Eastcheap.

The text of this ms. is that of the first American edition.

The library of the compiler contains one page of the manuscript of this book.

BRACEBRIDGE HALL
1822

BRACEBRIDGE HALL, / OR / THE HUMOURISTS. / A Medley, / BY / GEOFFREY CRAYON, GENT. / (rule) / Under this cloud I walk, Gentlemen. I am a traveler, who, having /surveyed most of the terrestrial angles of this globe, am hither arri- / ved, to peruse this little spot. / CHRISTMAS ORDINARY. / (rule) / IN TWO

BRACEBRIDGE HALL, continued

VOLUMES. / VOL. I. [II.] (short double rule) / NEW-YORK: / PRINTED BY C. S. VAN WINKLE, / No. 101 Greenwich Street. / (short rule) / 1822.

Collation: Vol. I: Flyleaf; (1), pre-title; (2), blank; (3), title-page; (4), copyright notice; (5), contents; (6), blank; (7), half-title; (8), blank; (9) – 16, author's note: THE AUTHOR; (17) – 348, text; flyleaf.

Vol. II: Flyleaf; (1), pre-title; (2), blank; (3), title-page; (4), copyright notice; (5), contents; (6), blank; (7), half-title; (8), blank; (9) – 351, text; (352), blank.

Number of flyleaves is doubtful, as all copies examined may have been rebound.

Page size: 9⅛ x 5⅜ inches.

Binding: Copy in the Library of Congress is bound in gray or gray brown boards and is probably not original binding. We have seen the original binding catalogued as boards, calf and half roan.

Published May 21, 1822. Some bibliographies state that it was published in New York and Philadelphia, but Foley gives only New York. We have only seen or seen described copies with the New York imprint.

In the second American edition, 1822, the text is that of the first English edition (see *infra*). This edition also has on page (9), Vol. I, an "Advertisement" giving the reason for the changes. This "Advertisement" has the ear-marks of having been written by Irving.

An edition was published in Paris in 1823; there was a revised edition published by Putnam on December 1, 1848, as Vol. VI of Irving's collected works. It follows the text of the English first edition in most or all of the variations.

BRACEBRIDGE HALL; / OR, / THE HUMORISTS. / (short rule) / BY GEOFFREY CRAYON, GENT. / (short rule) / Under this cloud I walk, gentlemen; pardon my rude assault. I / am a traveller, who, having surveyed most of the terrestrial angles of / this globe, and hither arrived to peruse this little spot. / CHRISTMAS ORDINARY. / IN TWO VOLUMES. / VOL. I. [II.] / LONDON: / JOHN MURRAY, ALBEMARLE-STREET. / (short rule) / 1822.

Collation: Vol. I: (i), title-page; (ii), printer's imprint; (iii) – iv, contents; (1), half-title; (2), blank; (3) – 14, author's note: THE AUTHOR; (15) – 393, text; (394), printer's imprint; flyleaf.

Vol. II: (i), title-page; (ii), printer's imprint; (iii) – iv, contents; (1), half-title; (2), blank; (3) – 403, text; (404), printer's imprint.

Page size: 9 x 5⅝ inches, irregular untrimmed.

Binding: Boards with blue paper sides and brown paper spine with white paper label printed in black: BRACEBRIDGE / HALL / BY / GEOFFREY CRAYON / (rule) / TWO VOLS. -24*s*. / VOL. I. [II.].

Only 1,000 copies of the first American edition were printed. While the English edition was in press, Irving made numerous alterations and its text therefore differs widely from the American edition. The English edition appeared May 23, 1822.

There are three states of the London 1822 edition. (This information comes from Mr. Webster.)

First state: Vol. I: before publication one leaf, p. 93–94, was substituted; there is therefore no cancelled leaf at this point. Vol. II: the text ends on p. 403, and the imprint is in the middle of p. (404). Bound in blue boards.

Second state: Vol. I: a cancelled leaf at p. 93–94. Vol. II: the text ends on p. 404, 21 lines having been added on p. 402–403. The imprint is now at the bottom of p. 404. A copy has also been noted with p. 333 misnumbered 281 on the inner corner of the text. Bound in brown boards.

Third state: Vol. I: no cancelled leaf; the imprint on p. (ii) has "Davison" correctly instead of "Davsion" as previously. Vol. II: as in the second state. Bound in blue boards.

It is to be expected that as copies of these states are found, there will be variations in the binding.

Copies: The New York Public Library contains a copy of the first American edition, and three copies of the first English edition. The collection of the compiler contains two copies of the first American edition (one probably in original binding); two copies of the first English state in original binding, one copy of the third English state, rebacked, and others.

Manuscripts: The New York Public Library contains the manuscript of many sketches or portions thereof from this book, manuscript of the revised edition, except as noted: Horsemanship (complete); Love Symptoms (complete); Falconry (complete); Hawking (incomplete); Village Worthies (complete); The Schoolmaster (complete); The School (complete); A Village Politician (complete); The Rookery (complete); May Day (complete, first edition except for quotation at beginning); The Manuscript (complete); Travelling (incomplete, first edition); Lovers' Troubles (incomplete); The Historian (incomplete); and The Wedding (incomplete).

The Library of Columbia University contains the following manuscript material: The Author (incomplete, first edition); The Hall (incomplete, first edition); The Busy Man (complete, first edition); The Family Servants (complete, first edition); The Widow (complete, revised edition); The Lovers (complete, first edition); Family Relics (complete, first edition); An Old Soldier (complete, first edition); The Widow's Retinue (complete, first edition); Ready-money Jack (complete, first edition); Bachelors (incomplete, revised edition); The Stout Gentleman (incomplete, revised edition); Forest Trees (complete, first edition); A Literary Antiquary (incomplete, revised edition); The Farm House (incomplete, first edition); Falconry (incomplete, first edition); Hawking (incomplete, first edition); St. Mark's Eve (incomplete, partly first and partly revised edition); Gentility (complete, revised edition); The Student of Salamanca (incomplete, revised edition); A Bachelor's Confession (complete, revised edition); English Gravity (complete, revised edition); Gipsies (complete, revised edition); May-day Customs (incomplete, revised edition); Annette Delarbre (incomplete, revised edition); Travelling (incomplete, first edition); Dolph Heyliger (incomplete, revised edition); Lovers' Troubles (incomplete, second revised edition).

TALES OF A TRAVELLER
1824

TALES / OF / A TRAVELLER, / PART 1. [2, etc.] / (French rule) / BY GEOFFREY CRAYON, GENT. / AUTHOR OF "THE SKETCH BOOK," "BRACEBRIDGE HALL," / "KNICKERBOCKER'S NEW-YORK." &C. / (French rule) / *PHILADELPHIA:* / H. C. CAREY & I. LEA, CHESNUT-STREET. / (Dotted rule) / 1824.

Collation: Part 1: Cover; (1), title-page; (2), copyright entry and printer's imprint; (3), contents; (4), blank; (5), title of first part and poetical quotation; (6), blank; (7) – 8, [introduction]; (9) – 165, text; (166), blank; flyleaf; cover.

Part 2: Cover; (1), title-page; (2), copyright entry and printer's imprint; (3), contents; (4), blank; (5), title of second part and poetical quotation; (6), blank; (7) – 212, text; cover.

Part 3: Cover; four pages of advertisements; (1), title-page; (2), copyright entry and printer's imprint; (3), contents; (4), blank; (5), title of third part; (6), blank; (7) – 135, text; (136), blank; cover.

Part 4: Cover; flyleaf; (1), title-page; (2), copyright entry and printer's imprint; (3), contents; (4), blank; (5), title of fourth part and poetical quotation; (6), blank; (7) – 161, text; (162), blank; flyleaf; cover.

Page size: 9¼ x 5¾ inches.

Binding: Brown paper covers. Covers are imprinted same as title-pages, but printed matter is enclosed in double rule.

Published in New York and Philadelphia in four parts appearing respectively August 24, September 7, September 25, and October 9, 1824.

An edition was published by L. Baudry, Paris, in 1824, in two volumes. The second American edition was published in 1825. A revised edition was published by Putnam in March, 1849, as Vol. VII of Irving's collected works. All three of these editions carry the introductory note as in the English edition (see *infra*), and the first two follow the text in all points compared.

The *first state* of Part 2 has on p. 99, l. 13, "at housand." In the *second state* this is correctly "a thousand."

TALES / OF / A TRAVELLER. / (rule) / BY GEOFFREY CRAYON, GENT. / (rule) / I am neither your minotaure, nor your centaure, nor your / satyr, nor your hyæna, nor your babion, but your meer tra- / veller, believe me. / BEN JONSON. / IN TWO VOLUMES. / VOL. I. [II.] / LONDON: / JOHN MURRAY, ALBEMARLE-STREET. / (short rule) / 1824.

Collation: Vol. I: (i), pre-title; (ii), printer's imprint; (iii), title-page; (iv), blank; (v) – xiv, TO THE READER; (xv) – xvi, contents; (1), sub-title: PART I / STRANGE STORIES [etc.]; (2), blank; (3) – 364, text; 364, printer's imprint. (Text includes half-titles mentioning the parts and individual tales.)

Vol. II: (i), pre-title; (ii), printer's imprint; (iii), title-page; (iv), blank; (v) – vi, contents; (1), sub-title: PART II / CONTINUED. / BUCKTHORNE / AND HIS FRIENDS.; (2), blank; (3) – 394, text; (395), blank (see *infra*); (396), printer's imprint.

TALES OF A TRAVELLER, continued

The *second state* contains a "notice" on p. (395) referring to "spurious" editions of Irving's work. Since its subject matter is such that, once having appeared, it would remain, copies containing the notice would seem to be the *second state* of the first edition.

Page size: 8⅞ x 5½ inches, irregular untrimmed.

Binding: Gray-brown boards and paper backs, some same color, some with green cloth spine; paper labels, printed in black; (rule) / TALES / OF A / TRAVELLER / (rule) / VOL. I. [II.] / (rule) / 24*s* / (rule).

The English edition was published August 25, 1824. Its introductory note, "To the reader" is not included in the first American edition. The text varies from that of the American edition.

Copies: The New York Public Library contains three copies of the first American edition, and one of the first English edition. The Huntington Library contains an uncut copy of the four parts in original wrappers.

The library of the American Antiquarian Society contains a set of the four parts in original wrappers.

The collection of the compiler contains a complete set of the first American edition, two copies of the first, and one of the second state of the English edition, and sundry volumes. The library of Dr. William G. Braislin contains a copy of the four parts of the American edition, in original wrappers, uncut, with Part 2 in the second state.

Manuscripts: The Huntington Library contains 185 pages of the manuscript of this book (HM 3183).

The New York Public Library contains one page of the manuscript of this book.

LETTERS OF JONATHAN OLDSTYLE
1824

LETTERS / OF / JONATHAN OLDSTYLE, GENT. / BY THE AUTHOR OF / THE SKETCH BOOK. / WITH A / BIOGRAPHICAL NOTICE. / (ornament) / New-York: / PUBLISHED BY WILLIAM H. CLAYTON. / Clayton & Van Norden, Printers. / (rule) / 1824.

Collation: Cover; (i), title-page; (ii), copyright notice; (iii) – x, Biographical notice; (3), half-title; (4), blank; (5) – 67, text; (68), blank; cover.

Page size: 9⅛ x 5¾ inches, irregular untrimmed.

Binding: Brown paper cover. Double-rule box, in which is printed: Price 50 Cents / (double rule) / LETTERS / OF / JONATHAN OLDSTYLE, GENT. / BY THE AUTHOR OF / THE SKETCH BOOK. / WRITTEN IN 1802. / New-York: / CLAYTON & VAN NORDEN, PRINTERS, / No. 64 Pine-street. / (short rule) / 1824.

In the fall of 1802 Irving wrote a series of nine letters under the above title, for the *Morning Chronicle* (a periodical edited and published by Peter Irving). They appeared in the following issues: no. 39, November 15, 1802, third page; no. 44, November 20, 1802, second page; no. 53, December 1, 1802, second and third pages; no. 56, December 4, 1802, second and third pages; no. 62, December 11, 1802, third page; no. 91, January 17, 1803, second page; no. 96, January 22, 1803, second page; no. 110, February 8, 1803, second page; no. 173, April 23, 1803, second and third pages. The pages of the *Morning Chronicle* are unnumbered, hence reference is given in this form. There were also two letters addressed to Jonathan Oldstyle, one signed "Philo Dramaticus" in the issue of February 1, 1803, and one signed, "Q-z" in the issue of June 7, 1803. According to a note in *Spanish Papers* Irving wrote only nine letters, among which these are not included, and there seems to be no reason to attribute them to Irving. The fourth letter, as reprinted in *Spanish Papers* in the 1866 and subsequent editions is incorrectly dated December 3, 1802. It was published in the issue of Dec. 4, 1802.

All but the first of these letters and the first paragraph of the second letter (i. e., the last eight letters) were reprinted, shortly after their appearance, in the *Chronicle Express,* New York, a semi-weekly periodical also edited and published by Peter Irving, in the numbers dated November 25, December 2, 6, 13, 1802, January 20, 24, February 10, and April 25, 1803.

There is a set of the *Chronicle Express* in the library of Mr. George S. Hellman. It contains nos. 1 to 116, November 25, 1802, to January 1, 1804, inclusive, and is probably the only complete file in existence, though occasionally single issues may be found. This copy was the property of Peter Irving and contains numerous corrections and notes in his hand. It is interesting to note that the first number contains the translation by Dr. Samuel Latham Mitchill of an Italian poem. Dr. Mitchill was the author of a book entitled *The Picture of New York. Knickerbocker's History of New York* was probably intended originally as a burlesque upon Dr. Mitchill's book.

A pirated edition of these letters appeared in 1824 as above. In this edition the first letter and the first paragraph of the second letter are omitted. The letters are numbered I to VIII, which thus should be II to IX. They are undated. In Vol. II of *Spanish and Miscellaneous Papers* published by G. P. Putnam, 1866, are published the first five of these letters, correctly numbered and dated, except as noted above.

LETTERS / OF / JONATHAN OLDSTYLE, GENT. / BY THE AUTHOR OF / THE SKETCH BOOK / WITH A / Biographical Notice. / (double rule) / LONDON: / EFFINGHAM WILSON, ROYAL EXCHANGE. / (rule) / 1824.

Collation: Cover; (i), title-page; (ii), printer's imprint; (iii) – x, BIOGRAPHICAL NOTICE; (1), half-title; (2), blank; (3) – 68, text; 68, printer's imprint; flyleaf.

Page size: 8⅝ x 5¾ inches.

Binding: Gray-brown paper wrappers, without lettering.

The *Spanish and Miscellaneous Papers* was published in England by Bell and Daldy, 1867, under the title *Biographies and Miscellaneous Papers.* It contains these Letters as in the American edition of the book.

Copies: The New York Public Library contains four copies of the first American (of which one is in wrappers, uncut), and one of the first English edition. There is a copy of the *Morning Chronicle* in the library of the New York Historical Society. The library of the Rev. Dr. Terry, The Henry E. Huntington Library, the library of Owen D. Young, Esq., each contains a copy of the first American edition, uncut, with the original wrappers. The collection of the compiler contains copies of both the first American and the first English edition in the original wrappers, uncut; one rebound copy, first American edition.

LIFE AND VOYAGES OF CHRISTOPHER COLUMBUS 1828

A / HISTORY / OF THE / LIFE AND VOYAGES / OF / CHRISTOPHER COLUMBUS. / (rule) / BY WASHINGTON IRVING. / (rule) / Venient annis secula seris, / Quibus Oceanus vincula rerum / Laxet, et ingens pateat tellus, / Tiphysque novus detegat orbes, / Nec sit terris ultima Thule. — *Seneca. Medea.* / (rule) / IN THREE VOLUMES. / VOL. I. [II., etc.] / (heavy rule) / G. & C. CARVILL, 108 BROADWAY, NEW-YORK. / (short rule) / 1828.

Collation: Vol. I: Flyleaf; (i), pre-title; (ii), blank; folded map; (some copies have the map before the pre-title); (iii), title-page; (iv), copyright notice and printer's imprint; (v) – xi, PREFACE; (xii), blank; (xiii) – xvi, contents; (1) – 399, text; (400), blank; flyleaf.

Vol. II: Flyleaf; (i), pre-title; (ii), blank; (iii), title-page; (iv), copyright notice and printer's imprint; (v) – viii, contents; (9) – 367, text; (368), blank; flyleaf.

Vol. III: Flyleaf; (i), pre-title; (ii), blank; (iii), title-page; (iv), copyright notice; (v) – viii, contents; (13) – 420, text; two flyleaves.

Page size: 9⅛ x 5¾ inches, irregular untrimmed.

Binding: Tan boards with red-brown cloth spine. White paper label printed in black: (double rule) / IRVING'S / LIFE / AND / VOYAGES / OF / COLUMBUS. / (rule) / VOL. I. [II., etc.] / (double rule).

Apparently published in February somewhat after the publication of the English edition. The second American edition, published in 1829, contained additional matter. A "Revised and Corrected Edition," copyright 1831, differs from both the English and American first editions. A revised edition was published by Putnam in three volumes, including *Voyages of the Companions of Columbus,* the first volume in 1848, the second in January, 1849, the third in February, 1849, as Vols. III, IV and V, of Irving's collected works. Vols. II and III contain folded maps different from those in the first edition. In Vols. I and II, in the first issue of this edition, a slip is inserted before the title-page containing a publisher's note, and the advertisements at the back are dated November, 1848. Later issues lack the inserted slip and the advertisements are undated. The advertisements in Vol. III are undated in both first and later issues. The preface contains additional matter, largely in the postscript, and the text differs from that of all preceding editions.

An abridgment in one volume was published in the United States in 1829. It contained an "advertisement" by Washington Irving not in the first edition. A revised edition of this abridgment

LIFE OF COLUMBUS, continued

was published in New York, 1831, omitting the "advertisement" and containing many changes and additions. It follows the text of the English 1830 abridgment, but does not contain the plates which appeared with the English edition. An edition, published in 1834, "abridged and arranged by the author, expressly for the use of schools," differs considerably in text from both of these. Another edition of the abridgment, n. d., copyright 1839, contains additional matter from this and other of Irving's works, and some evidently written for or by the publishers. This edition was apparently issued for school use and does not appear to contain any new matter or revisions by Irving.

Pierre Irving's *Life and Letters of Washington Irving* speaks of an octavo edition of this book "to range with Prescott's works," of which about two hundred and fifty copies were sold. No date is given for this edition, but as Irving's "Columbus" antedated all of Prescott's important works, it is evident that this does not refer to the first edition. There was also an edition published by Galignani, Paris, 1828, with paper covers, in four volumes with two maps. It follows the text of the first English edition.

A / HISTORY / OF THE / LIFE AND VOYAGES / OF / CHRISTOPHER COLUMBUS. / BY / WASHINGTON IRVING. / Venient annis / Sæcula seris, quibus Oceanus / Vincula rerum laxet, et ingens / Pateat tellus, Typhisque novos / Detegat Orbes, nec sit terris / Ultima Thule. / *Seneca, Medea.* / IN FOUR VOLUMES. / VOL. I. [II., etc.] / LONDON: / JOHN MURRAY, ALBEMARLE-STREET. / (rule) / MDCCCXXVIII.

Collation: Vol. I: (i) pre-title; (ii), printer's imprint on reverse; (i), title-page; (ii), blank; (iii) – viii, PREFACE; (i), half-title; (ii), blank; (ix) – xii, contents; (1) – 473, text; (474), blank, (475), printer's imprint; (476), blank.

Vol. II: (i), pre-title; (ii), printer's imprint; (iii), title-page; (iv), blank; (v) – viii, contents; (1) – 490, text; (491), printer's imprint; (492), blank.

Vol. III: (i), pre-title; (ii), printer's imprint; (iii), title-page; (iv), blank; (v) – viii, contents; (1) – 413, text; (414), printer's imprint.

Vol. IV: (i), pre-title; (ii), printer's imprint; (iii), title-page; (iv), blank; (v) – vii, contents; (viii), blank; (1) – 439, text; (440), blank; (441) – 489, index; (490), blank (491), blank; (492), printer's imprint.

Page size: 8⅞ x 5⅝ inches.

Binding: The following descriptions and comparisons are given to a considerable extent from information received in the first instance from Mr. F. D. Webster of Tunbridge Wells, England. They have been checked, and amplified from six copies of the book in the collection of the compiler.

The four volumes of the book contain two large folding maps different from those in the American edition. These apparently were placed somewhat at random. We have seen them both in the front of volume one, in the fronts of volumes one and two, in the front and back of volume one and in volumes three and four. (This last was in a copy which may have been rebound.) When placed in the front they may be inserted any where before the text. At this period especially, publishers frequently exchanged books in sheets and bound them in their own style. This may account for the variety in bindings, location of maps, and appearance of copies which vary from the issues described. (This information comes from Mr. Webster.)

There were at least three issues of this book varying in binding and otherwise.

First Issue

Vols. 1 and 2 are without the colon (:) after London in imprint on verso of half-title. Vols. 3 and 4 have the colon.

Vol. 1, p. 335. 33 is in numerals of a different font from the 5.

Vol. 2, p. 198, the 8 is in a smaller font of type than the other numerals; p. 490 is misnumbered 460.

Vol. 3. Imprint is on page (414); p. 374, the 7 in numeral is in larger font; p. 385–400, all numerals are in larger font than in rest of the volume.

Vol. 4, p. 428 is misnumbered 423. In the numerals of this volume in all copies of all issues that we have seen, two, possibly three, different fonts and sizes of type were used without any semblance of regularity from page to page, varied sizes frequently appearing in the same number. It is obviously impracticable to set out a description of every numeral of every issue, but an examination of some hundred or so pages of each copy disclosed a consistent variation between the first two issues and the third. In these two issues the following page numerals are small: 18, 2 in 26, 7 in 70, 76, 99; the following page numerals are large: 19, 9 in 89, 9 in 90, 7 in 257,

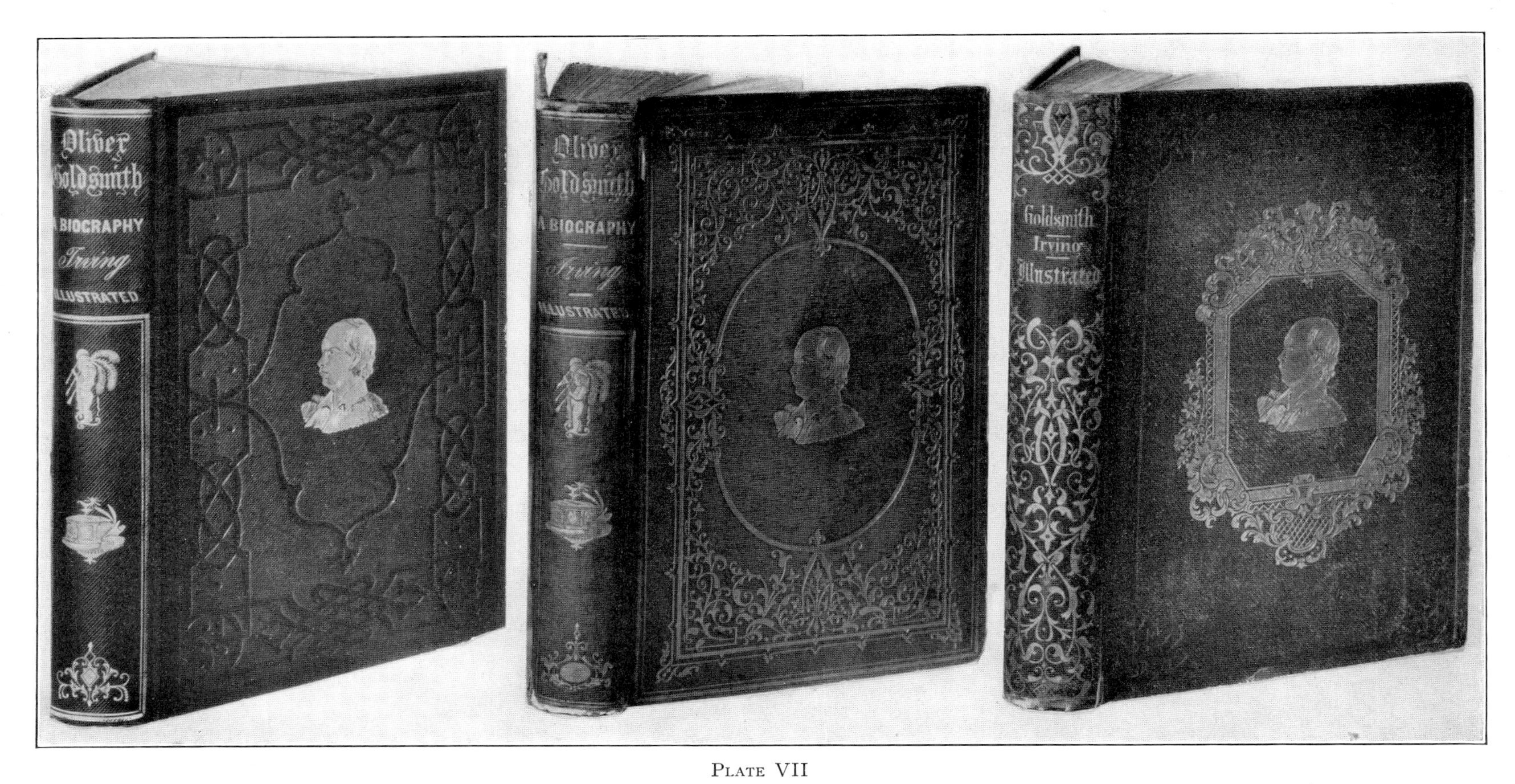

PLATE VII

Oliver Goldsmith. Three variant bindings: *left,* dark blue ribbed cloth, from the collection of Dr. William G. Braislin; *center,* red pebbled cloth, and, *right,* light blue pebbled cloth, from the collection of the compiler. (*Reduced*) The collection of Carroll A. Wilson, Esq., contains a copy in green pebbled cloth, which duplicates the stamping of the red copy in the *center,* above. [See also page 38.]

the 6's and 9 in pages 261 to 269 inclusive, 7 in 278, 79 in 279. The following bindings exist for this issue:

Gray-green boards, maroon cloth backstrips, paper labels. Gray-blue cloth, paper labels. Gray boards, figured green cloth backstrips, paper labels. Dark brown figured cloth, gilt lettered on spine, yellow end papers.

SECOND ISSUE

Vol. 2, p. 490 is correctly numbered. In all other points this issue is the same as the first, except the binding given as gray boards, paper labels. We have seen a copy (showing some evidence of being rebound though uncut), which coincides with this except that the binding is maroon cloth with black leather labels, printed in gold: (upper label) LIFE & / VOYAGES OF / COLUMBUS (lower label) VOL. / I. [II.]; and another copy in blue boards, gray paper backstrip and paper labels, coinciding with this except that in Vol. 1, p. 335, the numerals were all in the same font. In some copies Vol. 3, p. 167, is misnumbered 16.

THIRD ISSUE

Vols. 1 and 2 have a colon (:) after London in imprint on verso of half titles.

Vol. 1, p. 322 is misnumbered 232 (see *infra*); p. 335 all numerals are in the same font.

Vol. 2, p. 198 (see *infra*); p. 490 is correctly numbered.

Vol. 3, p. 374, the numeral 7 is in the same font as the others. Contents, pages VI to VIII, numerals are much larger than those used in previous issues; p. 78 is misnumbered 87. The imprint at end of the volume is on page (415), pages (414) and (416) being blank. p. 60 may be found with or without numerals.

Vol. 4, p. 428 is correctly numbered. Mr. Webster states, "practically the whole of the page numbering in this volume have been altered to smaller and more uniform figures." We have, however, found smaller and larger used indiscriminately, but find the following uniform variations in page numerals from the first two issues: the following numerals are smaller: 9 in 89, 9 in 90; both numerals are small and of the same size on pages 19, 26, 257, 278, 279; on pages 261 to 269 inclusive only the 6 in 260 is larger: the following numerals are larger: 18, 7 in 70, 76, 99. The following are the bindings: Blue boards, gray paper backstrips, paper labels. Blue boards, brown roan backstrips, paper labels.

We have seen a copy in gray-brown boards, red cloth backstrip, paper labels, and one in gray boards and backstrip (paper on the side and back all one piece), paper labels. In this last copy, Vol. 1, p. 332, is correctly numbered and the contents, (IX) to XII are placed before (III). and in Vol. 2, p. 198, 98 is in larger numerals. We have also seen a rebound copy of this issue which in Vol. 2, p. 198, all the numerals were the same size.

In all copies with paper labels, the labels are white paper printed in black: (rule) / LIFE / AND / VOYAGES / OF / COLUMBUS. / BY / WASHINGTON IRVING. / (short rule) / IN FOUR VOLS. / VOL. I. [II., etc.] / (short rule) / £2 2s. / (rule).

From the foregoing it seems probable that binding should not be taken as a determining factor of issue. Indeed we have been told of bindings different from all of those described. Copies coinciding with the other variances cited may however be placed as to issue with reasonable certainty, but it is obvious that copies exist which, while resembling a certain issue in general, may differ in one or two points from the description thereof.

There are slight differences between the texts of the English and American first editions.

The first English abridgment was published by John Murray in 1830; the advertisements in it are dated January, 1830. The text is that of the 1831 American edition.

Copies: The New York Public Library contains one complete copy of the first American edition, Vols. II and III of the first American edition, and three copies of the first English edition. The collection of the compiler contains a copy of the first American edition, six copies of the first English edition (all three issues) four of them in original bindings; and sundry others.

Manuscripts: Mr. B. J. Beyer has in his possession a set of printed sheets with several thousand annotations and 116 pages of ms. laid in, which together make the text for the revised edition of 1848–1849.

The library of Mr. Carl H. Pforzheimer contains the 1600-page printer's manuscript of the English edition, of which 52 pages and numerous notes are in Irving's hand.

At the American Art Association-Anderson Galleries, Inc., there was sold, on November 10, 1932, 204 pages of ms. notes for this book. These notes consisted of extracts from innumerable sources of information, used as a foundation work for *Columbus;* a number of rough drafts, and in a few instances finished drafts. Not all the notes were in Irving's hand nor in English; many notes were included which did not appear in final publication.

CONQUEST OF GRANADA

1829

A / CHRONICLE / OF THE / CONQUEST OF GRANADA. / (rule) / BY / FRAY ANTONIO AGAPIDA. / (rule) / IN TWO VOLUMES. / VOL. I. [II.] / (French rule) / Philadelphia: / CAREY, LEA & CAREY — CHESNUT-STREET. / (dotted rule) / 1829.

Collation: Vol. I: Flyleaf; two pages of advertisements, the second of which is numbered 2; (iii), title-page; (iv), copyright entry; (v) – viii, contents; (ix) – xii, introduction; (13) – 311, text; (312), blank; four pages of advertisements; flyleaf.

Vol. II: Flyleaf; (i), title-page; (ii), copyright entry; (iii) – vi, contents; (7) – 319, text and appendix; (320), blank; flyleaf.

Page size: 7¾ x 4½ inches, irregular untrimmed.

Binding: Boards with red cloth spine and white paper label printed in black: (double rule) / IRVING'S / CONQUEST / OF / GRANADA, / IN 2 VOLS. / (short rule) / VOL. I. [II.] / (double rule).

There was also a large-paper edition, identical with the above, except that the page size was 9 3/16 x 5⅞ inches. Some copies of this have two pages of advertisements in the front of Vol. I the same as those in the front of Vol. I of the smaller paper edition, and four pages of advertisements in the front of Vol. II, unnumbered and undated. Other copies have the four pages of advertisements at the end of Vol. I, and no advertisements at the end of Vol. II. Copies have been mentioned with the advertisements located as first stated, but those in Vol. II differently worded.

Published April 20, 1829. A revised edition was published by Putnam as Vol. XIV of the collected edition of Irving's works in 1850. It contained some additional matter in the text and an additional note in the introduction, which included much of the same material as an article by Irving in the May and October, 1830, numbers of the *London Quarterly Review.* An edition was published by A. and W. Galignani, Paris, 1829, in two volumes. The text is that of the first English edition.

A / CHRONICLE / OF THE / CONQUEST OF GRANADA. / FROM THE MSS. OF FRAY ANTONIO AGAPIDA. / BY / WASHINGTON IRVING. / IN TWO VOLUMES. / VOL. I. [II.] / LONDON: / JOHN MURRAY, ALBEMARLE-STREET. / MDCCCXXIX.

Collation: Vol. I: (i), pre-title; (ii), printer's imprint; (iii), title-page; (iv), blank; (v) – ix, INTRODUCTION; (x), blank; (xi) – xv, contents; (xvi), blank; (1) – 407, text; (408), printer's imprint.

Vol. II: (i), title-page; (ii), printer's imprint; (iii) – viii, contents; (1) – 421, text and appendix; (422), printer's imprint; two pages of advertisements, second page dated February, 1829.

Page size: 8¾ x 5½ inches, irregular untrimmed.

Binding: Gray-brown boards, brown paper spines with white paper labels, printed in black: (rule) / A / CHRONICLE / OF THE / CONQUEST / OF / GRANADA / BY / WASHINGTON IRVING / (rule) IN TWO VOLS. / VOL. I. [II.] / (rule) / 24s. / (rule).

The English edition was published on May 23, 1829. The text differs materially from that of the American edition.

Copies: The New York Public Library contains one copy of the first American and one of the first English edition. The Pierpont Morgan Library and the collection of the compiler contain a large paper copy of the American first edition and there are also in the collection of the compiler copies of the first American and English editions, all in original binding.

Manuscripts: The Pierpont Morgan Library contains manuscript pages 207 to 1014 of this book, being page 4, chapter 19, volume 1 to end of published book, lacking pages 394, 722 and 723, and containing a few unnumbered pages. Pages 211 to 216 are apparently omitted from the numbering without a break in the text. The library of the Rev. Dr. Roderick Terry contains sixteen pages of manuscript, comprising pages 247 to 257, Vol. I. of this book. We were unable to compare this with the Morgan manuscript to determine whether it was a duplication, omission or possibly a portion of the manuscript of the revised version.

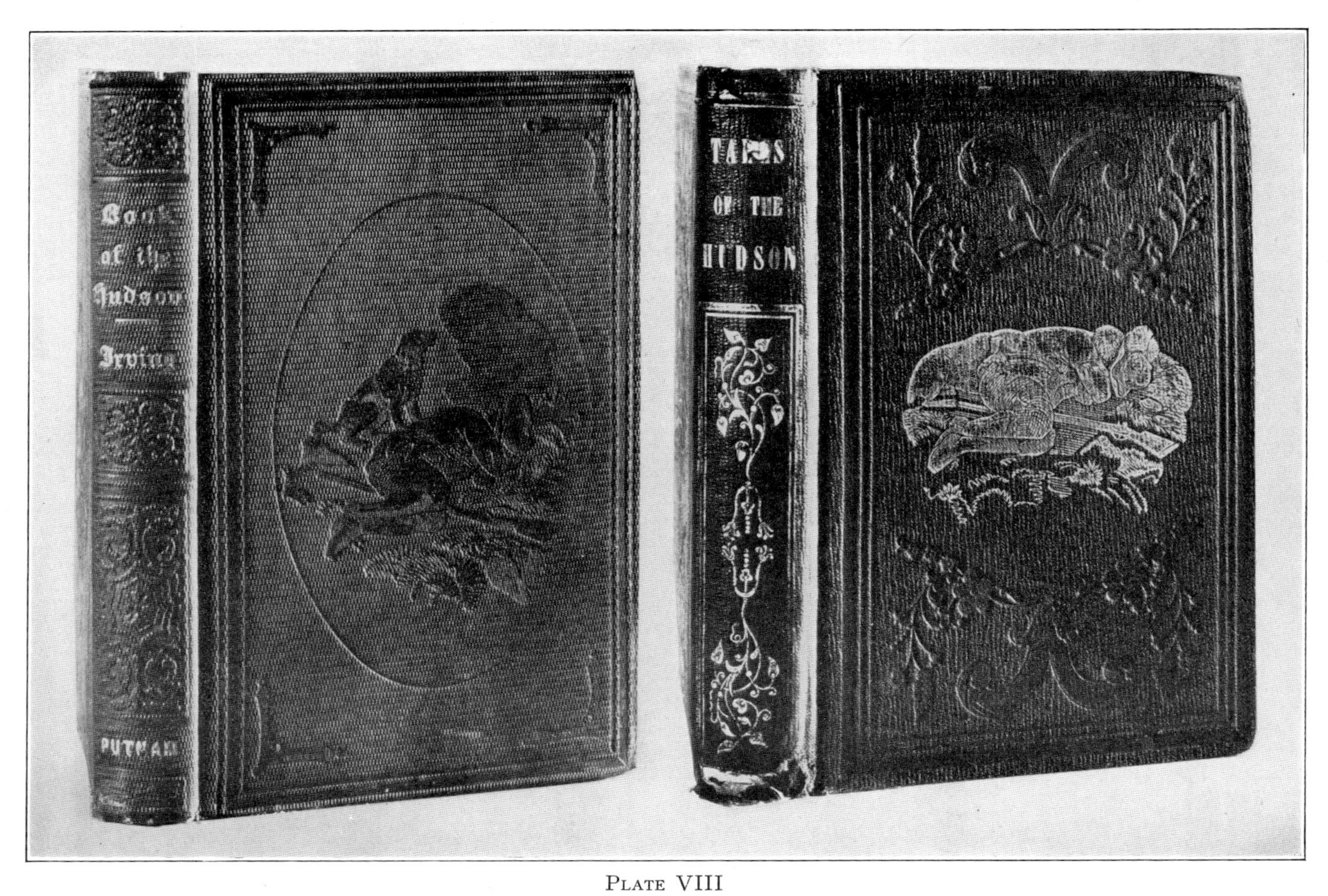

PLATE VIII

A Book of the Hudson, showing the bindings described in the collation, page 40. *Left,* Issue A; and, *right,* Issue B. (*Reduced*) In The New York Public Library. There are variations in these bindings and sheets. [See page 40.]

VOYAGES AND DISCOVERIES OF THE COMPANIONS OF COLUMBUS

1831

VOYAGES / AND / DISCOVERIES / OF / THE COMPANIONS OF COLUMBUS. / (short rule) / BY / WASHINGTON IRVING. / (short rule) / To declare my opinion herein, whatsoever hath heretofore been discovered by the famous tra- / vayles of Saturnus and Hercules, with such other whom the Antiquitie for their heroical /acts honoured as gods, seemeth but little and obscure, if it be compared to the victorious / labours of the Spanyards. *P. Martyr, Decad. III. c. 4. Lock's translation.* / (rule) / Philadelphia: / CAREY AND LEA — CHESNUT STREET. / 1831.

Collation: Flyleaf; (1), title-page; (2), copyright entry and printer's imprint; (3) – 7, INTRODUCTION; (8), blank; (9) – 350, text; two pages of advertisements; flyleaf.

Page size: 9 x 5¾ inches, irregular untrimmed.

Binding: Tan boards with red cloth spine. White paper label, printed in black: (double rule) / VOYAGES / AND / DISCOVERIES / OF THE / COMPANIONS / OF / COLUMBUS. / (short rule) / BY / *W. Irving.* / (double rule) /

We have seen copies, 9 1/16 x 5⅞ inches, with four pages of advertisements before the title-page, but there appears to be no indication which, if either, is the prior publication. These advertisements have a page size of 7¾ x 4⅜ inches, and are dated February, 1830. This also exists, size 9 3/16 x 5¾, with four pages of advertisements in front and two pages in back. At this period publishers were apt to insert advertisements rather at random, and probably copies in the same printing differed from each other in this respect. The page size of the advertisements in this case indicates that those before the title-page were not intended specially for this book.

The book was published unchanged as the third volume of the 1831 edition of the *Life and Voyages of Columbus,* i. e., it was numbered on the back Vol. III, but the title, both on the back and on the title-page, is given as *Life and Voyages of the Companions of Columbus.* A revised edition was published by Putnam in February, 1849, as Vol. III of *The Life and Voyages of Columbus* in the collected edition of Irving's works (Vol. V of the collected edition). It follows in text the first English edition in the main, but there are some revisions, changes, and many additions to the appendix.

This book was also published by A. & W. Galignani, Paris, 1831.

VOYAGES AND DISCOVERIES / OF THE / COMPANIONS OF COLUMBUS. / (rule) / BY / WASHINGTON IRVING. / (Decorative design of shield and helmet) / LONDON: / JOHN MURRAY, ALBEMARLE STREET. / MDCCCXXXI.

Collation: Publisher's slip (advertisement), inserted before the end-paper; twelve pages of advertisements dated DECEMBER, MDCCCXXX, numbered (1) – 12; engraving, "The Convent of La Rabida"; (i), title-page; (ii), quotation from P. Martyr as on title-page of American edition, printer's imprint; (iii) – ix, INTRODUCTION; (x), blank; (xi) – xviii, contents; (1) – 337, text and appendix; 337, printer's imprint; (338), advertisement; folded map.

Page size: 6⅛ x 3⅞ inches, irregular untrimmed.

Binding: Tan cloth, printed in black on spine: (two double rules) / VOYAGES / OF THE / COMPANIONS / OF / COLUMBUS. / (short rule) / 5*s.* / (four double rules) / FAMILY / LIBRARY. / No. XVIII. / (double rule). On front cover in double-rule border: THE / FAMILY LIBRARY. / No. XVIII. / (short rule) VOYAGES / OF THE / COMPANIONS OF / COLUMBUS. / (short rule) / LONDON: / JOHN MURRAY, ALBEMARLE STREET. / MDCCCXXXI. / *Price five shillings.*; on the back cover a list of other volumes of the Family Library. Also published in a black embossed leather binding, gold stamped on the back: VOYAGES / AND / DISCOVERIES, and with yellow end-papers and without the publisher's slip or advertisements in the front of the book; smaller size, gilt edges. Page size: 5¾ x 3¾ inches. An English bookdealer states that it was also issued in brown cloth with gold lettering on the back.

VOYAGES OF COMPANIONS OF COLUMBUS, continued

The texts of the American and English editions differ slightly both in the introduction and in the main body of the narrative. The variations in the English text are mainly revisions in the interests of style and accuracy, and would therefore indicate that the English text is later.

Copies: The New York Public Library contains three copies of the first American, and one of the first English edition. The collection of the compiler contains two copies, first American edition (the two sizes mentioned in the text); and four first English, in tan cloth and black leather bindings.

THE ALHAMBRA
1832

THE / ALHAMBRA: / A SERIES / OF / TALES AND SKETCHES / OF / THE MOORS AND SPANIARDS. / (rule) / BY THE AUTHOR / OF / THE SKETCH BOOK. / (rule) / IN TWO VOLUMES. / VOL. I. [II.] / (double rule) / Philadelphia: / CAREY & LEA. / (short rule) / 1832.

Collation: Vol. I: Flyleaf; (i), title-page; (ii), copyright entry; (iii) – iv, DEDICATION; (13) – 234, text; (235), contents; (236), blank; thirty-six pages of advertisements of much smaller page size, apparently two or three booklets of advertisements; flyleaf.

Vol. II: Flyleaf; (1), title-page; (2), blank; (3), contents; (4), blank; (5) – 236, text; two flyleaves.

Page size: 7¾ x 4¾ inches, irregular untrimmed.

Binding: Tan boards with dark red or purple cloth spine, white paper label, printed in black: (double rule) / THE / ALHAMBRA. / BY THE AUTHOR / *of the* / SKETCH BOOK. / (short rule) / *In Two Volumes.* / VOL. I. [II.] / (double rule).

A revised edition was published by Putnam in 1850 as Vol. XIV of the revised edition of Irving's works, containing "many alterations and additions." An edition was issued in Paris in 1832 by Baudry. It follows the text of the English edition.

THE / ALHAMBRA. / BY GEOFFREY CRAYON, / AUTHOR OF "THE SKETCH BOOK," "BRACEBRIDGE HALL," / "TALES OF A TRAVELLER," &C. / IN TWO VOLUMES. / VOL. I. [II.] / LONDON: / HENRY COLBURN AND RICHARD BENTLEY, / NEW BURLINGTON STREET. / 1832.

Collation: Volume I: (i), pre-title; (ii), printer's imprint; (iii), title-page; (iv), blank; (v) - vi, dedicatory preface; (vii) – viii, contents; (1), sub-title; (2), blank; (3) – 333, text; 333, printer's imprint; (334), blank; flyleaf. The versos of the sub-titles are blank, and whenever the article ends on the right-hand page, the following left-hand page is left blank. All of these sub-title pages, blank pages and the first pages of the individual articles are unnumbered.

Volume II: (i), advertisements; (ii), blank; (iii), pre-title; (iv), printer's imprint (different from that in volume I); (v), title-page; (vi), blank; (vii), contents; (viii), blank; (1), sub-title; (2), blank; (3) – 299, text; (300), printer's imprint (different from that in volume I); four unnumbered pages of advertisements.

Page size: 8 15/16 x 5 ⅝ inches.

Binding: Dark gray boards, paper spines, paper labels, printed in black: (double rule) / THE / ALHAMBRA / BY / GEOFFREY CRAYON / (short rule) / Vol. I. [II.] / (double rule).

Another edition was issued in England by the same publishers, in the same year, page size: 7⅝ x 4⅝ inches, as given by one English dealer; according to another, the size is 7⅞ x 5 inches. The larger size is probably more accurate. In this edition, however, there are two titles, "Discipline," by Mrs. Brunton, and "The Prairie," by Cooper, listed in the advertisements at the end as numbers XVI and XVII respectively. These titles do not appear in the lists in the first edition which end with number XV. Page 148 is misprinted 184.

Copies: The New York Public Library contains one copy each of the first American and first English editions. The collection of the compiler contains copies of both English and American first editions in original bindings and a rebound copy of later English edition of the same year.

Manuscripts: The New York Public Library contains one page of the manuscript of this book.

PLATE IX

The Crayon Miscellany, No. 1, showing the two issues of the labels: *left,* the first issue; and, *right,* the second. In The New York Public Library.

THE CRAYON MISCELLANY
1835

1.

A TOUR ON THE PRAIRIES

(See Plate VII)

THE / CRAYON MISCELLANY. / (double rule) / BY THE AUTHOR OF THE SKETCH BOOK. / (double rule) / No. 1. / CONTAINING / A Tour on the Prairies. / (double rule) / Philadelphia: / CAREY, LEA, & BLANCHARD. / (dotted rule) / 1835.

Collation: Flyleaf; (i), title-page; (ii), copyright entry and printer's imprint; (iii), ADVERTISEMENT; (iv), blank; (v), half-title; (vi), copyright entry and printer's imprint; (vii) – xv, introduction; (xvi), blank; (17) – 274, text; (275) and (276), blank; flyleaf; several pages of advertisements. We have seen copies with twelve, twenty-four, and thirty-six pages of advertisements. (The advertisements in this and the following volume are undated and seem to have been inserted as convenient. The page termed title-page is a general title-page for all three volumes of the *Crayon Miscellany;* the page termed half-title relates only to the individual volume in which it appears.

Page size: 7 $^{1}/_{16}$ x 4 $^{5}/_{16}$ inches.

Binding: Blue cloth with white paper label on spine, printed in black: (double rule) / THE / CRAYON / MISCELLANY. / (short rule) / A / TOUR / ON THE / PRAIRIES. / BY THE AUTHOR OF / THE / Sketch Book. / (double rule). The American edition was published in April, 1835. The introduction is entirely different from and longer than the preface to the English edition. It expresses Irving's feelings of pleasure on returning to the United States. This was not contained in the English edition. This omission was one of the causes of the accusation made against Irving of being an Anglophile.

There were two different papers used in this volume, and two issues of the labels. Both textures of paper may be found with each label. White paper and dark-cream paper were used; the white paper has not been found in any other volumes of the *Miscellany;* the dark-cream paper is used throughout, so that the inference would be that the white paper was an earlier printing. The *second issue* label is larger and has single rules at top and bottom and reads / MISCELLANY / *No. 1 / etc.*

2.

ABBOTSFORD AND NEWSTEAD ABBEY

THE / CRAYON MISCELLANY. / (double rule) / BY THE AUTHOR OF THE SKETCH BOOK. / (double rule) / No. 2. / CONTAINING / Abbotsford / AND / Newstead Abbey. / (double rule) / PHILADELPHIA: / CAREY, LEA, AND BLANCHARD. / (dotted rule) / 1835.

Collation: Flyleaf; (1), title-page; (2), copyright entry and printer's imprint; (3), half-title; (4), blank; (5)–230, text; several pages of advertisements; flyleaf. We have seen copies with twenty-two, twenty-six, thirty-two, and thirty-six pages of advertisements. An unopened copy at the Yale University Library shows that the first ten pages of advertisements were an integral part of the last signature. This, with one complete signature (12 p.) would make the twenty-two pages of advertisements. It is probable that additional leaves or sections of signatures made up the other groups of advertisements.

Page size: 7 $^{1}/_{16}$ x 4 $^{5}/_{16}$ inches.

Binding: Blue cloth with white paper label on spine, printed in black: (double rule) / THE / CRAYON / MISCELLANY. / No. 2. / (rule) / ABBOTSFORD / AND / NEWSTEAD / ABBEY. / BY THE AUTHOR OF / THE / Sketch Book. / (double rule).

Copies also exist with the advertisements after the flyleaf; the collation would then be: (231)–(232), blank; several pages of advertisements.

In some copies page (4) repeats the entry and imprint on page (2). There is no evidence of priority.

The American edition was published May 30, 1835. The *Tour* and *Abbotsford* were published by Putnam in May, 1849, as Vol. IX of Irving's collected works. The text is that of the first American edition, but the introduction contains only the first few paragraphs as in the *Tour,* omitting the part which caused the controversy referred to above.

THE CRAYON MISCELLANY, continued

3.

LEGENDS OF THE CONQUEST OF SPAIN

THE / CRAYON MISCELLANY. / (double rule) / BY THE AUTHOR OF THE SKETCH BOOK. / (double rule) / No. 3. / CONTAINING / LEGENDS / Of the Conquest of Spain. / (double rule) / PHILADELPHIA: / CAREY, LEA & BLANCHARD. / 1835.

Collation: flyleaf; (i), blank; (ii), publisher's note regarding "BEAUTIES OF WASHINGTON IRVING" on verso; (i), title-page; (ii), copyright entry and printer's imprint; (iii), half-title; (iv), copyright entry and printer's imprint; (v) – ix, PREFACE; (x), blank; (11) – 276, text; eight pages of advertisements numbered (1) to 8.

Page size: 7 1/16 x 4 5/16 inches.

Binding: Blue cloth with white paper label on spine, printed in black: (double rule) / THE / CRAYON / MISCELLANY. / No. 3. / (rule) / LEGENDS / OF THE / CONQUEST / OF / SPAIN. / BY THE AUTHOR OF / THE / Sketch Book. / (double rule).

The American edition was published in October, 1835. Republished with additional collected and cognate material as Vol. I of *Spanish Papers* in 1866. These three books were also published by A. and W. Galignani, Paris, 1835. The text of *A Tour on the Prairies* is that of the first English edition.

The blank leaf (i) – (ii) may also be found after the title-page.

1.

A TOUR ON THE PRAIRIES

MISCELLANIES. / BY / THE AUTHOR OF "THE SKETCH-BOOK." / No. I. / CONTAINING / A TOUR ON THE PRAIRIES. / (rule) / LONDON: / JOHN MURRAY, ALBEMARLE STREET. / MDCCCXXXV.

Collation: (i), title-page; (ii), printer's imprint; (iii), half-title; (iv), blank; (v) – vi, PREFACE; (vii) – xiii, contents; (xiv), blank; (1) – 335, text; (336), printer's imprint. Title-pages and half-titles as in American edition.

Page size: 8 x 4⅞ inches, irregular untrimmed.

Binding: Boards covered in tan gray rough paper, same paper spine with white paper label printed in black: (double rule) / TOUR / ON THE / PRAIRIES. / BY / THE AUTHOR / OF THE / SKETCH BOOK. / (double rule).

The English edition was published in March, 1835. It varies slightly in text from the American edition and its preface is entirely different from the Introduction to the American edition.

2.

ABBOTSFORD AND NEWSTEAD ABBEY

MISCELLANIES. / BY / THE AUTHOR OF "THE SKETCH-BOOK." / No. II. / CONTAINING / ABBOTSFORD, AND NEWSTEAD ABBEY. / (rule) / LONDON: / JOHN MURRAY, ALBEMARLE STREET. / MDCCCXXXV.

Collation: (i), pre-title; (ii), printer's imprint; (iii), title-page; (iv), blank; (v), half-title; (vi), blank; (vii), contents; (viii), blank; (1), sub-title; (2), blank; (3) – 290, text; 290, printer's imprint.

Page size: 7¾ x 4⅞ inches, irregular untrimmed.

Binding: Tan gray rough paper boards, same paper spine with white paper label printed in black: (double rule) / ABBOTSFORD / AND / NEWSTEAD / ABBEY. / BY / THE AUTHOR / OF THE / SKETCH-BOOK. / (double rule).

The English edition was published May 1, 1835. It varies slightly in text from the American edition.

3.

LEGENDS OF THE CONQUEST OF SPAIN

MISCELLANIES. / BY / THE AUTHOR OF "THE SKETCH-BOOK." / No. III. / CONTAINING / LEGENDS OF THE CONQUEST OF SPAIN. / (rule) / LONDON: / JOHN MURRAY, ALBEMARLE STREET. / MDCCCXXXV.

Collation: (i), title-page; (ii), printer's imprint; (iii), half-title; (iv), blank; (v) – xi, PREFACE; (xii), blank; (xiii) – xviii, contents; (xix), sub-title; (xx), blank; (1) – 340, text; 340, printer's imprint.

Page size: 7¾ x 4⅞ inches, irregular untrimmed.

Binding: Gray boards, maroon cloth spine, with white paper label printed in black: (double rule) / LEGENDS / OF THE / CONQUEST / OF SPAIN. / BY / THE AUTHOR / OF THE / SKETCH BOOK. / (double rule).

The English edition was published in December, 1835. Its text is apparently identical with that of the American edition except that the publisher's note contained in the American edition is omitted.

Copies: The New York Public Library contains a complete copy, two copies of Vol. I, one of Vol. II, and one of Vol. III, of the first American edition; and a complete copy of the first English edition. The collection of the compiler contains all first American and English editions in original bindings, and sundry additional volumes.

Manuscripts: The New York Public Library contains one page of the manuscript of this book and two pages of corrected proof with author's manuscript additions, on the subject of mementoes of Boabdil.

ASTORIA
1836

ASTORIA, / OR / ANECDOTES OF AN ENTERPRISE / BEYOND THE / ROCKY MOUNTAINS. / BY WASHINGTON IRVING. / IN TWO VOLUMES. / VOL. I. [II.] / PHILADELPHIA: / CAREY, LEA, & BLANCHARD. / 1836.

Collation: Vol. I: Flyleaf; (1), title-page; (2), copyright entry and printer's imprint; (3) – 6, INTRODUCTION; (vii) – xii, contents; (13) – 285, text; (286), blank; flyleaf.

Vol. II: Flyleaf; folded map; (i), title-page; (ii), copyright entry and printer's imprint; (iii) – viii, contents; (9) – 279, text and appendix; (280), blank; 1 – 6; (7), advertisements; 8, publisher's memorandum regarding books advertised; flyleaf.

Page size: 8 $^{11}/_{16}$ x 5⅜ inches.

Binding: Red figured cloth, stamped in gold on spine: ASTORIA / BY / W. IRVING / (French rule) / VOL. 1. [2.]

It was also published in light blue cloth of the same design as the red cloth; in brown cloth both of the same and of a different design; and in plain blue cloth. The Henry E. Huntington Library and Art Gallery catalogues another variant binding of green cloth, which may possibly be the same as the blue, as this latter has a greenish tinge. Some copies of the blue binding have map before title-page in Vol. I instead of Vol. II, and page (2) in Vol. I blank. There appears to be no evidence of priority in any of these bindings.

The first American edition was published in October, 1836.

A revised edition was published by Putnam in 1849 as Vol. VIII of the collected edition of Irving's works. It contains a map different from that in the first edition. The text is apparently unchanged except that one paragraph has been added at the end, referring to the settlement of the United States-Canada boundary question.

This book was also published in one volume by A. and W. Galignani, Paris, 1836.

ASTORIA; / OR, / ENTERPRISE BEYOND / THE ROCKY MOUNTAINS. / BY WASHINGTON IRVING. / AUTHOR OF "THE SKETCH BOOK," "THE ALHAMBRA," &C. / IN THREE VOLUMES. / VOL. I. [II., etc.] / LONDON: / RICHARD BENTLEY, / NEW BURLINGTON STREET. / (short rule) / 1836.

Collation: Vol. I: Pre-title; blank; (i), title-page; (ii), printer's imprint; (iii) – viii, INTRODUCTION; (ix) – xvi, contents; (1) – 317, text; 317, printer's imprint; (318), blank; two pages of advertisements.

Vol. II: (i), title-page; (ii), printer's imprint; (iii) – ix, contents; (x), blank; (1) – 320, text; 320, printer's imprint.

ASTORIA, continued

Vol. III: (i), title-page; (ii), printer's imprint; (iii) – vii, contents; (viii), blank; (1) – 294, text and appendix; 294, printer's imprint.

The copy from which collation was made was apparently in original condition with nothing missing. It did not contain a pre-title either in Vol. II or Vol. III. The only other information which I have on pre-title pages is a catalogue description of a copy with the pre-title to Vols. II and III missing. I believe that these volumes never contained any pre-title. An English book dealer consulted confirms this opinion. An early issue has Vol. I, page 96 misnumbered 86. In all copies seen the numeral "3" in the pagination of Vol. II, page 308, is defective.

Page size: 7 9/16 x 4¾ inches, irregular untrimmed.

Binding: Gray boards, maroon cloth spine with white paper label printed in black: (double rule) / ASTORIA. / BY / WASHINGTON IRVING. / Author of / "The Sketch Book," / "The Alhambra," &c. &c. / (short rule) / IN THREE VOLS. / VOL. I. [II., III.] / (double rule).

The first English edition was published in October, 1836, simultaneously with American publication; the text is apparently identical with that of the American edition.

Manuscripts: There is in the possession of a gentleman who does not wish his identity made public, the following portions of the manuscript of this book:

Chapter 5. Manuscript pages 1–24 inclusive, page 18, however, being missing, corresponding (with the exception of the part represented by the missing page 18) to pages 54–65 inclusive, of Vol. I of the printed book. Chapter 14. Manuscript pages 8–14 inclusive, corresponding to pages 145–147 inclusive, of Vol. I of the printed book. Chapter 15, complete. Thirty-four manuscript pages, consisting of one unnumbered page on which is the chapter heading, two unnumbered pages, one page numbered 3 to 30, and pages 31–60 inclusive, corresponding to 148–162 of Vol. I of the printed book. Chapter 16. Twenty-one pages of manuscript, several of them being two pages or parts of pages pasted together, consisting of one unnumbered page, on which is the chapter heading, page 1, one page numbered 3 to 10, page 11, one page numbered 12 and 13, pages 14–28 inclusive, page 30 (or 31, the number being corrected), corresponding to pages 163–171 inclusive, the bottom of 172 to the top of 173, the middle of 173 to near the bottom of 173 of Vol. I of the printed book. Chapter 30. Manuscript pages 2–6 inclusive, corresponding from the middle of page 282 to near the bottom of 284 of Vol. I of the printed book.

The New York Public Library contains the following portions of the manuscript: Vol. I, the following chapters and pages of the first edition text: Ch. VI, p. 66–79; Ch. VII, p. 80–88; Ch. VIII, p. 89–95; Ch. X, p. 101–112; Ch. XI, p. 113–123; Ch. XII, p. 124–130; Ch. XIII, p. 131–140; Ch. XIV, p. 141–143; Ch. XVI, p. 173–174; Ch. XVII, p. 182–186; Ch. XVIII, p. 187–197; Ch. XX, p. 207–217; Ch. XXI, p. 218–225; Ch. XXII, p. 230; Ch. XXIII, p. 236–238; Ch. XXIV, p. 242; Ch. XXV, p. 247–251; Ch. XXVI, p. 252–256; Ch. XXVII, p. 261–266; Ch. XXIX, p. 281.

Copies: The New York Public Library contains three copies of the first American and one of the first English edition.

The collection of the compiler contains three copies of the first American (the variant bindings) and two of the first English edition.

THE ROCKY MOUNTAINS
1837

(Practically all editions of this book, except the first and one other American, bear the title *Adventures of Captain Bonneville*)

THE / ROCKY MOUNTAINS: / OR, / SCENES, INCIDENTS, AND ADVENTURES / IN THE FAR WEST; / DIGESTED FROM THE JOURNAL OF CAPTAIN B. L. E. BONNEVILLE, / OF THE ARMY OF THE UNITED STATES, AND ILLUSTRATED / FROM VARIOUS OTHER SOURCES, / BY WASHINGTON IRVING. / IN TWO VOLUMES. / VOL. I. [II.] / PHILADELPHIA. / CAREY, LEA, & BLANCHARD. / 1837.

Collation: Vol. I: Flyleaf; folded map; (1), title-page; (2), copyright entry and printer's imprint; (3) – 9, INTRODUCTORY NOTICE; (10), blank; (xi) – xvi, contents; (17) – 248, text; twelve pages of advertisements, seven of which contain the introduction to and part of the table of contents of Astoria; flyleaf. In some copies containing the same number of advertisements, the text of these advertisements differs. There is only a brief notice of Astoria and there are other variations. I assume that these advertisements were of a later date (although they may have been inserted at the same time) as it is probable that the more extended notice of Astoria would be earlier than the mere mention. However, it may with equal force be thought that the reproduction of part of Astoria would be more convenient later and that therefore advertisements containing this would have been printed subsequently to those containing a mere notice.

Vol. II: Flyleaf; folded map; (i), title-page; (ii), copyright entry and printer's imprint; (iii) - vii, contents; (viii), blank; (9) - 248, text and appendix; flyleaf.

Page size: $7\,^{9}/_{16}$ x 4½ inches.

Binding: Blue cloth with white paper label on spine printed in black: (double rule) / THE / ROCKY / MOUNTAINS: / OR, / ADVENTURES / IN THE / FAR WEST. / (rule) / BY / WASHINGTON / IRVING. / *In Two Vols.* / VOL. I. [II.] / (rule) / WITH MAPS. / (double rule).

An edition in four parts with paper covers was published in 1843. A "revised" edition in one volume with one map was published in June, 1849, by Putnam as Vol. x of the collected edition of Irving's works. The introductory notice is dated 1843, but is the same as that of the first edition. The text is apparently the same as that of the first American edition.

An edition in one volume was published by Baudry in Paris, in 1837, without maps. In it, chapter XVI of Vol. II (of American first) was broken into two chapters. The book was entitled *Irving's Adventures of Captain Bonneville* and followed the text of the English edition.

ADVENTURES / OF / CAPTAIN BONNEVILLE, / OR / SCENES / BEYOND THE / ROCKY MOUNTAINS OF / THE FAR WEST. / (short rule) / BY WASHINGTON IRVING. / AUTHOR OF / "THE SKETCH-BOOK," "THE ALHAMBRA," "ASTORIA," &C. / IN THREE VOLUMES. / VOL. I. [II., etc.] / LONDON: / RICHARD BENTLEY, / NEW BURLINGTON STREET. / (short rule) / 1837.

On the title-pages of Vols. II and III "The Sketch Book" is not hyphenated.

Collation: Vol. I: Pre-title; title-page, printer's imprint on verso; (1) - 4, contents; (5) - 18, INTRODUCTORY NOTICE; (19), (dedication); (20), blank; (21) - 303, text and appendix; 303, printer's imprint; (304), blank.

Vol. II: Pre-title; title-page, printer's imprint on verso; (1) - 4, contents; (5) - 292, text; 292, printer's imprint.

Vol. III: Pre-title; title-page, printer's imprint on verso; (1) - 4, contents; (5) - 302, text and appendix; 302, printer's imprint.

Page size: 7¾ x 4⅞ inches.

Binding: Grey boards with white paper label on spine, printed in black: (double rule) / ADVENTURES / OF / CAPTAIN / BONNEVILLE. / BY / WASHINGTON IRVING. / AUTHOR OF / "The Sketch Book." / IN THREE VOLUMES / VOL. I. [II., III.] / (double rule)

The English edition contains one or two trifling variations in text.

Copies: The New York Public Library contains a copy of the first American and a copy of the first English edition.

The collection of the compiler contains two copies each of the first American and English editions, all except one copy of the English edition in original bindings.

LIFE OF OLIVER GOLDSMITH

1840

(See Plate VIII)

THE / LIFE / OF / OLIVER GOLDSMITH, / WITH / SELECTIONS FROM HIS WRITINGS. / BY / WASHINGTON IRVING. / IN TWO VOLUMES. / VOL. I. [II.] / NEW-YORK: / HARPER & BROTHERS, 82 CLIFF-STREET. / (short rule) / 1840.

Collation: Vol. I: (iii), blank; (iv), engraved portrait of Goldsmith; (v), title; (vi), copyright entry; (vii) - viii, contents; (9) - 323, text; (324), blank.

Irving's biography occupies pages (9) - 186 of Vol. I.

Vol. II: Flyleaf; title-page, printer's imprint on verso; (i) - v, contents; (vi), blank; (7) - 313, text; (314), blank; flyleaf.

Page size: $6\,^{1}/_{16}$ x 3¾ inches.

Binding: This book was issued in two bindings (probably simultaneously). In one form it was bound in tan cloth. On the front outside cover was printed in black, inside a double-rule border: HARPERS' / FAMILY LIBRARY. / No. CXXI. [CXXII.] / (rule) / THE / LIFE AND WRITINGS / OF / OLIVER GOLDSMITH. / BY / WASHINGTON IRVING. / IN TWO VOLUMES. / VOL. I. [II.] / (rule) / NEW-YORK: / PUBLISHED BY HARPER & BROTHERS, / No. 82 CLIFF-STREET. On the back outside cover was printed a list of the books included in the library. The spine was printed in black with seven double rules between the second and third of which is printed: IRVING'S / LIFE AND WRITINGS / OF / OLIVER GOLDSMITH. / (short rule) / IN TWO VOLS. / VOL. I. [II.] /. Between the sixth and seventh double rule is printed: FAMILY / LIBRARY. / No. CXXI. [CXXII.]. The other binding was a dark brown embossed cloth. Nothing was printed on the covers, but the spine bore an ornamental design in

LIFE OF GOLDSMITH, continued

gold in which was printed in gold: THE / FAMILY / LIBRARY. / No. 121 [122] and at the bottom in gold: IRVING'S / GOLDSMITH / IN TWO VOLS. / VOL. I. [II.]

This work was written three times in varying forms. In 1825 Galignani, Paris, published an edition of Goldsmith's Works in four volumes, for which Irving wrote an introductory Life of Goldsmith. In 1830 J. Crissy and J. Grigg published in Philadelphia an edition of the miscellaneous works of Goldsmith in one volume, which contained the same prefatory life. In 1837 Baudry, Paris, also issued an edition in four volumes with the same introductory life. The two Paris editions are identical in text, type and pagination, differing practically only in their title-pages. It is therefore probable that they were printed from the same plates. All three of these editions state on the title-page, "edited by Washington Irving," but in none of them is the Life otherwise credited to him. In 1840 Harper and Bros., as a part of Harper's Family Library published an edition of selections from Goldsmith's works in two volumes, collated above, which included a biography of Goldsmith by Washington Irving. For this Irving rewrote the *Life* in the Paris and Philadelphia editions, altering it very materially. This is usually accepted as the first edition of Irving's *Life of Goldsmith.*

Rewritten, altered, and much enlarged, and with a preface added, this book was published by Putnam in 1849 as Vol. XI of the collected edition of Irving's works entitled Oliver Goldsmith as below: OLIVER GOLDSMITH: / A BIOGRAPHY. / BY / WASHINGTON IRVING. / NEW-YORK: / GEORGE P. PUTNAM, 155 BROADWAY. / LONDON: JOHN MURRAY. / 1849.

Collation: Yellow end-paper; (i), pre-title; (ii), blank; (iii), title-page; (iv), copyright entry and printer's imprint; (v) – xiii, contents; (xiv), blank; (xv) – xvi, PREFACE; (17) – 382, text; (383), publisher's announcement; (384), blank; 16 pages of advertisements, the thirteenth of which is dated July, 1849; yellow end-paper. Copies have been seen with thirty-six pages of advertisements, with the first page dated July, 1849; and also p. 25–36 only, plus two unnumbered leaves, the first of which bears the usual date.

There is a general title-page referring to the collected edition, followed by a title-page for the specific book. It seems best to term the former a pre-title and the latter the title-page. Collation above is that of title-page. Pre-title reads: THE WORKS / OF / WASHINGTON IRVING. / NEW EDITION, REVISED. / (rule) / VOL. XI. / OLIVER GOLDSMITH. / (rule) / NEW-YORK: / GEORGE P. PUTNAM. / 1849.

Page size: 7 7/16 x 5 1/8 inches.

Binding: Green embossed cloth, gold stamped on spine: IRVING'S / WORKS / (rule) / GOLDSMITH / PUTNAM (*at bottom*).

There was also an illustrated edition of this book published in 1849: OLIVER GOLDSMITH: / A BIOGRAPHY. / BY / WASHINGTON IRVING. / (Portrait of Oliver Goldsmith) / WITH ILLUSTRATIONS. / NEW-YORK: / GEORGE P. PUTNAM, 155 BROADWAY. / LONDON: JOHN MURRAY. / 1849.

Collation: Yellow coated end-paper; frontispiece; (1), title-page; (2), copyright entry and printer's imprint; (3) and (4), PREFACE; (5) – 12, contents; 13 – 15, facsmile of letter by Goldsmith; 16, illustration; (17) – 382, text; (383), publisher's announcement; flyleaf; yellow coated end-paper. Gilt edges.

Page size: 8 3/8 x 6 inches.

Binding: Blue cloth, gold and blank embossed on both covers. Imprinted on spine, in gold within gold ornamental design: Goldsmith / Irving / (rule) / Illustrated. T. e. g.

This was also published in red cloth, with gold embossed design on both covers and gold ornamental design on back, both however differing from those of the blue cloth binding.

There was evidently considerable variation in the binding of this illustrated edition of Goldsmith. In addition to the two bindings mentioned (red and light blue) there was a green binding which duplicated the stamping on the red binding. All three of these were pebbled cloth. There was also a dark-blue ribbed cloth binding, with different stamping and somewhat taller. Only two copies of this latter have been seen: one in the library of Dr. William G. Braislin, and one at Yale University Library. The Braislin copy has the signature of William Cullen Bryant on the title-page; since it was an uncut copy, it is not impossible that they were specially bound for presentation purposes, though there is no proof that such was the case. The library of Alfred L. Rose, Esq., contains a copy in contemporary tooled black leather, with all edges gilt and goffered.

OLIVER GOLDSMITH: / A BIOGRAPHY. / BY / WASHINGTON IRVING. / (wavy rule) / LONDON: / JOHN MURRAY, ALBEMARLE STREET. / 1849.

Collation: Yellow end-paper; (i), pre-title; (ii), blank; (iii), title-page; (iv), printer's imprint; (v) – vi, PREFACE; (vii) – xv, contents; (xvi), blank; (17) – 382, text; (383), printer's imprint; (384), blank; yellow end-paper.

Page size: 7 x 4 3/4 inches.

Binding: Red embossed cloth, front and back sides blind stamped with decorative designs and in circle in center MURRAY'S COLONIAL & HOME LIBRARY. Spine blind stamped with decorative design and at top printed in gold: IRVING'S / LIFE OF / GOLDSMITH, and at bottom MURRAY.

The text, type, and pagination of text of the English edition is identical page for page with that of the American edition and it is probable therefore that they were printed from the same type or plates. Contents and preface, however, are transposed and pagination thereof correspondingly changed. A publisher's list is printed on the yellow end-papers.

Published (November, 1849?).

Manuscripts: The New York Public Library contains the manuscript of the 1849 edition of the book, bound in two volumes. They contain 512 pages, of which approximately 175 are partially or entirely in type. Apparently in preparing the work, Irving inserted in his manuscript the printed portions of the earlier life which he retained, and supplied the additions and revisions in script.

Copies: The New York Public Library contains two copies of the first American edition, and others.

The library of Carroll A. Wilson, Esq., contains a copy of the green binding; the library of Dr. William G. Braislin contains a copy of the dark-blue ribbed cloth, as does Yale University Library.

The collection of the compiler contains copies of all American and English editions, in original bindings, and red and light-blue cloth copies of the illustrated edition.

BIOGRAPHY OF MARGARET DAVIDSON
1841

BIOGRAPHY / AND / POETICAL REMAINS / OF THE LATE / MARGARET MILLER DAVIDSON. / BY WASHINGTON IRVING. / (rule) / Thou wert unfit to dwell with clay, / For sin too pure, for earth too bright! / And death, who call'd thee hence away, / Placed on his brow a gem of light! / MARGARET TO HER SISTER. / (rule) / PHILADELPHIA: / LEA AND BLANCHARD. / 1841.

Collation: Yellow end-paper; three flyleaves; (i), pre-title; (ii), blank; (iii), title-page; (iv), copyright entry and printer's imprint; (v) – vii, contents; (viii), blank; (9) – 359, text, of which pages (9) – 152 are occupied by the biography by Irving; (360), blank; eight pages of advertisements; three flyleaves; yellow end-paper.

Page size: 7 $^{9}/_{16}$ x 4 $^{11}/_{16}$ inches.

Binding: Black embossed cloth with gilt decorative design on sides, printed on spine: MEMOIR / OF / MARGARET / DAVIDSON / BY / W. IRVING.

LIFE / AND / POETICAL REMAINS / OF / MARGARET M. DAVIDSON. / BY WASHINGTON IRVING. / Thou wert unfit to dwell with clay, / For sin too pure, for earth too bright! / And Death, who call'd thee hence away, / Placed on his brow a gem of light! / MARGARET TO HER SISTER. / LONDON: / TILT AND BOGUE, FLEET STREET. / MDCCCXLIII.

Collation: Yellow end-paper; (i), pre-title; (ii), blank; frontispiece, Margaret and her Mother; (iii), title-page; (iv), printer's imprint; (v) – viii, contents; (9) – 350, text, of which pages (9) – 171 are occupied by the biography by Irving; 350, printer's imprint; 18 pages of advertisements, of which the last fifteen are numbered 2 to 16; yellow end-paper.

Page size: 6¾ x 4¼ inches.

Binding: Purple cloth, blind embossed with decorative design on covers.

Copies: The New York Public Library contains a copy of the first American edition.

The collection of the compiler contains two copies of the first American and one of the first English edition, in original bindings.

A BOOK OF THE HUDSON
1849

(See Plate IX)

[*Issue A*]

A / BOOK OF THE HUDSON. / COLLECTED FROM THE VARIOUS WORKS OF / Diedrich Knickerbocker. / EDITED BY GEOFFREY CRAYON. / NEW YORK: / G. P. PUTNAM, 155 BROADWAY. / 1849.

Collation: Yellow end-paper, two flyleaves; (i), pre-title; (ii), blank; (iii), title-page; (iv), copyright notice and printer's imprint; (v), contents; (vi), blank; (vii) – viii, INTRODUCTION;

A BOOK OF THE HUDSON, continued

(11) – 215, text; (216), blank; (1) – (16), advertisements, [p. (1) – 15 dated March, 1849; p. (16) dated November, 1848]; flyleaf.

Page size: 6⅛ x 4 $^{3}/_{16}$ inches.

Binding: Green figured cloth, blind stamped front and back with sleeping figure of Rip Van Winkle, gun, and dog sitting behind him, this figure enclosed within an oval; further ornamental devices at the corners, and, surrounding all, a triple-rule border. On the spine, within an ornamental device in blind, is stamped in gold, old English letters: Book / of the / Hudson / (rule) / Irving / (*at bottom, in roman*) PUTNAM.

Printer and stereotyper, R. Craighead.

[*Issue B*]

A / BOOK OF THE HUDSON. / COLLECTED FROM THE VARIOUS WORKS OF / Diedrich Knickerbocker. / EDITED BY / GEOFFREY CRAYON / NEW-YORK: / G. P. PUTNAM, 155 BROADWAY. / 1849.

Collation: Flyleaf; (i), pre-title; (ii), blank; (iii), title-page; (iv), copyright notice and printer's imprint; (v), contents; (vi), blank; (vii) – viii, INTRODUCTION; (9) – 283, text; (284), blank; flyleaf.

Page size: 5 $^{13}/_{16}$ x 4 $^{3}/_{16}$ inches.

Binding: Blue figured cloth, blind stamped on front with ornamental devices at top and bottom, between which, in gold, an ensemble wholly different from that of *Issue A*. Rip is still asleep, his hat has slipped further off his head; his clothes and gun have been changed, and the dog now slumbers with his head on Rip's side. This and the ornamental devices above and below, enclosed in a triple-rule border, blind stamped.

On the back, the stamping on the front is duplicated in blind. On the spine, between a double rule (above) and an ornamental device (below) running to the bottom, both in gold, is stamped in gold roman letters: TALES / OF THE / HUDSON

Printer and stereotyper, John F. Trow.

There are further differences between the two issues: there is the expected difference in typeface and lay-out from beginning to end. *Issue A* is in smaller type, on better paper; but *Issue B* has no advertisements, and contains four two-color lithographs, of which one is an extra title-page. *Issue B* has an error in the table of contents: *Communipaw,* page 9, is listed as page 7.

Priority is not at all certain; deduction would seem to indicate *Issue A* as the earlier. In the *Morning Courier and New York Inquirer* for April 15, 1849, appears the first mention of this book, when Mr. Putnam announces "This day is published..." It is described as "a neat little volume" and no mention of illustration is made. This, at a time when publishers, Putnam included, made much of any illustrations leads to the surmise that the issue had none, and that *Issue B* with its lithographs, its gold stamping, its lack of advertisements and its, in general, more fancy get-up, was a later issue, probably designed for the holiday trade of 1849.

There is, however, no hard and fast rule that may be laid down. Copies have also been seen with the contents of *Issue A* in the binding of *Issue B,* and with this order reversed and the binding of *Issue A* on the illustrated contents. One copy has been seen in a different binding, of dark olive-green cloth, with the blind stamping of *Issue A* in gold, and otherwise as *Issue B*. The other conjecture, so far unsubstantiated, would be that there were both "plain and fancy" editions simultaneously, and that things were occasionally mixed.

This book is a selection of Irving's writings, edited by him, and with the introduction added. Of the two paragraphs of the introduction, the first was reprinted, with some changes, from the *Knickerbocker Magazine,* March, 1839, and appeared here for the first time in book form. (Later published, further revised, in Vol. 2 of the *Spanish Papers.*) The second paragraph was here published for the first time. It is also the first appearance of "Communipaw" in book form, and the text thereof is entirely different from that of the article of the same name in the *Knickerbocker Magazine* and the *Spanish Papers,* though the material is similar. "Guests from Gibbet Island" is reprinted, with slight revision, from the *Knickerbocker Magazine,* October, 1839; "Peter Stuyvesant's Voyage up the Hudson" is reprinted from *Knickerbocker's History of New York;* "The Chronicle of Bearn Island" probably appears here for the first time. "The Legend of Sleepy Hollow" is reprinted from the *Sketch Book;* "Dolph Heyliger" from *Bracebridge Hall;* "Rip Van Winkle" from the *Sketch Book;* and "Wolfert Webber" from *Tales of a Traveller.*

Manuscripts: The New York Public Library contains 6 pages of the manuscript "Communipaw." It is an excerpt from a longer manuscript, also in The New York Public Library, never published in full.

Copies: The New York Public Library contains copies of both issues; the collection of the compiler contains copies of both issues.

LIFE OF MAHOMET
1850

MAHOMET / AND / HIS SUCCESSORS. / BY / WASHINGTON IRVING. / IN TWO VOLUMES. / VOL. I. [II.] / NEW-YORK: / GEORGE P PUTNAM, 155 BROADWAY. / M.DCCC.L.

Collation: Vol. I: Yellow end-paper; white flyleaf; pre-title, verso blank; title-page; copyright entry and printer's imprint on verso; (i) – vii, contents; (viii), blank; (ix) – xi, PREFACE; (xii), blank; (13) – 373, text and appendix; (374), blank; 36 pages of advertisements dated July, 1849; yellow end-paper.

Vol. II: Yellow end-paper; (i), pre-title; (ii), blank; (iii), title-page; (iv), copyright entry and printer's imprint; (i) – viii, contents; (ix) – xii, PREFACE; (13) – 500, text; yellow end-paper.

There is a general title-page referring to the collected edition followed by a title-page for the specific book. It seems best to term the former a pre-title and apply the term title-page to the latter. Pre-title reads: THE WORKS / OF / WASHINGTON IRVING. / (rule) / MAHOMET AND HIS SUCCESSORS. / VOL. XII. [XIII.] / (rule) / NEW-YORK: / GEORGE P. PUTNAM. / 1850.

Page size: 7 $^{7}/_{16}$ x 5⅛ inches.

Binding: Green embossed cloth printed in gold on spine: IRVING'S / WORKS / (rule) / MAHOMET [in Vol. II. MAHOMET'S / SUCCESSORS] / PUTNAM *(at bottom)*.

This work was published as Vols. XII and XIII of the collected edition of Irving's works. Although entitled on both pre-title and title-pages "Mahomet and His Successors," and although the pre-titles state "in two volumes" and are respectively numbered Vol. I and Vol. II, the first volume contains only the life of Mahomet and the second only that of his successors. Further, the back of the book is entitled, for the first volume "Mahomet" and for the second "Mahomet's Successors." Vol. I is copyrighted 1849 and advertisements and preface are dated 1849 and Vol. II, 1850, but several authorities consulted give 1850 as the correct date of the first edition of both volumes.

LIVES OF MAHOMET / AND / HIS SUCCESSORS. / BY WASHINGTON IRVING. / IN TWO VOLUMES. — VOL. I. / LONDON: / JOHN MURRAY, ALBEMARLE STREET. / 1850. (All enclosed in single-rule border.)

Collation: Vol. I: Yellow end-paper; flyleaf; (i), title-page; (ii), blank; (iii), sub-title: LIFE / OF / MAHOMET. / BY WASHINGTON IRVING. / LONDON: / JOHN MURRAY, ALBEMARLE STREET. / 1850. (All enclosed in single-rule border); (iv), printer's imprint; (v) – vii, PREFACE; (viii), blank; (ix) – xv, contents; (xvi), blank; (13) – 373, text; 373, printer's imprint; (374), publisher's note of following volume; 2 pages of advertisements, unnumbered; 16 pages of advertisements numbered (1) to 16, the first and (eleventh) pages dated January, 1850. Yellow end-paper. The 16 pages of advertisements are printed in black and red.

Vol. II: Yellow end-paper; (i), sub-title: LIVES / OF THE / SUCCESSORS OF MAHOMET. / BY WASHINGTON IRVING. / LONDON: / JOHN MURRAY, ALBEMARLE STREET. / 1850. (All enclosed in single-rule border); (ii), blank; (iii), title-page; (iv), printer's imprint; (v) – viii, PREFACE; (ix) – xvi, contents; (13) – 500, text; 500, printer's imprint; 16 pages of advertisements numbered (1) to 16, the first and (tenth) dated July, 1850; yellow end-paper.

Copies may also have the advertisements in Vol. II dated October, 1849, or January, 1850. Those dated January duplicate the advertisements in Vol. I.

Page size: 8¾ x 5⅝ inches.

Binding: Green embossed cloth printed in gold on spine: *(at top)* MAHOMET / AND HIS / SUCCESSORS / (short rule) / I. [II.] *(in middle)* WASHINGTON / IRVING / *(at bottom)* LONDON / JOHN MURRAY.

Text printed from same plates as American edition. This probably accounts for the numbering of the introductory pages extending to (xvi) and xvi respectively in the English edition, extending only to (xii) and xii in the American edition, and the text commencing with (13).

Vol. I was announced as "now ready" and Vol. II as "in March" in John Murray's "List of books," dated January, 1850. The dates of the English publication therefore would be: Vol. I, 1849; Vol. II, March, 1850.

Both of these volumes were also published in a smaller format by George Routledge & Co., London, 1850. The publications by Murray are, however, the first English editions.

Copies: The New York Public Library contains two copies of the first American edition, and Vol. I of the first English edition.

The collection of the compiler contains a copy of the first American, two copies of the first English edition, in original bindings, except one copy of English edition.

LIFE OF WASHINGTON
1855–1859

LIFE / OF / GEORGE WASHINGTON. / BY / WASHINGTON IRVING. / IN THREE VOLS. (see below) / VOL. I. [II., etc.] / NEW YORK: / G. P. PUTNAM & CO., 10 PARK PLACE. / 1855. (see below)

Title-pages of all five volumes are the same except that only Vols. I and II carry the line "In Three Vols.," and the dates of the volumes are respectively 1855, 1855, 1856, 1857, 1859. Some copies of Vol. II are dated 1856.

Collation: Vol. I: Tan end-paper; frontispiece; (i), title-page; (ii), copyright entry; (iii) – v, PREFACE; (vi), blank; (vii) – xvi, contents; xvi, list of illustrations; (1) – 504, text and appendix; tan end-paper. Some copies have the imprint of R. Craighead on (ii).

Vol. II: Tan end-paper; frontispiece; (i), title-page; (ii), copyright entry and printer's imprint; (iii) – xii, contents; xii, list of illustrations; 1 – 518, text; (519), (note of error in text); (520), blank; tan end-paper.

Vol. III: Yellow end-paper; flyleaf; frontispiece; (i), title-page; (ii), copyright entry and printer's imprint; (iii), (author's note); (iv), blank; (v) – xiv, contents; xiv, list of illustrations; 1 – 523, text; (524), blank; inserted slip with note by publisher, and one by author; yellow end-paper.

Vol. IV: Yellow end-paper; flyleaf; frontispiece; (i), title-page; (ii), copyright entry and printer's imprint; (iii) – x, contents; x, list of illustrations; 1 – 518, text; yellow end-paper. Copies also exist with four pages of undated advertisements in front; and ten pages in back, also undated, numbered 1–6, 21, 12, [13?], [14?].

Vol. V: Tan end-paper; white flyleaf; frontispiece (two facing plates); (i), title-page; (ii), copyright entry and printer's imprint; (iii) – iv, PREFACE; (v) – xii, contents; 2-page facsimile of letter from Washington to Franklin; 1 – 456, text, appendix, and index; tan end-paper.

Page size: 9⅛ x 5 13/16 inches.

Binding: Blue embossed cloth printed in gold on spine: LIFE / OF / WASHINGTON. / (rule) / IRVING. / VOL. I. [II., etc.] (*in center of back*) / Putnam. (*at bottom of back*).

Although originally intended to appear in three volumes, this work was extended, as explained in the preface and note in Vol. III, to five volumes. These were published in April or May, 1855, December, 1855, July, 1856, May, 1857 and April, 1859. A limited quarto edition of 110 copies was also published. Text was apparently printed from the same plates but it is enclosed in a single-rule border and printed on heavier paper. The volumes are dated 1855, 1856, 1856, 1857 and 1859. All copies that we have seen or seen catalogued contain a large number of additional engraved illustrations. These illustrations were published separately by Putnam and this separate publication also included additional engraved title-pages. (The set in the collection of the compiler has these title-pages only for four volumes, and it may be that these were all that were issued.) The lists of illustrations in this edition, however, only mention the same illustrations as the lists in the trade edition. The copy of the limited quarto edition in the collection of the compiler does not contain the engraved title-pages. A list of Putnam publications, without date but evidently issued in 1861, lists this quarto edition with "102 plates and numerous woodcuts"; it also lists the separate publication of the illustrations — "102 engravings on steel and 40 engravings on wood." The trade edition may be taken as a first edition.

We have heard rumors of a one-volume edition in English published at Seville, Spain, about 1860 or earlier. This, of course, is not impossible, but at the time of printing no such copy had materialized.

LIFE / OF / GEORGE WASHINGTON. / BY / WASHINGTON IRVING. / IN THREE VOLUMES. / VOL. I. / COMPRISING HIS EARLY LIFE, EXPEDITIONS, AND CAMPAIGNS. / LONDON: / HENRY G. BOHN, / YORK STREET, COVENT GARDEN. / 1855.

LIFE / OF / GEORGE WASHINGTON. / BY / WASHINGTON IRVING. / IN THREE VOLUMES. / VOL. II. / THE AMERICAN WAR, INVASION OF CANADA, &C. / LONDON: / HENRY G. BOHN, YORK STREET, COVENT GARDEN. / 1856.

LIFE / OF / GEORGE WASHINGTON. / BY / WASHINGTON IRVING. / VOL. III. / THE AMERICAN WAR / DURING THE YEARS 1777, 1778, and 1779. / LONDON: / HENRY G. BOHN, YORK STREET, COVENT GARDEN. / 1856.

LIFE / OF / GEORGE WASHINGTON. / BY / WASHINGTON IRVING. / VOL. IV. / CONCLUSION OF THE AMERICAN WAR, ETC. / LONDON: / HENRY G. BOHN, YORK STREET, COVENT GARDEN. / 1857.

LIFE / OF / GEORGE WASHINGTON. / BY / WASHINGTON IRVING. / VOL. V. / CONCLUSION, WITH GENERAL INDEX. / LONDON: / HENRY G. BOHN, YORK STREET, COVENT GARDEN. / 1859.

Collation: Vol. I: Two leaves and inside front cover fancy paper with advertisements; (i), pre-title; (ii), blank; engraving of Stuart portrait of Washington, facing title-page; (iii), title-page; (iv), printer's imprint; (v) – vii, PREFACE; (viii), blank; (ix) – xvi, contents; (1) – 348, text; 348, printer's imprint; four blank pages; three leaves and inside back cover fancy paper with advertisements.

Vol. II: Three leaves and inside front cover fancy paper with advertisements; (i), pre-title; (ii), blank; (iii), title-page; (iv), printer's imprint; (v) – xii, contents; 349–715, text; (716), printer's imprint; three leaves and inside back cover fancy paper with advertisements.

Vol. III: Three leaves and inside front cover fancy paper with advertisements; publisher's notice, verso blank; pre-title, verso blank; (i), title-page; (ii) printer's imprint; (iii), note by Irving; (iv), blank; (v) – xii, contents; (xiii), half-title; 716–1080, text; printer's imprint, verso blank; three leaves and inside back cover fancy paper with advertisements.

Vol. IV: Three leaves and inside front cover fancy paper with advertisements; (i), pre-title; (ii), blank; (iii), title-page; (iv), printer's imprint; (v) – xi, contents; (xii), blank; 1081 – 1444, text; 1444, printer's imprint; three leaves and inside back cover fancy paper with advertisements.

Vol. V: Three leaves and inside front cover fancy paper with advertisements; (possible pre-title? Copy examined apparently unmutilated and without pre-title); engraving of tomb of Washington, facing title-page; (i), title-page; (ii), printer's imprint; (iii) – iv, PREFACE; v – xii, contents; 1445–1752, text, appendix, and index; 1752, printer's imprint; three leaves and inside back cover fancy paper with advertisements.

Page size: 7⅛ x 4½ inches, untrimmed.

Binding: Light green paper boards with title enclosed in decorative border: On outside front cover: AUTHORIZED EDITION, PRICE *2s. 6d.* / (double rule) / LIFE / OF / GEORGE WASHINGTON. / BY WASHINGTON IRVING. / (wavy rule) / EARLY LIFE, / EXPEDITIONS INTO THE WILDERNESS, / AND / CAMPAIGNS ON THE BORDER. (*and correspondingly in the other volumes*) / (wavy rule) / London: / Henry G. Bohn, York Street, Covent Gardens. / 1855. [etc.] On outside back cover: advertisement of Wolfert's Roost and Complete Works of Irving. Spine printed in black, enclosed in single rule: (rule) / (decorative design) / (double rule) / WASHINGTON / IRVING'S / LIFE / OF / GEORGE / WASHINGTON / (double rule) / (decorative design) / (double rule) / VOL. I. [etc.] / (short rule) / EARLY / LIFE (*correspondingly in other volumes*). These last two lines are not certain as back of Vol. I was destroyed in copy from which collation was made. / (double rule) / PRICE / *2s. 6d.* The binding, advertisements, etc., are similar in all five volumes.

Manuscripts: The Pierpont Morgan Library contains ms. pages 462–479 of Vol. V (printed pages 308–318) and pages 62 and 462 of Vol. IV (printed pages 41 and 354, respectively).

The library of the Rev. Dr. Roderick Terry contains 13 pages (some not full pages, but all consecutive) ms. of Vol. IV, chapter XXIII (printed pages 310–319).

The New York Public Library contains ms. 14 pages, Vol. I, chapter V (complete), written pages 42–56 (printed pages 47–63); ms. 28 pages, Vol. V, chapters I, II and III (complete), written pages 1–25, plus 3 pages of chapter headings (printed pages 1–20); ms. 17 pages, Vol. V, chapter XXXI, written pages 406–418, plus 4 unnumbered pages and one page chapter headings (printed pages 272–281); ms. 1 page, Vol. V, chapter XIV (printed page 104).

The library of Mr. Boies Penrose, Jr., of Devon, Pa., contains the ms. of Vol. IV, chapter XX, printed pages 257–278 inclusive, approximately 35 pages of ms.

The library of Mr. Carl H. Pforzheimer contains the manuscript of Chapter XXII, Vol. IV.

The library of Mr. Harry M. Bland contains the sheet of the "Life" eulogizing Hamilton.

The Henry E. Huntington Library and Art Gallery contains the following manuscripts: ms. 92 pages, Vol. IV, chapter IX (HM 3190); ms. 46 pages, Vol. V, chapters XXIX and XXX (HM 3160); ms. 16 pages, Vol. IV, chapter XXXIII (HM 3170); ms. 14 pages, Vol. V, chapter XXXIII (HM 3161).

Copies: The New York Public Library contains five copies of the first American edition.

The collection of the compiler contains copies of the American and first English editions, in original bindings; the American limited edition, and the separate plates.

WOLFERT'S ROOST

1855

WOLFERT'S ROOST / AND / OTHER PAPERS, NOW FIRST COLLECTED. / BY / WASHINGTON IRVING. / NEW YORK : / G. P. PUTNAM & CO., 12 PARK PLACE. / 1855.

Collation: Yellow end-paper; flyleaf; (1), blank; (2), frontispiece; (3), illustrated title-page; (4), blank; (5), title-page; (6), copyright entry and printer's imprint; (7) and 8, contents; (9) – 383, text; (384), blank; (1) – 12, advertisements dated at 10 PARK PLACE, Feb'y., 1855; yellow end-paper.

Page size: 7 7/16 x 5⅛ inches.

Binding: Green embossed cloth. Size is the same as and binding similar to the collected edition of Irving's works. An ornamental design, however, is stamped in gold on the front side and the blind stamping of the entire cover varies slightly. No volume number is given to this book and it carries on the spine, gold stamped: WOLFERT'S / ROOST / (rule) / IRVING / (*at bottom*) PUTNAM. We are informed that it was also issued in red cloth, gilt edges, for gift purposes.

The book was published in February, 1855. The entire contents are articles reprinted from periodicals or books:

Wolfert's Roost. From the *Knickerbocker Magazine,* April, 1839. (Extensively revised.)

The Birds of Spring. From the *Knickerbocker Magazine,* May, 1839. (Slightly revised.)

The Creole Village. From the *Magnolia* (an annual), 1837.

Mountjoy. From the *Knickerbocker Magazine,* November and December, 1839.

The Bermudas. From the *Knickerbocker Magazine,* January, 1840.

The Widow's Ordeal. From the *Magnolia,* 1837.

The Knight of Malta. From the *Knickerbocker Magazine,* February, 1840.

A Time of Unexampled Prosperity. From the *Knickerbocker Magazine,* April, 1840. This was later reprinted, as No. v of the series "Reading on the Rail," issued in 1864, under the imprint of *The Rebellion Record,* New York.

Sketches in Paris in 1825. From the *Knickerbocker Magazine,* November and December, 1840.

A Contented Man. Place and date of previous publication have not been determined.

Broek; or the Dutch Paradise. From the *Knickerbocker Magazine,* January, 1841.

Guests from Gibbet-Island. From the *Knickerbocker Magazine,* October, 1839, and reprinted, with slight changes, in *A Book of the Hudson.*

The Early Experiences of Ralph Ringwood. From the *Knickerbocker Magazine,* August and September, 1840.

The Seminoles. From the *Knickerbocker Magazine,* October, 1840.

The Count Van Horn. From the *Knickerbocker Magazine,* March, 1840.

Don Juan — A Spectral Research. From the *Knickerbocker Magazine,* March, 1841.

Legend of the Engulphed Convent. From the *Knickerbocker Magazine,* March, 1840.

The Phantom Island. From the *Knickerbocker Magazine,* July, 1839.

Recollections of the Alhambra. From the *Knickerbocker Magazine.*

WOLFERT'S ROOST / AND OTHER TALES. / NOW FIRST COLLECTED. / BY / WASHINGTON IRVING. / LONDON : / HENRY G. BOHN, YORK STREET, COVENT GARDEN. / 1855.

Collation: (i), Pre-title; (ii), blank; plate: Hinchcliff etching of Irving, facing title; (iii), title-page; (iv), printer's imprint; (v) – vi, contents; (1) – 280, text; 280, printer's imprint.

Page size: 7⅛ x 4⅜ inches.

Binding: Green boards with title enclosed in decorative triple rule: Fine Edition, Price 1s. 6d. / (irregular rule) / Washington Irving's / Wolfert's Roost, / and other tales. / (rule) / Complete in one volume. / (rule) / London: / Henry G. Bohn, York Street, Covent Garden. / (rule) / 1855. / (These lines are probably also printed in capitals.) List of Bohn's Standard Library on end-papers front and back with two extra sheets each (making seven pages of advertisements front and seven back). This binding is uniform with that of the first edition of Irving's *Life of Washington.*

An English bookdealer states that the following is the first English edition, basing his opinion on the words "Author's Edition" on the title-page. I have also seen this listed as first English edition in American catalogues:

CHRONICLES OF WOLFERT'S ROOST / AND OTHER PAPERS / BY WASHINGTON IRVING. / AUTHOR'S EDITION. / EDINBURGH: THOMAS CONSTABLE AND CO. / S. LOW, SON, & CO.; HAMILTON, ADAMS, & CO., LONDON. / JAMES M'GLASHAN, DUBLIN. / MDCCCLV.

Collation: Yellow end-paper; (1) – 4, advertisements (1, 2 and 3 unnumbered); (5), announcement; (6), blank; (i), pre-title; (ii), blank; (iii), title-page; (iv), printer's imprint; (v) – vi, contents; (1) – 351, text; (352), printer's imprint; four pages of advertisements; yellow end-paper.

Page size: 7 x 4¾ inches.

Binding: Brown cloth gold and blind embossed on front cover, blind embossed on back cover, printed in gold on spine: WOLFERT'S ROOST / AND / OTHER PAPERS / (short rule) / WASHINGTON IRVING, *at bottom, blind stamped,* (rule) / CONSTABLE'S / MISCELLANY / IV / (rule).

In the *second issue* there is one page of advertisements at the front, on the verso of which is an announcement that Vol. VII of the series is in press. There are no advertisements in back. In the *first issue,* p. (5), the announcement concerns Vol. V.

Manuscripts: The library of the Rev. Dr. Roderick Terry contains: Complete ms. of "Paris at the Restoration" (the last of the "Sketches in Paris in 1825"), 14 pages or part pages, some consisting of two part pages inlaid on one leaf. Complete ms. of "English and French Character" (the fourth of "Sketches in Paris in 1825") 8 pages. Complete ms. of "The Legend of the Engulphed Convent," 17 pages, some being two part pages inlaid on one leaf. Complete ms. of "The Three Kings of Bermuda" (without the introductory portion entitled "The Bermudas"), 14 pages, some consisting of two part pages inlaid on one leaf. Introduction only to "The Knight of Malta," 4 pages of manuscript. One page of manuscript from one of the articles, not definitely located.

The library of Owen D. Young, Esq., contains the complete manuscript of "Communipaw," 21 pages.

The Henry E. Huntington Library and Art Gallery contains The Seminoles (Introductory section), 13 pages of manuscript (HM 2118); The Conspiracy of Neamantha, 24 pages of manuscript (HM 3172); The Early Experiences of Ralph Ringwood, 58 pages of manuscript.

The New York Public Library contains 68 of 93 pages of the manuscript of "Mountjoy"; 13 pages of the manuscript of "The Count Van Horn" (incomplete); 1 page of manuscript, not definitely located, from another portion of the book.

Copies: The New York Public Library contains three copies of the first American and one of the first English edition.

The collection of the compiler contains several copies of the first American, one each of the Edinburgh first and second issues, and one of the London edition, in original bindings.

Posthumous Works

Beginning shortly after Irving's death and continuing to the present time there have been published several volumes containing articles previously unpublished in book form, diaries, notebooks, letters, notes made in preparation of his works and similar material. Those which have appeared to date are given in the following pages. It is probable that there will be further similar publications from time to time, as certain Irving material still remains in manuscript form.

SPANISH PAPERS

1866

SPANISH PAPERS AND OTHER / MISCELLANIES, HITHERTO UNPUBLISHED / OR UNCOLLECTED. / BY / WASHINGTON IRVING. / ARRANGED AND EDITED BY / PIERRE M. IRVING. / IN TWO VOLUMES. / VOL. I. [II.] / (Decorative design) / NEW YORK: / G. P. PUTNAM; HURD AND HOUGHTON. / 1866.

Collation: Vol. I: Yellow end-paper; white flyleaf; engraving of Wilkie portrait of Irving, facing title-page; (i), title-page; (ii), copyright entry and printer's imprint; (iii) – v, PREFACE BY THE EDITOR; (vi), blank; (vii) – xv, contents; (xvi), blank; (1), subtitle; (2), blank; (3) – 5, PREFACE (by Irving to Legends of the Conquest of Spain, which book is included in this volume); (6), blank; (7) – 466, text; two white flyleaves; yellow end-paper. Between each article is a

SPANISH PAPERS, continued

subtitle with verso blank. Where any article ends on the right-hand page, the following left-hand page is blank.

Vol. II: Orange end-paper; white flyleaf; (5), title-page; (6), copyright entry and printer's imprint; (7), contents; (8), blank; (9), subtitle; (10), [editor's note]; (11) – 487, text; (488), blank; white flyleaf; orange end-paper. Two subtitles, (162) and (302), contain editor's note.

Page size: 7 7/16 x 5⅛ inches.

Binding: Green ribbed cloth, same color as the collected edition of Irving's works. Gold stamped decorative design on top and on bottom of spine. Inside of top design gold stamped: IRVING'S / WORKS / (rule) / SPANISH / PAPERS / (rule) / VOL. I. [II.] Some copies have the stamp of J. B. Lippincott, Philadelphia, at the bottom, and the cloth is different. In both forms a rule border is blind stamped on the sides, but they differ. It is possible that the Lippincott stamping was put only on copies sold by that firm.

CONTENTS OF VOLUME I.

The Legend of Don Roderick, from *Legends of the Conquest of Spain.*

Legend of the Subjugation of Spain, from *Legends of the Conquest of Spain.*

Legend of Count Julian and His Family, from *Legends of the Conquest of Spain,* but including one or two notes not in that book.

The Legend of Pelayo. Parts of this had been published in the *Knickerbocker Magazine,* January, 1840, and in *Spirit of the Fair, 1864.* This portion of the text is somewhat revised and new matter is included.

Abderahman. Previously published in the *Knickerbocker Magazine,* May, 1840, but revised by Irving in 1847, though not published at that time.

Chronicle of Fernan Gonzalez, Count of Castile. From unpublished manuscript.

Chronicle of Fernando the Saint, from unpublished manuscript.

Spanish Romance, published in the *Knickerbocker Magazine,* September, 1839.

CONTENTS OF VOLUME II.

Letters of Jonathan Oldstyle (*q. v.*). The last four letters published in the *Morning Chronicle* and in the 1824 edition of *Jonathan Oldstyle* are omitted.

Biographical Sketches

Captain James Lawrence, from the *Analectic Magazine* of August, 1813, including an explanatory note by Irving from the *Analectic Magazine* of September, 1813.

Lieutenant Burrows, from the *Analectic Magazine,* November, 1813.

Commodore Perry, from the *Analectic Magazine,* December, 1813.

Captain David Porter, from the *Analectic Magazine,* September, 1814.

Thomas Campbell, from the *Analectic Magazine,* March, 1815, omitting the last paragraph and having added the letter to Harper & Brothers published in the preface to the American edition of Beattie's *Life of Campbell,* 1841.

Washington Allston, from Duyckinck's *Encyclopedia of American Literature.*

Conversations with Talma, from the *Knickerbocker Gallery,* 1855.

Margaret Miller Davidson, from the collection of her poems published in 1841.

Reviews and Miscellanies

Review of the Works of Robert Treat Paine, from the *Analectic Magazine,* March, 1813.

Review of the Poems of Edwin C. Holland, from the *Analectic Magazine.*

Review of Wheaton's "History of the Northmen," from the *North American,* 1832.

Review of the Conquest of Granada, an explanatory article published by Irving under the name of Fray Antonio Agapida in the *London Quarterly Review,* May and October, 1830.

Letter to the Editor of the Knickerbocker Magazine, from *Knickerbocker Magazine,* March, 1839. One paragraph of this letter was reprinted, with omissions and slight changes, in *A Book of the Hudson;* the entire letter is here reprinted as it originally appeared.

Sleepy Hollow, from the *Knickerbocker Magazine,* May, 1839.

National Nomenclature, from the *Knickerbocker Magazine,* August, 1839.

Desultory Thoughts on Criticism, from the *Knickerbocker Magazine,* August, 1839.

Communipaw, from the *Knickerbocker Magazine,* September, 1839.

Conspiracy of the Cocked Hats, from the *Knickerbocker Magazine,* October, 1839.

Letter from Granada, from the *Knickerbocker Magazine,* July, 1840.

The Catskill Mountains, from *Home Book of the Picturesque.* This volume was apparently published in 1852 but possibly 1851, and not in 1850 as is stated in the editor's note.

BIOGRAPHIES / AND / MISCELLANEOUS PAPERS / BY / WASHINGTON IRVING / *Author of "The Sketch Book," "Life of George Washington,"* &c &c / COLLECTED AND ARRANGED / BY / PIERRE IRVING / LONDON / BELL AND DALDY / YORK STREET COVENT GARDEN / 1867.

Collation: Red brown end-papers; (i), title-page; (ii), printer's imprint; (iii), ADVERTISEMENT; (iv), blank; (v) – xi, contents; (xii), blank; (1) – 519, text; (520), printer's imprint; red brown end-papers.

Page size: 7¼ x 4⅛ inches (irregular untrimmed).

Binding: Purple cloth, with blind stamped design on sides and printed in gold on spine: (rule) / BIOGRAPHIES / AND / MISCELLANEOUS / PAPERS / (short rule) / *WASHINGTON IRVING* / (rule) / *At bottom of back*: (rule) / BELL & DALDY. / (rule).

This book included the entire contents of the two volumes of the American edition of *Spanish Papers,* except that the preface by Pierre Irving is omitted and the publisher's "advertisement" inserted instead, and that articles which had previously appeared in *Legends of the Conquest of Spain* are also omitted.

This is apparently the first English edition of this book, but English catalogues mention an edition also published in 1867 by Low.

Manuscripts: The Henry E. Huntington Library and Art Gallery contains 18 p. of "Conversations with Talma" (HM 3147).

The New York Public Library contains 2 p. ms. of The Conspiracy of the Cocked Hats (incomplete).

There is in the possession of a gentleman who does not wish his name made public, the following portions of the manuscript of this book: The Legend of Pelayo (incomplete). Manuscript pages 1–51 inclusive, and 56–72 inclusive, corresponding to pages 209 to the middle of 238, and the middle of 240 to 241 of Vol. I of the printed book.

Fernando, the Saint (incomplete). Manuscript pages 1–97 inclusive, 98 and 100. Page 100 is a fragment of a sentence apparently not consecutive, and the page appears to be improperly numbered. This corresponds to pages 353 to near the end of 415, the first thirteen chapters and the first two paragraphs of the fourteenth chapter of the printed book.

Fernan Gonzalez (complete). 108 pages of manuscript, corresponding to pages 278–350 of Vol. I of the printed book.

In the above manuscripts, the chapter headings are in a different handwriting, probably that of Pierre Irving, the editor of the book.

The Library of Columbia University contains the manuscript of Abderahman. It forms part of an unpublished manuscript. (*Vide* section "Unpublished Writings.")

Copies: The New York Public Library contains two copies of the first American edition.

The collection of the compiler contains copies of the first American edition in both bindings, and of the Bell & Daldy English edition.

LETTERS TO BREVOORT

1915

THE LETTERS OF / WASHINGTON IRVING (*in red*) / TO / HENRY BREVOORT (*in red*) / EDITED, WITH AN INTRODUCTION, BY / GEORGE S. HELLMAN / "*Sub Sole / Sub Umbra / Virens*" / *IN TWO VOLUMES / VOLUME ONE* [*TWO*] / NEW YORK / G. P. PUTNAM'S SONS (*in red*) / The Knickerbocker Press / 1915

Collation: Vol. I: Light buff end-paper; white flyleaf; (note of limited edition signed by publishers), verso blank; reproduction, on Japan paper, of Newton's portrait of Irving; (i), title-page; (ii), copyright entry and printer's imprint; iii–ix, PUBLISHERS' NOTE; (x), blank; xi–lii,

LETTERS TO BREVOORT, continued

INTRODUCTION; liii–lvii, contents; (lviii), blank; 1, subtitle; (2), blank; (3) – 198, text; folded facsimile of one page of a letter by Irving; white flyleaf; light buff end-paper.

Vol. II: Light buff end-paper; white flyleaf; note of limited edition signed by publishers, verso blank; engraved portrait of Irving on Japan paper facing title-page; (i), title-page; (ii), copyright entry and printer's imprint; iii–ix, contents; (x), blank; 1, half-title; (2), blank; 3–248, text; folded facsimile of one page of a letter by Irving; two white flyleaves; light buff end-paper.

Page size: 9 5/16 x 5⅞ inches, irregular untrimmed.

Binding: Light gray paper covered boards with decorative designs stamped in gilt on sides and black leather label on spine, printed in gilt: (double rule) / LETTERS / OF / IRVING / TO / BREVOORT / 1 [2] (enclosed in circle) / (double rule). Each volume has paper dust covers of the same color as the cover and imprinted the same but in blue. Both volumes were issued in a box with a paper label. The edition was limited to 255 sets.

A trade edition of this work was published in one volume in 1918. A companion edition of Brevoort's *Letters to Irving* in two volumes, limited to 310 sets, was issued by the same publishers in 1916. It is generally similar to the *Letters to Brevoort,* but the first volume only was signed by the publishers.

These letters by Irving are in various public and private libraries mentioned in the introduction. Many of those owned by Mr. George S. Hellman and Mr. Isaac N. Seligman have, since the publication of these volumes, been given to The New York Public Library.

Copies: The New York Public Library contains two copies of this book, and several copies of the *Letters to Irving.*

The collection of the compiler contains copies of the limited and trade editions; and a copy of Brevoort's *Letters to Irving.*

JOURNALS OF WASHINGTON IRVING
1919

THE / JOURNALS / OF / WASHINGTON / IRVING / (HITHERTO UNPUBLISHED) / (scroll design) / EDITED BY / WILLIAM P. TRENT / AND / GEORGE S. HELLMAN / PRINTED FOR MEMBERS ONLY / THE BIBLIOPHILE SOCIETY / BOSTON MCMXIX

The title-page is engraved on Japan paper and the text thereof is enclosed in an elaborate decorative design.

Collation: Vol. I: Two flyleaves; (i), subtitle; (ii), blank; (iii), engraved page on Japan paper with seal of Bibliophile Society and note of limited edition; (iv), blank; frontispiece reproduction of Newton's portrait of Irving followed by an illustration; (v), engraved title-page on Japan paper; (vi), copyright entry; vii–xvi, FOREWORD; xvii–xxv, INTRODUCTION; (xxvi), blank; (1) – (2), list of the journals; 3–225, text; (226), blank; two flyleaves. The volume contains numerous illustrations, some on the numbered pages of the text and others of full-page size inserted and not included in the pagination, as follows: facing frontispiece and facing pages viii, x, xiv, 8, 10, 12, 14, 16, 130 and 133 (these last two pages being unnumbered but included in the pagination), 172 (facsimile of page of diaries). Most of these illustrations are reproductions of original sketches by Irving.

Vol. II: Two flyleaves; (1), subtitle; (2), blank; (3), engraved page on Japan paper with seal of Bibliophile Society and note of limited edition; (4), blank; portrait of Irving; (5), engraved title-page on Japan paper; (6), copyright entry; 7–199, text; (200), blank; 2 flyleaves; full-page illustration not included in pagination facing page 119.

Vol. III: Two flyleaves; subtitle, verso blank; engraved page on Japan paper with seal of Bibliophile Society and note of limited edition, verso blank; portrait of Irving followed by illustration; engraved title-page on Japan paper, copyright entry on verso; 1–220, text; three flyleaves; full-page illustrations not included in pagination facing p. 100, 196, 198.

Vols. II and III, like Vol. I, contain numerous less-than-full-page illustrations on numbered pages.

Page size: 9 x 6¼ inches, irregular uncut on sides and bottom, but top trimmed and gilded.

Binding: Tan boards with brown cloth spine, printed in gold on spine / *(at top)* JOURNALS / OF / WASHINGTON / IRVING / (rule) / VOL. I [II., etc.] *(in middle)* seal of Bibliophile Society. *(at bottom)* THE / BIBLIOPHILE / SOCIETY / 1919

Manuscripts: The manuscript of most of these Journals is in the Seligman Collection in The New York Public Library. It comprises twenty Note Books or Journals. The library of the Rev. Dr. Roderick Terry contains 9 p. ms., 1822, apparently published in this book.

Copies: The New York Public Library contains four copies of this book.

The collection of the compiler contains a copy of this book.

NOTES OF TRAVEL IN EUROPE
1921

NOTES AND JOURNAL / OF / TRAVEL IN EUROPE / 1804–1805 / BY / WASHINGTON IRVING / (double rule) / *With an Introduction by William P. Trent and / Title-page and Illustrations in Aquatint / Designed and Engraved by / Rudolph Ruzicka* / (double rule) / IN THREE VOLUMES / VOLUME I [II., etc.] / New York / THE GROLIER CLUB / (rule) / 1921.

Collation: Vol. I: (i), pre-title; (ii), blank; half-title with illustration in colored aquatint, verso blank; (iii), title-page; (iv), copyright entry; (v), contents; (vi), blank; (vii), list of illustrations for all three volumes; (viii), blank; (ix)–xlii, INTRODUCTION; (xliii)–xliv, NOTE; (1), subtitle; (2), blank; colored aquatint; (3) – 167, text and notes; (168), blank; facing page (3) is an aquatint illustration.

Vol. II: (i), pre-title; (ii), blank; half-title with illustrations in colored aquatint, verso blank; (iii), title-page; (iv), copyright entry; (v), contents; (vi), blank; (vii), subtitle; (viii), blank; (1)–188, text and notes; facing page (67) is an aquatint illustration.

Vol. III: (i), pre-title; (ii), blank; half-title with illustration in colored aquatint, verso blank; (iii), title-page; (iv), copyright entry; (v), contents; (vi), blank; (vii), subtitle; (viii), blank; (1)–199, text, notes and index; (200), publisher's note of limited edition; facing page (87) is an aquatint illustration.

Page size: 6 13/16 x 4 5/16 inches, irregular uncut on sides and bottom, but top trimmed and gilded.

Binding: Blue cloth with decorative border in gilt on sides and decorative rules and emblems on spine in gilt and gilt stamped between second and third rule: *Notes / of Travel / in / Europe.* Between fourth and fifth rules: *Washington / Irving* Between fifth and sixth rules *1* [*2*, etc.] (enclosed in circle.)

The edition was limited to 230 sets, boxed.

Manuscripts: The manuscripts stated in the table of contents as Vol. I, July 1, 1804, to January 23, 1805, and as Vol. IV, May 17, 1805, to October 18, 1805, of Irving's Journals are in The New York Public Library; that stated in the table of contents as Vol. II, January 24, 1805, to April 13, 1805 (129 pages), is in the library of the Rev. Dr. Roderick Terry.

Copies: The New York Public Library contains three copies of this book.

The collection of the compiler contains one copy of this book.

ABU HASSAN AND THE WILD HUNTSMAN
1924

These are companion books issued in an edition limited to 455 copies and enclosed in a green cloth slip case with label.

ABU HASSAN (*in red*) / BY / WASHINGTON IRVING / (HITHERTO UNPUBLISHED) / WITH AN INTRODUCTION BY / GEORGE S. HELLMAN / (seal in blue) / PRINTED EXCLUSIVELY FOR MEMBERS OF / THE BIBLIOPHILE SOCIETY (*in red*) / BOSTON MCMXXIV.

Collation: Two flyleaves; (1), pre-title; (2), blank; (3), seal of Bibliophile Society, etc., on parchment paper; (4), blank; (5), title-page; (6), copyright entry and printer's imprint; 7–18, introduction; (19), half-title; (20), blank; (21), characters of the play; (22), blank; 23–83, text; (84), blank; three flyleaves.

Page size: 9½ x 6⅜ inches, irregular untrimmed except top which is gilt.

Binding: Green cloth sides, white imitation vellum spine, printed in gold: ABU / HASSAN / (rule) /IRVING (at bottom) 1924.

THE WILD HUNTSMAN (*in red*) / BY / WASHINGTON IRVING / (HITHERTO UNPUBLISHED) / WITH AN INTRODUCTION BY / GEORGE S. HELLMAN / (seal in

ABU HASSAN AND THE WILD HUNTSMAN, continued

blue) / PRINTED EXCLUSIVELY FOR MEMBERS OF / THE BIBLIOPHILE SOCIETY (*in red*) / BOSTON MCMXXIV

Collation: Two flyleaves; (1), pre-title; (2), blank; (3), seal of Bibliophile Society, etc., on parchment paper; (4), blank; (5), title-page; (6), copyright entry and printer's imprint; 7–19, introduction; (20), blank; (21), half-title; (22), blank; (23), characters of the play; (24), blank; 25–113, text; (114), blank; two flyleaves.

Page size and binding uniform with above volume, except the title on spine, as follows: THE / WILD / HUNTS- / MAN / (rule) / IRVING (at bottom) 1924.

Manuscripts: The New York Public Library, Hellman Collection, contains the mss. of these plays, approximately 72 p. and 100 p. respectively.

Copies: The New York Public Library contains three copies of each of the above titles.

The collection of the compiler contains copies of each title.

AN UNWRITTEN DRAMA OF LORD BYRON
1925

AN UNWRITTEN DRAMA / OF LORD BYRON / By / Washington Irving / With an Introduction by / THOMAS OLLIVE MABBOTT, Ph. D. / (publisher's emblem) / CHARLES F. HEARTMAN / Metuchen, New Jersey / 1925

Collation: (i), pre-title; (ii), note of limited edition; (iii), title-page; (iv), publisher's note; (v)–(vii), INTRODUCTION; (viii), blank; (ix)–(xiii), text; (xiv), blank; flyleaf.

Page size: 9⅜ x 6⅜ inches, irregular untrimmed.

Binding: Mottled green and tan boards, with white paper label on front printed in black within a double-ruled border: An Unwritten Drama / OF / Lord Byron / (decoration) / BY / WASHINGTON IRVING

This is the first separate publication of this article, limited to 51 copies. It was first published in *The Gift* for 1836.

It is stated by Prof. Mabbott in the introduction that this was the source for Edgar Allan Poe's "William Wilson."

Copies: The New York Public Library contains two copies of this book, and two of *The Gift*.

The collection of the compiler contains a copy of this and *The Gift*.

WASHINGTON IRVING DIARY. SPAIN 1828–29
1926

WASHINGTON IRVING / DIARY / SPAIN 1828–1829 / EDITED FROM THE MANUSCRIPT IN / THE LIBRARY OF THE SOCIETY BY / CLARA LOUISA PENNEY / Corresponding Member of The Hispanic / Society of America / (seal of Society) / THE HISPANIC SOCIETY / OF AMERICA / NEW YORK / 1926

Collation: Yellow end-paper; (i), pre-title; (ii), blank; frontispiece map; (iii), title-page; (iv), copyright entry and printer's imprint; (v), contents; (vi), blank; vii, list of illustrations; (viii), blank; ix–xviii, INTRODUCTION; (1), subtitle; (2), blank; 3–142, text, notes, references and index; yellow end-paper. Decorative seals and illustrations and a few words are printed on the end papers.

Page size: 6 7/16 x 4¼ inches. Printed on light tan paper, with rounded corners and red edges.

Binding: Tan cloth, printed in red at the top of the front side: HISPANIC NOTES / & MONOGRAPHS / (seal). At the bottom of the side is printed: CATALOGUE SERIES. The spine is printed in red at the top: WASHINGTON / IRVING / DIARY / (rule) / PENNEY and at the bottom: THE HISPANIC / SOCIETY OF / AMERICA. The book carries a tan paper jacket printed in red on both sides, back and both inside flaps.

Manuscript: The manuscript of this book is in the library of the Hispanic Society of America, New York.

Copies: The New York Public Library contains one copy of this book.

The collection of the compiler contains one copy of this book.

IRVING'S SKETCH BOOK NOTES 1817
IRVING'S TOUR IN SCOTLAND 1817
1927

These two volumes are companion books, published together in a box covered with light blue paper. The edition was limited to 525 copies.

NOTES / WHILE PREPARING / SKETCH BOOK / &C. / 1817 / BY / *WASHINGTON IRVING* / (decorative rule) / *Edited with a Critical Introduction by* / STANLEY T. WILLIAMS / (seal) / *NEW HAVEN* / YALE UNIVERSITY PRESS / *MDCCCCXXVII*

The title-page is enclosed in decorative border.

Collation: Two flyleaves; (i), pre-title; (ii), blank; (iii), blank; (iv), frontispiece (front cover of ms.); (v), title-page; (vi), copyright entry and printing note; (vii), contents; (viii), blank; (ix), list of illustrations; (x), blank; (xi), *ACKNOWLEDGMENT;* (xii), blank; (1) – 42, INTRODUCTION; (43)–97, text and index; (98), blank; (99), note of limited edition; (100), blank; two flyleaves. Two pages of ms. reproduced between pages 64 and 65.

Page size: 8 x 5 inches, irregular untrimmed.

Binding: Light blue boards, black cloth spine printed in gold: *Irving's / Sketch / Book / Notes /* 1817 Seal stamped in gold at bottom of back.

TOUR / IN / SCOTLAND / 1817 / AND / OTHER MANUSCRIPT NOTES / BY / *WASHINGTON IRVING* / (decorative rule) / *Edited with a Critical Introduction by /* STANLEY T. WILLIAMS / (seal) / *NEW HAVEN* / YALE UNIVERSITY PRESS / *MDCCCCXXVII*

The title-page is enclosed in decorative border.

Collation: Two flyleaves; (i), pre-title; (ii), blank; (iii), blank; (iv) and (v), double-page map; (vi), blank; (vii), title-page; (viii), copyright entry and printing note; (ix), contents; (x), blank; (xi), list of illustrations; (xii), blank; (xiii), *ACKNOWLEDGMENT;* (xiv), blank; (1)–18, INTRODUCTION; (19), half-title; (20), blank; (21)–146, text, notes and index; (147), note of limited edition; (148), blank; two flyleaves. Facsimiles opposite pages 26, 36, 52, 68, 72.

Page size and binding same as preceding. Title in gold on spine: *Irving's / Tour / in / Scotland* / 1817 Seal in gold at bottom.

Manuscripts: The manuscript of the Sketch Book Notes, one volume, is in Yale University Library; that of the Tour in Scotland, two volumes, is the property of Mr. Preston Davie, Tuxedo Park, New York.

Copies: The New York Public Library contains a copy of each of the above titles.

The collection of the compiler contains one copy of each of the above titles.

LETTERS FROM SUNNYSIDE AND SPAIN
1928

LETTERS / FROM SUNNYSIDE AND SPAIN / BY / WASHINGTON IRVING / EDITED BY / STANLEY T. WILLIAMS / (publisher's device) / NEW HAVEN / YALE UNIVERSITY PRESS / 1928.

Collation: (i), pre-title; (ii), blank; frontispiece; (iii), title-page; (iv), copyright entry; (v) – vi, PREFACE; (vii), CONTENTS; (viii), blank; (1), sub-title; (2), blank; (3) – 80, text.

Page size: 8⅝ x 5⅝ inches.

Binding: Blue cloth, stamped in gold on spine: (rule) / Letters / from / Sunnyside / and Spain / (French) / Irving / (dotted rule) / at the bottom of the spine, the seal of the Press. The sides are blind stamped with a border rule.

In addition to the frontispiece the book contains two illustrations, fac-similes of letters by Irving. Most of the text is reprinted from the *Yale Review,* April, 1927, and October, 1927; a few letters and explanatory comments have been added.

Copies: The New York Public Library contains a copy, as does the collection of the compiler.

POEMS

1931

THE POEMS OF / WASHINGTON IRVING / (decoration) / *Brought together from various sources by* / WILLIAM R. LANGFELD / (decoration) / NEW YORK / THE NEW YORK PUBLIC LIBRARY / 1931

Collation: (1), title-page; (2), printer's imprint; 3, [introduction]; 4–19, text; 20, blank.

Page size: 10 x 7 inches.

Binding: Issued in light blue wrappers, printed same as the title-page.

The pamphlet was reprinted from the *Bulletin* of The New York Public Library, November, 1930.

Of this edition, twenty-eight copies were specially bound for presentation by the compiler.

Copies: The New York Public Library contains several copies of this, as does the collection of the compiler.

JOURNAL OF WASHINGTON IRVING (1823–1824)

1931

JOURNAL OF / WASHINGTON IRVING / (1823–1824) / EDITED BY / STANLEY T. WILLIAMS / (seal) / CAMBRIDGE / HARVARD UNIVERSITY PRESS / 1931

Collation: Light cream end-papers; (i), pre-title; (ii), imprint of English publisher; portrait of Irving; (iii), title-page; (iv), copyright entry and publisher's imprint; (v), acknowledgment to owner of manuscript; (vi), blank; (vii), Contents; (viii), blank; ix–xvii, introduction; (xviii), blank; (1), half-title; (2), blank; 3–(257), text; (258), blank; (259), subtitle; (260), blank; 261–278, Index; (279) and (280), blank; light cream end-papers.

Page size: 7¾ x 5 1/16 inches.

Binding: Dark red cloth, sides stamped in blank, spine printed in gilt: JOURNAL / OF / WASHINGTON / IRVING / (1823–1824) / (rule) / WILLIAMS and at bottom, seal in gilt. Cream colored paper dust cover printed in black, title, author and publisher on front outside and back, list of publications back outside, publisher's note inside front flap.

Manuscript: The library of the Rev. Dr. Roderick Terry contains the manuscript of this book.

Copies: The New York Public Library contains a copy of this book.

The collection of the compiler contains a copy of this book.

LETTERS TO MRS. WILLIAM RENWICK

Undated

LETTERS FROM WASHINGTON IRVING / TO MRS. WILLIAM RENWICK, AND / TO HER SON, JAMES RENWICK, / PROFESSOR OF NATURAL PHILOSOPHY / AT COLUMBIA UNIVERSITY, WRITTEN / BETWEEN SEPTEMBER 10TH, 1811 / AND APRIL 5TH, 1816. / (French rule) / *Printed for private distribution.*

Collation: (1), Cover with title; (2), inside cover, blank; 3–4, introductory explanation; 5–34, text; (35), inside back cover, with note on letter of April 5, 1816; (36), outside cover, blank.

Page size: 8½ x 5 9/16 inches.

Binding: Light blue paper wrapper.

This booklet was printed privately and not put on sale.

Manuscript: The Library of Columbia University contains the manuscript of this book.

Copy: The New York Public Library contains a copy.

BOOKS WHICH IRVING EDITED OR TO WHICH HE CONTRIBUTED

It is difficult in some cases to determine whether certain books should be listed as separate works by Irving, in which case they should receive full descriptions and collations, or whether they should be included under the heading above. Of such doubtful cases we are including with the separate works The Life of Lawrence, The Biography of Margaret Davidson, the various forms of the Life of Goldsmith, and The Poetical Works of Thomas Campbell; others are listed below. Contributions to annuals are listed with contributions to periodicals.

BRYANT, WILLIAM CULLEN. Poems, by William Cullen Bryant, an American. Edited by Washington Irving. London: J. Andrews, 1832. xii, 235 p. 12°.

This contains an introductory letter by Irving, p. iii–vi. He also altered line 3, stanza 1, line 1, stanza 2, line 9, stanza 4, line 11, stanza 5, of one of the poems, *The Song of Marion's Men,* page 79, which he thought would be offensive to British readers. This alteration, together with the variations between the English and American introductions to *The Rocky Mountains,* gave rise to the charge of being an Anglophile, to which reference has been made. He made a number of other alterations in the book.

Copies: The New York Public Library; Library of Congress; collection of the compiler.

CAMPBELL, THOMAS. The Poetical Works of Thomas Campbell. Including several pieces from the original manuscript, never before published in this country. To which is prefixed a biographical sketch of the author, by a gentleman of New-York. Printed for Philip H. Nicklin & Co., Baltimore. Also, for D. W. Farrand and Green, Albany; D. Mallory and Co., Boston; Lyman and Hall, Portland; and E. Earle, Philadelphia. Fry and Kammerer, Printers, 1810. 296 p. 12°.

This edition includes an introductory Life written by Irving. This work appeared in two distinct editions, of one and two volumes respectively. Irving's *Life* occupies pages vi–xliii of the one-volume edition, and pages (7)–41 of vol. 1 of the two-volume edition. Enlarged and revised, this *Life* was published in the *Analectic Magazine* in March, 1815. An edition of the *Poetical Works of Thomas Campbell,* published by Edward Earle at Philadelphia, in 1815, contains the *Life* as published in the *Analectic Magazine.* Foley lists this Earle edition as Philadelphia, 1815, with an undated title-page. It also appeared with the same publisher and printer, but with the title-page dated Philadelphia, 1815. The *Life* occupies pages (1)–24 of the undated edition, and pages v–xxvii of the dated edition. It is not clear which of these is the prior issue. William L. Stone's *The Poetry and History of Wyoming,* New York: Wiley and Putnam, 1841, contains, pages (iii) – xxiv, a further revision of this *Life,* several paragraphs being added. An edition of Beattie's *Life of Campbell* published by Harper & Bro. in two volumes contains an introductory letter by Irving on Thomas Campbell, vol. 1, p. xi–xvi. The exact date of this edition is not certain: we have seen only a copy dated 1855. It contains no copyright entry, nor is there any indication to show that it is a second printing or a second or later edition. The *Life* is reprinted in *Spanish Papers,* vol. II, as it appeared in the *Analectic Magazine,* except for the omission of the last paragraph. It includes, however, this letter.

Copies: Both The New York Public Library and the Library of Congress have copies of both the one-volume and the two-volume 1810 edition. Mr. Albert A. Bieber of Manasquan, N. J., has copies of both editions in the original bindings, boards and calf respectively.

The collection of the compiler contains copies of the other titles mentioned in the preceding paragraph.

Additional information will be found on p. 13–14.

DUYCKINCK, EVERT AUGUSTUS, AND GEORGE L. DUYCKINCK. Cyclopædia of American Literature; embracing personal and critical notices of authors, and selections from their writings . . . New York: C. Scribner, 1855. 2 v. illus. 4°.

Article on Washington Allston, vol. 2, p. 14–16. Republished in *Spanish Papers,* Vol. 2.

Copies: The New York Public Library; Library of Congress; collection of the compiler.

BOOKS WHICH IRVING EDITED OR TO WHICH HE CONTRIBUTED, continued

HARRIMAN, FLORENCE JAFFRAY (HURST). From Pinafores to Politics, by Mrs. J. Borden Harriman. New York: Henry Holt and Company, 1923. 4 p.l., 359 p. illus. 8°.

The Lay of the Sunnyside Ducks, a poem, appears on p. 22–23.
Copies: The New York Public Library; Library of Congress; collection of the compiler.

HARRISON, GABRIEL. The Life and Writings of John Howard Payne. Albany, N. Y.: Joel Munsell, 1875. ix, 410 p., 2 ports. f°.

Contains two poems by Irving: A Song, p. 397, and Signs of the Times, p. 398.
Copies: The New York Public Library; Library of Congress; collection of the compiler.

THE HOME BOOK OF THE PICTURESQUE; or, American Scenery, Art, and Literature. Comprising a series of essays by Washington Irving, W. C. Bryant, Fenimore Cooper . . . etc. With thirteen engravings on steel, from pictures by eminent artists . . . New York: G. P. Putnam, 1852. 4 p.l., [7] – 8 p., 2 l., 188 p., 13 pl. 4°.

Contains Irving's essay The Catskill Mountains, p. 71–78. Reprinted in his *Spanish Papers,* Vol. II.
Copies: The New York Public Library; Library of Congress; collection of the compiler.

IRVINGIANA: a memorial of Washington Irving. New York: Charles B. Richardson, 1860. lxiv p. illus. f°.

This volume contains several unpublished letters by Irving and a number of letters previously published in various periodicals, but appearing here for the first time in book form. Among these is one of special interest on Ichabod Crane, reprinted from the Kinderhook, N. Y., *Sentinel.*
Copies: The New York Public Library and the collection of the compiler contain copies; the library of Dr. Roderick Terry contains an extra-illustrated copy.

THE KNICKERBOCKER GALLERY: a testimonial to the editor of the Knickerbocker Magazine [i. e., Lewis Gaylord Clark] from its contributors. With forty-eight portraits on steel . . . engraved expressly for this work. New-York: S. Hueston, 1855. 1 p.l., (i)x – xiv, 15–505 p., 49 ports. 8°.

Contains Irving's Conversations with Talma, p. 15–22. Republished in the *Atlantic Souvenir* for 1859 and also in his *Spanish Papers,* Vol. II.
Copies: The New York Public Library; Library of Congress; collection of the compiler.

MEMORIAL OF JAMES FENIMORE COOPER. New York: G. P. Putnam, 1852. 106 p. illus. 8°.

Contains a letter by Irving regarding Cooper, p. 7.
Copies: The New York Public Library; Library of Congress; collection of the compiler.

PAULDING, WILLIAM IRVING. Literary Life of James K. Paulding. Compiled by his son, William I. Paulding. New York: Charles Scribner and Company, 1867. 1 p.l., xiii, 15–397 p., 1 port. 8°.

This work quotes, on page 120, a part of one of Irving's letters, portions of which are included in Pierre Irving's *Life and Letters,* Vol. I, p. 455.
Copies: The New York Public Library; Library of Congress; collection of the compiler.

PONS, FRANÇOIS RAYMOND JOSEPH DE. A Voyage to the Eastern Part of Terra Firma, or the Spanish Main, in South-America, during the Years 1801, 1802, 1803, and 1804 . . . Translated by an American gentleman. New-York: I. Riley and Co., 1806. 3 v. 8°.

This was edited and partly translated by Irving.
Copies: The New York Public Library; Library of Congress; collection of the compiler.

Letters from Washington Irving may be found in innumerable biographies of contemporary authors or in books on literary topics dealing with the period of his work. It is obviously impossible to note all of these, but several may be mentioned here. James Grant Wilson's *Life and Letters of Fitz Green Halleck*, New York, 1869, gives quotations from a speech by Irving, p. 397–398, in greater fullness than the report of the same in Pierre Irving's *Life and Letters*, and also one or two anecdotes and remarks not found in the latter. Donald G. Mitchell in his *American Lands and Letters*, New York, 1897, p. 321–322, prints for the first time a letter by Irving. The same writer's *Dream Life*, New York, 1863, contains in the preface a letter by Irving in full, only part of which is quoted in Pierre Irving's *Life and Letters*. William Watson Waldron, in his *Washington Irving and Contemporaries, in Thirty Life Sketches*, New York: W. H. Kelley & Co., n. d., prints many letters or portions of letters, in the "sketches," and also a series of nine letters to himself. The latter, as well as several of the former, are printed for the first time. Robert E. Spiller's *The American in England*, New York, 1926, contains on p. 281 portions of a letter, no part of which had been previously published.

On the first of the four pages of advertisements in the front of volume 2 of the first edition of Poe's *Tales of the Grotesque and Arabesque* (Philadelphia: Lea and Blanchard, 1840 [actually published 1839]) there are quoted opinions of Poe's work, two of them being extracts from letters from Washington Irving. In Poe's *The Literati*, first edition (New York: J. S. Redfield, 1850) in the introductory memoir by Rufus Griswold, short portions of these two letters are quoted, differing slightly from the advertisement. In *The Life of Edgar Allan Poe*, by George E. Woodberry (New York: Houghton Mifflin Company, 1909) the second of these letters is quoted in full, Vol. 2, p. 216–217. It is dated Newburg, Nov. 6, 1839, and agrees with the Griswold quotation except one word. It also refers to a previous letter, on page 213 of the same volume, some of the phrases of which are apparently duplicated in the later one. The collection of the compiler contains first editions of *Tales of the Grotesque and Arabesque* (imperfect) and of *The Literati*. The Griswold memoir also quotes from and comments upon memoranda prepared by Poe for a sketch of his life in 1843, Poe's version of the second letter, which differs slightly and which he says is "a characteristic instance of perversion in the reproduction of compliments."

CONTRIBUTIONS TO PERIODICALS AND ANNUALS

American Literature

Washington Irving's First Stay in Paris. By Stanley T. Williams. Vol. 2, No. 1, March, 1930, p. 15–20.

Published in part in Pierre M. Irving's *Life and Letters of Washington Irving*, Vol. I, p. 144–147.

New Verses by Washington Irving. By John Howard Birss. Vol. 4, No. 3, November, 1932, p. 296.

The Analectic Magazine

This periodical was edited by Irving for a short time in 1813. He also contributed to it the following articles:

Review of the Works of Robert Treat Paine. March, 1813, p. 249–266.

Reprinted in *Spanish Papers*, Vol. II, p. 303–324.

Biography of Captain James Lawrence. August, 1813, p. 122–139.

Reprinted in *Spanish Papers*, Vol. II, p. 37–58.

Captain Lawrence. [Note to the previous article.] September, 1813, p. 222–223.

Reprinted in *Spanish Papers*, Vol. II, p. 58–59. This and the preceding article, together with other matter not by Irving, were published in book form in 1813.

The Lay of the Scottish Fiddle: a Tale of Havre de Grace. [A review.] September, 1813, p. 223–230.

Biographical Notice of the late Lieutenant Burrows. November, 1813, p. 396–403.

Reprinted in *Spanish Papers*, Vol. II, p. 60–69.

CONTRIBUTIONS TO PERIODICALS AND ANNUALS, continued

Biographical Memoir of Commodore Perry. December, 1813, p. 494–510.

Reprinted in *Spanish Papers,* Vol. II, p. 70–90.

Traits of Indian Character. February, 1814, p. 145–156.

Reprinted, with considerable revision, in the *Sketch Book* in all English editions, and in all American editions beginning with the fourth.

[Review of] Odes, Naval Songs, and other occasional Poems. By Edwin C. Holland. March, 1814, p. 242–252.

Reprinted in *Spanish Papers,* Vol. II, p. 325–338.

Philip of Pokanoket. An Indian Memoir. June, 1814, p. 502–515.

Reprinted, with considerable revision, in the *Sketch Book* in all English editions, and in all American editions beginning with the fourth.

Lord Byron. July, 1814, p. 68–72.

Biographical Memoir of Captain David Porter. September, 1814, p. 225–243.

Reprinted in *Spanish Papers,* Vol. II, p. 91–114.

A Biographical Sketch of Thomas Campbell. March, 1815, p. 234–250.

Reprinted (except one paragraph) in *Spanish Papers,* Vol. II, p. 115–135.

The Atlantic Souvenir

On Passaic Falls. [A poem.] Written in the year 1806. The Atlantic Souvenir, 1827. Philadelphia [cop. 1826]. 24°. p. 146–148.

This poem was later republished in *The New-York Book of Poetry,* New-York: George Dearborn, 1837, p. 105–106, omitting stanzas 5, 6, 7, and 10, and with some slight changes in punctuation.

The Dull Lecture. [A poem.] The Atlantic Souvenir, 1828. Philadelphia [cop. 1827]. 24°. p. 294.

Reprinted in *Irvingiana,* New York, 1860, p. xliii.

Bulletin of The New York Public Library

The Poems of Washington Irving. Brought together from various sources for the first time by William R. Langfeld. Vol. 34, No. 11, November, 1930, p. 763–779.

Reprinted separately. (See p. 52.)

The Cornhill Magazine

Written in the Deepdene Album. [A poem, written June 24th, 1822.] Vol. 1, May, 1860, p. 582.

Reprinted in Pierre M. Irving's *Life and Letters of Washington Irving,* New York, 1862–64, Vol. II, p. 85–86.

Forget-Me-Not, Philadelphia

Ellen. A sketch from "Scenes and Thoughts." Forget-me-not. Philadelphia: Judah Dobson, 1828. 24°. p. 300–302.

Friendship's Offering: — A Christmas, New Year and Birthday Present for 1849

The Haunted Ship. Friendship's Offering . . . for 1849. Boston: Phillips and Sampson, 1849. 12°. p. 326–330.

Galignani's Messenger, Paris

Irving contributed to this periodical two articles in 1824, one on the death of Louis XVII, the other on Byron.

The Gift, Philadelphia

An Unwritten Drama of Lord Byron. The Gift . . . for 1836. Philadelphia: E. L. Carey & A. Hart [pref. 1835]. 16°. p. 166–171.

This article was republished as a separate volume in 1925. (See p. 50.)

The Knickerbocker, or New-York Monthly Magazine

To the Editor of the Knickerbocker. Vol. 13, No. 3, March, 1839, p. 206–210.

First paragraph reprinted with some changes in *A Book of the Hudson;* reprinted in full with further revision in *Spanish Papers,* Vol. II, p. 417–424.

A Chronicle of Wolfert's Roost. Vol. 13, No. 4, April, 1839, p. 317–328.

Reprinted, with extensive revision, in *Wolfert's Roost,* p. 9–29.

The Birds of Spring. Vol. 13, No. 5, May, 1839, p. 434–437.

Reprinted, with slight revision, in *Wolfert's Roost,* p. 30–37.

Sleepy Hollow. Vol. 13, No. 5, May, 1839, p. 404–411.

Reprinted in *Spanish Papers,* Vol. II, p. 425–439.

Recollections of the Alhambra. Vol. 13, No. 6, June, 1839, p. 485–494.

Reprinted, with extensive revision, in *Wolfert's Roost,* p. 366–383.

The Enchanted Island. Vol. 14, No. 1, July, 1839, p. 26–38.

Reprinted, with extensive revision, in *Wolfert's Roost,* p. 341–365, under the title The Phantom Island.

National Nomenclature. Vol. 14, No. 2, August, 1839, p. 158–162.

Reprinted in *Spanish Papers,* Vol. II, p. 440–446.

Desultory Thoughts on Criticism. Vol. 14, No. 2, August, 1839, p. 175–178.

Reprinted in *Spanish Papers,* Vol. II, p. 447–452.

Spanish Romance. Vol. 14, No. 3, September, 1839, p. 225–231.

Reprinted in *Spanish Papers,* Vol. I, p. 455–466.

Communipaw. Vol. 14, No. 3, September, 1839, p. 257–262.

Reprinted in *Spanish Papers,* Vol. II, p. 453–462.

Conspiracy of the Cocked Hats. Vol. 14, No. 4, October, 1839, p. 305–309.

Reprinted in *Spanish Papers,* Vol. II, p. 463–470.

Guests from Gibbet-Island. Vol. 14, No. 4, October, 1839, p. 342–350.

Reprinted, with slight revision, in *A Book of the Hudson* and in *Wolfert's Roost,* p. 234–248.

Mountjoy. Vol. 14, No. 5, November, 1839, p. 402–412; No. 6, December, 1839, p. 522–538.

Reprinted in *Wolfert's Roost,* p. 49–99.

The Bermudas. Vol. 15, No. 1, January, 1840, p. 17–25.

Reprinted in *Wolfert's Roost,* p. 100–114.

Pelayo and the Merchant's Daughter. Vol. 15, No. 1, January, 1840, p. 65–70.

Reprinted, with slight revision and much addition, in *Spanish Papers,* Vol. I, p. 209–244.

CONTRIBUTIONS TO PERIODICALS AND ANNUALS, continued

To the Editor of the Knickerbocker. [Letter on international copyright.] Vol. 15, No. 1, January, 1840, p. 78–79.

The Knight of Malta. Vol. 15, No. 2, February, 1840, p. 108–118.
Reprinted in *Wolfert's Roost,* p. 130–150.

Legend of the Engulphed Convent. Vol. 15, No. 3, March, 1840, p. 234–237.
Reprinted in *Wolfert's Roost,* p. 334–340.

The Count Van Horn. Vol. 15, No. 3, March, 1840, p. 241–249.
Reprinted in *Wolfert's Roost,* p. 305–321.

A Time of Unexampled Prosperity. Vol. 15, No. 4, April, 1840, p. 303–324.
Reprinted in *Wolfert's Roost,* p. 151–191.

Abderahman. Vol. 15, No. 5, May, 1840, p. 427–440.
Reprinted, much revised, in *Spanish Papers,* Vol. I, p. 245–273.

The Taking of the Veil, and The Charming Letoriéres. Vol. 15, No. 6, June, 1840, p. 513–521.

Letter from Granada. Vol. 16, No. 1, July, 1840, p. 57–61.
Reprinted in *Spanish Papers,* Vol. II, p. 471–479.

The Early Experiences of Ralph Ringwood. Vol. 16, No. 2, August, 1840, p. 152–165; No. 3, September, 1840, p. 258–266.
Reprinted in *Wolfert's Roost,* p. 249–288.

The Seminoles. Vol. 16, No. 4, October, 1840, p. 339–347.
Reprinted, with slight revision, in *Wolfert's Roost,* p. 289–304.

Sketches in Paris in 1825. Vol. 16, No. 5, November, 1840, p. 425–430; No. 6, December, 1840, p. 519–530.
Reprinted, with slight revision, in *Wolfert's Roost,* p. 192–218.

Broek: or The Dutch Paradise. Vol. 17, No. 1, January, 1841, p. 55–58.
Reprinted in *Wolfert's Roost,* p. 226–233.

Don Juan: a Spectral Research. Vol. 17, No. 3, March, 1841, p. 247–253.
Reprinted in *Wolfert's Roost,* p. 322–333.

American Researches in Italy. Vol. 18, No. 4, October, 1841, p. 319–322.

THE LITERARY WORLD, NEW YORK

Correction of a misstatement respecting "Astoria," by Washington Irving. [Letter to the editor respecting the statement that he had received $5,000 from Astor for writing "Astoria."] Vol. 9, No. 251, November 22, 1851, p. 408.

THE MAGNOLIA, NEW YORK

The Widow's Ordeal, or A Judicial Trial by Combat. The Magnolia for 1837. New-York: Bancroft & Holley [cop. 1836]. 12°. p. 257–274.

This was originally intended for a miscellany edited by Allan Cunningham, called *The Anniversary.* The article, however, did not appear at this time, since the second volume of *The Anniversary* was never published.
Reprinted in *Wolfert's Roost,* p. 115–129.

The Creole Village. A Sketch from a Steamboat. The Magnolia for 1837. New-York: Bancroft & Holley [cop. 1836]. 12°. p. 315–326.

Reprinted in *Wolfert's Roost,* p. 38–48.

Contains first use of the phrase, "the almighty dollar." In the reprint in *Wolfert's Roost* there is added a short, humorous note mentioning this.

According to Pierre M. Irving, *Life and Letters of Washington Irving,* v. 3, p. 99, Irving also contributed to the *Magnolia* "The Happy Man," which was later reprinted in *Wolfert's Roost* as "The Contented Man." It does not, however, appear in either the 1836 or 1837 issues of the *Magnolia.* All subsequent issues of this publication are merely reprints of one or the other of these two issues.

The Morning Chronicle, New York

The Letters of Jonathan Oldstyle, nine in number, were published in this paper in 1802 and 1803. Eight of these were republished in 1824. The first five were reprinted in *Spanish Papers,* Vol. ii, p. 11–33. For detailed information regarding this series see the entry under *Letters of Jonathan Oldstyle* in the section: Chronological List of Works.

North American Review

[Review of] Wheaton's History of the Northmen. Vol. 35, No. 77, October, 1832, p. 342–371.

Reprinted in *Spanish Papers,* Vol. ii, p. 339–377.

The Plaindealer, New York

[Letter to the editor of the Plaindealer, on the charge made against him of being an Anglophile.] Vol. 1, No. 9, January 28, 1837, p. 131.

Washington Irving's Apology to William Cullen Bryant. [Letter dated February 16, 1837.] Vol. 1, No. 12, February 18, 1837, p. 186–187.

The Quarterly Review

[Review, or rather explanation, of his Conquest of Granada.] Vol. 43, No. 85, May, 1830, p. 55–80.

Reprinted in *Spanish Papers,* Vol. ii, p. 378–416.

[Review of] A Year in Spain. By a Young American [Alexander Slidell]. Vol. 44, No. 88, February, 1831, p. 319–342.

Scribner's Magazine

Correspondence of Washington Irving and John Howard Payne (1821–1828). Edited by Payne's grandnephew, Thatcher T. Payne Luquer. Vol. 48, No. 4, October, 1910, p. 461–482; No. 5, November, 1910, p. 597–616.

The Spirit of the Fair, New York

The Story of Pelayo. A fragment. (Now published for the first time.) No. 11, April 16, 1864, p. 126; No. 12, April 18, 1864, p. 138–139.

Reprinted in *Spanish Papers,* Vol. i.

Yale Review

Washington Irving's Religion. By Stanley T. Williams. Vol. 15, No. 2, January, 1926, p. 414–416.

This hitherto unpublished letter, written to Emily Foster and dated August 23, 1825, was in the possession of Dr. A. S. W. Rosenbach at the time of its publication.

CONTRIBUTIONS TO PERIODICALS AND ANNUALS, continued

Unpublished Letters of Washington Irving. Sunnyside and New York Chronicles. By Stanley T. Williams. Vol. 16, No. 3, April, 1927, p. 459–484.

Published for the first time from the manuscripts in the Yale University Library.

Letters of Washington Irving. Spanish Fêtes and Ceremonies. By Stanley T. Williams. Vol. 17, No. 1, October, 1927, p. 99–117.

Published from manuscripts in the Yale University Library.

These letters, and those in the April, 1927, issue, were reprinted in *Letters from Sunnyside and Spain.*

PLAYS

In addition to the two plays published by the Bibliophile Society, previously listed, which Irving wrote, he also revised or altered to a greater or less extent several of the plays of John Howard Payne, or collaborated with him in their composition. The exact extent of Irving's work in this connection is somewhat uncertain. Information may be found in biographies of Irving, in his notebooks and journals, and in letters exchanged between Irving and Payne. These references are frequently indefinite and casual, and do not invariably indicate whether Irving actually collaborated or whether he merely gave friendly opinions or occasional suggestions. In the following list are included all those plays in which it seems reasonably certain that Irving had a hand. Among these it is certain that Irving wrote a considerable portion, by himself or with Payne, of *Richelieu* and *Charles the Second,* that he had much to do with *Azendai,* and that he eliminated much of Payne's first draft of the *Spanish Husband.*

RICHELIEU: a domestic tragedy, founded on fact . . . Now first printed from the author's manuscript. New York: E. M. Murden, 1826. 79 p. 16°.

CHARLES THE SECOND; OR, THE MERRY MONARCH . . . London: Printed for Longman, Hurst, Rees, Orme, Brown, and Green, 1824. 66 p. 8°.

Also published in London by T. Dolby [1824]; and in 1829 by Neal & Mackenzie, Philadelphia and New York. Reprinted, with changes, several times and included by A. H. Quinn in his *Representative American Plays,* New York, 1917.

MARRIED AND SINGLE. Written about 1823.

AZENDAI. Written about 1823.

THE SPANISH HUSBAND. Performed in London May 25, 1830 and in New York November 1, 1830.

In *Washington Irving, Esquire,* by George S. Hellman, there is a reference to "The Spanish Hero," but this is probably a misprint for this play.

MAZEPPA. Performed in New York June 22, 1833, probably its first performance.

PETER SMINK. London: Thomas Haile Lacy, n. d. Performed in London July 8, 1822, and in New York October 14, 1826.

NORA; or, The Girl of Erin. Performed in London February 1, 1826.

It is probable, though less certain, that Irving did some work on *The Guilty Mother* and *Le Contrebandier.*

Copies: The Library of Congress possesses copies of both the London, 1824, editions of *Charles the Second,* and the New York, 1826, edition of *Richelieu.* The Library of the University of Pennsylvania contains copies of the London: Longman, etc., 1824, and the Philadelphia and New York: Neal and Mackenzie, 1829, editions of *Charles the Second.* The Harvard University Library contains copies of the Longman, etc., London, 1824 (imperfect), the Neal & Mackenzie, 1829, Philadelphia and New York, and the London: Dolby [1824] editions of *Charles the Second,* the Lacy, London, n.d., edition of *Peter Smink* and the New York, 1826, edition of *Richelieu.* The collection of the compiler contains a copy of the Longman, etc., London, 1824, edition of *Charles the Second* and two copies, one uncut and unbound, of the Murden, New York, 1826, edition of *Richelieu.*

UNPUBLISHED WRITINGS

While several of Irving's diaries and notebooks have been published, there still remain a number in manuscript form. There are also in the possession of collectors and institutions several unpublished manuscripts. Unpublished letters are numerous, both in private and public hands. Many of these are naturally of slight importance, but some are of biographical or of general interest. The following list of unpublished manuscript material written by Irving includes, it is believed, all that is of real importance, although there are many letters and pages or small portions of manuscript which it is impracticable to enumerate.

The New York Public Library

a. *In the Seligman Collection.*

Journal, August 5 to November—, 1804.
Notebooks or journals 1805–6, principally concerning London and Paris.
Numerous letters.
Notes for Knickerbocker's History of New York, 1807–8, 1808–9.
Notebook 1817.
Notebook 1818.
Notebook 1818 (another book).
Notebook 1824–5.
Notebook 183–?
Notebook 1844.
Eleven pages, Essay on Communipaw. A portion of this was published in the first chapter of Communipaw in *The Book of the Hudson.*
Notebook containing extracts of poetry and prose, hint for a tale or farce, etc.
Notes for the Life of Washington (two books).
Notes for the study of Arabic.
Notes for the Life of Mahomet.
Notes relative to Charles Martel, etc.
Eighty-six pages. Translation of Sahagun's Conquest of Mexico. Chapters 1 to 29. This manuscript lacks the last chapter which Irving translated.
Journal July 1, 1804 to January 23, 1804.
Journal August 5 to November—, 1804.
Journal December 23, 1804 to May—, 1805.
Journal May 17 to October 18, 1805.
Journal July to August, 1829. Part of this was published in *Journals of Washington Irving,* New York, 1919.
Journal January 6, 1830 to July 2, 1831.

b. *In the Hellman Collection.*

Two pages, anecdote of Admiral Harvey, incomplete.
One page, notes for the Life of Washington.
One page, notes for The Alhambra.
One page, notes for one of the Spanish historical works.
Many letters.

UNPUBLISHED WRITINGS, continued

c. In the General Library Collection.

Several letters.

COLUMBIA UNIVERSITY LIBRARY

Three hundred and six pages, a portion of the Chronicle of the Ommiades. A portion of this, the story of Abderahman, was published in *Spanish Papers.*

Two letters.

THE HENRY E. HUNTINGTON LIBRARY AND ART GALLERY

Notebook, sixty-three pages, c. 1810 (HM 3171).

Notebook, sixty-six pages, c. 1840, containing notes for the Origin of the White, the Red and the Black Man (HM 3150).

Notebook, twenty-one pages, c. 1840, containing notes for the Conspiracy of Neamathla (HM 3151).

Notes, four pages, copied by Irving from an article in the *British Review and Critical Literary Magazine* (HM 580).

Contract with Marsh, Capen and Lyon for the publication of the *Life and Voyages of Christopher Columbus.* D. S. four pages, March 1, 1839 (HM 7126).

Twenty-six letters. (HL 851, HL 854, HL 105, HL 106, HL 856, HL 858, HL 857, HL 859, HL 860, HL 861, HL 862, HL 863, HM 7130, HL 848, HL 849, HL 850, HL 853, HL 852, HM 7129, HL 864, HL 855, HM 3146, HL 865, HM 2626, HM 7128, HM 7127.)

LIBRARY OF WILLIAM R. LANGFELD

Twenty letters.

Three pages, translation of Sahagun's *Conquest of Mexico,* chapter 30 (numbered 29 and corrected).

Sixteen pages, portion of rough draft of the "Chronicle of Fernando the Saint," published in *Spanish Papers,* fourteen pages a part of Chapter VI and two pages a part of Chapter XX, both differing in text from the published version, the latter, however, in but a word or two.

Passport signed while in the American Legation at London. Corrected galley proof of letter published in the Plaindealer. Two pages of unidentified manuscript (of different works), which may or may not have been published.

One page and a fraction, "Notes of a visit to the Tower [of London]."

Two pages, headed Chapter LX, apparently a part of one of the unpublished Spanish chronicles — "Prince Abredahman," "Cruelty of Alarkin," etc.

Five pages, headed "Finding of the book of S. Gregory," apparently notes or extracts from works on Spanish topics consulted by Irving.

LIBRARY OF THE REV. DR. RODERICK TERRY

Four pages concerning the publication of The Sketch Book, evidently for use as biographical material.

Four pages of an article concerning a tour in North Wales.

Four pages on Holyrood House (possibly published in part or entirely in *Abbotsford*).

Two pages, Wolfert's Roost (possibly published in part or entirely in *Wolfert's Roost*).

Four pages, Notes on the poet Rogers.

Two pages concerning travels in Derbyshire.

Two pages, Notes on Little Britain.

Two pages, part of an article on Gog and Magog.

Four pages, part of a diary.

One page, expense account.

Two pages concerning Westminster Abbey, either a part of *The Sketch Book* or notes for that work.

Four-page letter to Mrs. Sarah Van Wart describing Tarrytown. (Probably the same letter published in part in *Life and Letters of Washington Irving,* by Pierre Irving, New York, 1863, Vol. 3, p. 153–155.)

The items listed above are bound together in one volume.

Twenty-six pages, notes, memoranda, copies of letters, etc., for the *Life of Washington.*

Notebook, 39 pages, memoranda on the Arthurian Legends.

Fifteen pages, notes for *Knickerbocker's History of New York.*

Twenty-three pages, notes and text of an unfinished tale, Polly Holman's wedding.

Notebook, 48 pages, conversation with Wm. P. Duval, the original of Ralph Ringwood in the tale of that title.

Three notebooks on the Arabs, in preparation for the *Life of Mahomet.* Approximately eighty, sixty-eight and seventy-six (of which twelve are blank) pages, respectively.

Notebook, approximately sixty pages, on Spanish topics.

Three pages, notes for *The Alhambra.*

Two pages, notes, only one of which was used, for *The Alhambra.*

Two pages, Proverbs, etc.

Four pages on The Empire of the West.

Two pages, Notes on London.

Two pages, An Almanack Worker, An Inn of Court Man, A New Scholar.

Two pages relative to the burning of Washington by the British.

Eleven pages, Story Told by Peter the Venerable Abbot.

Eleven pages on Christmas, apparently unpublished.

Ten pages, Biographical Notes.

UNPUBLISHED WRITINGS, continued

Approximately seventy-five to one hundred letters, some few of which have been published.

Of great interest, also, is the last will of Washington Irving contained in this library.

YALE UNIVERSITY LIBRARY

One hundred and sixty letters (approximately).

Letters to Prince Dolgorouki.

Official Report on the "Armistead Case" 1834.

Notebook 1810.

Notebook 1818.

Fragment of Irving's Diary relating to his love for Mathilda Hoffman.

Six pages of an article on Sir David Wilkie, the Painter.

LIBRARY OF OWEN D. YOUNG, ESQ.

Three pages, An appreciation of Newton, the painter.

In the possession of a gentleman who does not desire his name to be made public are the following manuscripts, which have been kept together with portions of the manuscript of *Spanish Papers,* Vol. I. It is probable that they are a portion of the material from which Pierre Irving made his selection for inclusion in that book, and are apparently complete and unpublished.

Eighteen pages, two pages of which have, written on the reverse and crossed off, matter not sequential with the rest of the text, entitled "The Seven Sons of Lara," subtitle "Don Garcia Fernandez."

Nineteen pages entitled "Chronicle of Don Garcia Fernandez."

There were sold at The American Art Association Anderson Galleries, Inc., on March 29th, 1932, the following unpublished items. Included are several parcels of manuscript which are rough or first drafts of material published in different form in books by Irving.

Thirty-five pages, not complete, rough draft manuscript of a Legend of the family feud between Spanish cavaliers in the tenth century.

Fifteen pages, rough draft manuscript of a portion of Chapter I of the *Life of Mahomet.*

Twenty-four pages, complete rough draft manuscript of the History of the Moorish Invasion of France and the defeat of the Moors by Charles Martel.

Six pages, a description of the Tague River from its source to the sea.

About one hundred pages, notes used in writing the *Life of Mahomet.*

About sixty-five pages, notes and memoranda for *The Alhambra,* together with ten pages, original manuscript of "The Cave of Salamanca," used as a note to "The Enchanted Soldier" in *The Alhambra,* omitting some material used in the published book and containing some not included therein and apparently differing in text.

Sixteen pages, notes containing "Consular Information."

One page, note concerning Fernando Perez del Pulgar, at end of Chapter XCI of the *Conquest of Granada,* with additions; twelve pages, rough draft manuscript Notes for Spanish Legendary Tales; about forty pages, Notes on Philip V of Spain, Anecdotes, etc., used by Irving but not in his autograph.

There were sold at the American Art Association Anderson Art Galleries, Inc., on Nov. 10, 1932, the following manuscripts apparently all unpublished. Sixteen pages, manuscript of "Chronicle of Fernando the Saint," differing in many respects from published version, Chapter I, nearly all of Chapter II, first part of Chapter VI.

About two hundred pages manuscript, notes used in writing the *Life and Voyages of Christopher Columbus,* about twenty pages of which are not in Irving's handwriting but were used in writing the book, including rough drafts of some matters not used in the book.

Fourteen pages, rough draft manuscript "French Romance."

Seven pages, leaves from Irving's diary, April 25–26, 1821, describing his meeting with John Howard Payne, etc.

Eight pages, complete narrative of "The Log House Hotel."

About 65 pages, notes, rough drafts and final versions of portions of the opening chapters of *Mahomet and His Successors.*

Twenty-four pages, Notes on "The Tower of London."

Five pages, Legend of the Midnight Hatter.

Five pages, Notes for *Spanish Papers.*

Sixteen pages, notes for *The Alhambra,* used in writing the chapter on "Poets of Moslem Andalus."

There were sold at the American Art Association Anderson Art Galleries, Inc., on April 26, 1933, the following items:

A series of twenty-five autograph letters to Charles R. Leslie, some undoubtedly unpublished, perhaps all.

Diary and memorandum book, over one hundred and fifty pages, March 1 to April 6, 1828, dealing with his tours from Madrid to Granada and the Alhambra, etc., and containing fifteen pencil sketches. This is apparently unpublished and covers the period immediately preceding that of the Washington Irving Diary, Spain 1828–9, published in 1926.

Autograph manuscript of a legend of Spain, four pages, complete; portions of manuscript, apparently *Bracebridge Hall,* eight pages; and other odd leaves of manuscript — altogether seventeen pages. As these were not personally seen by the compilers, they cannot state definitely whether or not it is unpublished material, but it is probable that at least part of it has not been published.

Autograph manuscript description of "My Uncle," twelve pages, apparently unpublished.

WORKS ASCRIBED TO IRVING

The following works have been attributed to Irving, but are not generally accepted as having been written by him:

LITERARY PICTURE GALLERY, and Admonitory Epistles to the Visitors of Ballston Spa. Ballston Spa, 1808. 12°.

FRAGMENT OF A JOURNAL of a Sentimental Philosopher, during his Residence in the City of New York. New York: E. Sargeant, 1809. 38 p. 8°.

Copy: The New York Public Library possesses a copy of this work.

A WORD IN SEASON touching the Present Misunderstanding in the Episcopal Church. By A. Layman. New York, 1811. 8°.

BRIEF REMARKS on the "Wife" of Washington Irving . . . New-York: Printed by Grattan and Banks, 1819. 16 p. 8°.

Copies: The New York Public Library and Dr. Roderick Terry each possesses a copy of this book.

SALMAGUNDI. SECOND SERIES . . . Philadelphia: M. Thomas; New York: J. Haly and C. Thomas, 1819–20. 3 v. 16°.

Issued irregularly, May 30, 1819 – Sept. 2, 1820, in 15 numbers.

This is a Paulding item; Irving contributed nothing to it.

Copy: The New York Public Library contains a copy; the collection of the compiler contains numbers 1, 3, 6, 7, 9, 10 in original wrappers uncut, and numbers 4–10 in bound volumes.

THE MANUSCRIPT of Diedrich Knickerbocker Junior. New York, 1824. 76 p. 8°.

TRANSLATIONS OF WORKS BY IRVING

Irving's fame and popularity abroad were prodigious. The following section lists something under two hundred and twenty-five items, representing fifteen different languages, including the Czech, Greek, Icelandic, Polish, Russian, Yiddish, and Welsh, in addition to the Scandinavian and central European tongues. Each of Irving's works up to and including *Wolfert's Roost* was translated, with the exception of the *Biography of Lawrence* and the *Book of the Hudson.*

The popularity of the man is due in part to the great interest he created because he was the first to teach a somewhat incredulous Continent that America could produce a Man of Letters and a gentleman. The literary output of the country had been, before the time of Irving, of a less polished nature, and the sort that would not commend itself to the interest of older nations with vast cultural stores of their own. Cooper, following shortly on Irving's heels, was likewise received with great acclaim; but Irving it was who first taught Europe that our writers could produce worthwhile work.

National interests are curiously reflected in the long list of translations. The Czechs translated the *Sketch Book,* in 1904; the Greeks preferred biography, and read the lives of Columbus and Mahomet in their own tongue; Icelandic became the vehicle not for one of Columbus' voyages, as might have been expected, but for *The Alhambra.* The Poles, like the Greeks, were interested in Mahomet; and the Russians selected various short sketches for periodical presentation. The Welsh claimed only Oliver Goldsmith. Other lands took a generous assortment of his work, with emphasis in Spain on Columbus (though not his companions) and *The Alhambra.* The interest of the Scandinavians is particularly noteworthy, as is that of the Dutch. Both these groups were impartial, and eager to read whatever the American could offer.

The *Sketch Book* and *The Alhambra* were equally popular, with a list of forty-three translations for the former and forty-six for the latter. This foreign taste echoes our native partiality for the *Sketch Book,* a partiality shared with the English; appreciation of *The Alhambra* abroad outdistances the native reception.

Thus, if the cosmopolitan character of an audience be any guide, Irving has been one of America's most-loved writers.

SALMAGUNDI

Swedish

Bref från den hjeltemodiga Mustapha Rub-a-Dub Keli Kahn, under hans fångenskap i New-York t. sina vänner i Tripolis. Stockholm: Beijer, 1872. 78 p. 2. ed. 12°.

Authority: Svensk bok-katalog, 1866–1875, p. 104.

KNICKERBOCKER'S HISTORY OF NEW YORK

French

Histoire de New-York, depuis le commencement du monde jusqu'à la fin de la domination hollandaise...par Diedrick Knickerbocker... Ouvragé traduit de l'anglais... Paris: A. Sautelet et Cie, 1827. 2 v. 12°.

Copy: The New York Public Library (NBX).

German

Die Handschrift Diedrich Knickerbockers der jüngern; aus dem Englischen. Leipzig: Rein, 1825. 8°.

Authority: C. G. Kayser, Vollständiges Bücher-Lexicon, Theil 6, Romane, p. 70.

Humoristische Geschichte von New-York, von Anbeginn der Welt bis zur Endschaft der holländischen Dynastie...von Dietrich Knickerbocker. (Verfasser des Skizzenbuchs.) Aus dem Englischen übersetzt... Frankfurt am Main: Johann David Sauerländer, 1829. 1 p.l., (1)6–298 p., 3 l. 24°.

Copy: The New York Public Library (NBX).

Dietrich Knickerbocker's humoristische Geschichte von New-York... New York, 1851. [Philadelphia: Schäfer & Koradi.] 256 p. illus. 8°.

Authority: C. G. Kayser, Vollständiges Bücher-Lexicon, Heft 11, p. 518.

Dietrich Knickerbocker's humoristische Geschichte von New-York, von Anbeginn der Gründung der Colonie durch Hendrick Hudson, bis zur Endschaft der holländischen Dynastie... New-York: Koch & Co., n. d. 2 p.l., 11–164, 7, 53 (1), v, viii–xvii p. illus. 12°.

The History of New York ends on p. 164. Following it are: p. 1–7: Der kecke Dragoner; p. 1–53: Rip Van Winkle [and other stories, mainly from the *Sketch Book*]; p. 53(1) – xvii: Die aristokratischen Einwanderer.

Copy: Columbia University Library.

THE SKETCH BOOK

Czech

Washington Irving: Náčrty. (The Sketchbook.) Výbor povídek a črt. Z Angličiny přeložil karel mušek. Prague: J. Otty, 1904. 1 p.l., (1)4–171(1) p. 24°.

Copy: Circulation Department, The New York Public Library.

Dutch

Schetsen en portretten, in Engeland en Amerika, naar het leven geteekend door Geoffrey Crayon, (Washington Irving.)... Uit het Engelsch. Leeuwarden: Steenbergen van Goor, 1823. (i)iv–xi p., 1 l., 236 p. 8°.

Copy: Library of Congress.

Rip Van Winkle

Rip Van Winkle... Antwerpen: G. Janssens, n. d. 32 p. 12°. (Keurboeking voor reizegers. no. 3.)

Authority: Dr. Maurice Chazin.

Rip Van Winkle... Teekeningen van A. Rackham. Antwerpen, 1906. 4°.

Authority: Dr. Maurice Chazin.

French

Complete Text

Esquisses morales et littéraires, ou, Observations sur les mœurs, les usages, et la littérature des Anglois et des Américains...traduites de l'anglois sur la 4e édition, par MM. Delpeux et Villetard... Paris: C. Le Tellier fils, 1822. 2 v. illus. 8°.

Copies: Library of Congress; Bibliothèque Nationale.

Voyage d'un Américain à Londres, ou Esquisses sur les mœurs anglaises et américaines; traduit de l'anglais de M. Irwin [*sic!*] Washington... Paris: Ponthieu, 1822. 2 v. 8°.

Copies: The New York Public Library (NBQ); Library of Congress; Bibliothèque Nationale.

Esquisses morales et littéraires, ou Observations sur les mœurs, les usages et la littérature des Anglois et des Américains; par M. Washington Irving. Traduites de l'anglois sur la quatrième édition, par MM. Delpeux et Villetard... Paris: Constant Le Tellier fils, 1827. 2 v. 2. ed. 12°.

Copies: The New York Public Library (NBY); Bibliothèque Nationale.

Voyage d'un Américain à Londres, ou Esquisses sur les mœurs anglaises et américaines. Traduit de l'anglais de M. Washington Irving ... Paris: Ponthieu, 1829. 2 v. 2. ed. 8°.

Copy: Bibliothèque Nationale.

...Le Livre d'esquisses. Traduit de l'anglais par Théodore Lefebvre. Paris: Poulet-Malassis, 1862. 388 p. 18°.

Copy: Bibliothèque Nationale.

...Le Livre d'esquisses. Traduction française littérale. Paris: Possielgue frères, 1885. 468 p. 18°. (Alliance des maisons d'éducation chrétienne.)

Copy: Bibliothèque Nationale.

Rip Van Winkle

Le Flacon de Rip. (Conte traduit d'Irving.) Par Henry Vesseron. Sedan: J. Laroche, 1867. 24 p. 12°.

Copy: Bibliothèque Nationale.

Translations, continued

The Sketch Book — French, continued

RIP VAN WINKLE. Par Washington Irving. Traduction exacte, par le major L. Du Bos... Philadelphia: Claxton, Remsen & Haffelfinger, 1877. xix, 21–64 p. 16°.
Copy: Library of Congress.

...RIP, la légende du dormeur. [Notice par Charles Simond.] Paris: H. Gautier [1891]. 36 p. 18°. (Nouvelle bibliothèque populaire à 10 centimes. Number 257.)
Copy: Bibliothèque Nationale.

...RIP...traduit par Léonora C. Herbert. Paris: J. Rouff [1905]. 125 p. illus. 16°.
Copy: Bibliothèque Nationale.

RIP VAN WINKLE, par Washington Irving, illustré par Arthur Rackham. Paris: Hachette, 1906. x, 69 p. illus. 4°.
Copy: Bibliothèque Nationale.

RIP VAN WINKLE, par Washington Irving. Adaptation française par M. Fernand Gillard... Paris: Larousse, n.d. 45 p. illus. 16°. (Les Livres roses pour la jeunesse. Number 142.)
Copy: Bibliothèque Nationale.

The Legend of Sleepy Hollow

REID, MAYNE. La Baie d'Hudson... Paris, 1878. 4°.
Contains Le Val dormant, récit arrangé par B. H. Révoil.
Copy: Bibliothèque Nationale.

Selections

CONTES américains, traduits de l'anglais de M. Irving, Miss Sedgwick [Paulding et Flint] ... Paris: A. Auffray, 1832. 240 p. 16°.
Copy: Bibliothèque Nationale.

CONTES, morceaux et anecdotes tirés de W. Irving, Gally Knight, W. Scott, etc., suivis de quelques poésies... Paris: Derache, 1840. vi, 88 p. 8°.
Includes Rip Van Winkle and The Spectre bridegroom.
Copy: Bibliothèque Nationale.

Le FIANCÉ-FANTÔME. Traduit de l'anglais par L. Bocquet. Paris et Bruxelles: Éditions de la Renaissance de l'Occident, 1921. 24 p. 8°.
Authority: Dr. Maurice Chazin.

GERMAN

GOTTFRIED CRAYON'S Skizzenbuch; aus dem Englischen des Washington Irving, übersetzt von S. H. Spiker. Berlin: Duncker und Humblot, 1825. 2 v. 12°.
Authority: C. G. Kayser, Völlstandiges Bücher-Lexicon, Theil 6, Romane, p. 70.

GOTTFRIED CRAYONS Skizzenbuch... Uebersetzt und herausgegeben von Chr. A. Fischer u. a. Frankfurt-am-Main, 1826. 6 v. 12°.
Authority: C. G. Kayser, Vollständiges Bücher-Lexicon, Theil 6, Romane, p. 70.

GOTTFRIED CRAYON'S Skizzenbuch. 2. sorgfältig verbesserte Auflage. Frankfurt-am-Main: Sauerländer, 1846. illus. 16°. (Ausgewählte Schriften. Hrsg. von J. V. Adrian. Theil 1.)
Authority: C. G. Kayser, Vollständiges Bücher-Lexicon, Theil 9, p. 473.

GOTTFRIED CRAYONS Skizzenbuch. Aus dem Englischen. 3., sorgfältig verbesserte Auflage. Frankfurt am Main: Sauerländer, 1870. 382 p. 8°.
Authority: C. G. Kayser, Vollständiges Bücher-Lexicon, Theil 17, p. 550.

SKIZZENBUCH von Washington Irving. Deutsch von Jenny Piorkowska. Leipzig: Violet, 1876. 381 p. 8°. (Hausbibliothek ausländischer Classiker. Bd. 4.)
Authority: C. G. Kayser, Vollständiges Bücher-Lexicon, Theil 19, p. 531.

WASHINGTON IRVING'S Skizzenbuch. Uebersetzt, mit Biographie und Anmerkungen herausgegeben von K. T. Gaedertz. Leipzig [1882]. 481 p. 8°. (Universal Bibliothek. Bd. 1031–1034.)
Copy: British Museum.

Das SKIZZENBUCH von Geoffrey Crayon, Esquire. Wortgetreu nach H. R. Mecklenburgs Grundsätzen aus dem Englischen übersetzt von R. T. Berlin: H. R. Mecklenburg, 1884–85. 192 p. 32°.
Authorities: C. G. Kayser, Vollständiges Bücher-Lexicon, Bd. 23, p. 557; Hinrichs' Verzeichniss der Bücher, July/Dec., 1884, p. 203, July/Dec., 1885, p. 221.

GOTTFRIED CRAYONS Skizzenbuch von Washington Irving. Gesamt-Ausgabe. Halle a. d. S.: Otto Hendel [1888?]. vii(i), 339 p., 1 port. 16°.
Copy: The New York Public Library (NBQ).

Rip Van Winkle

RIP VAN WINKLE. Illustriert durch 50 Aquarelle von Arthur Rackham. Leipzig: E. A. Seemann, 1905. 47 p. 4°.
Authority: C. G. Kayser, Vollständiges Bücher-Lexicon, Bd. 33, p. 1049.

RIP VAN WINKLE. Übersetzt von R. Diehl. Wiesbaden, 1909. 35 p. 8°. (Wiesbadener Volksbücher. Nr. 124.)
Authority: C. G. Kayser, Vollständiges Bücher-Lexicon, Bd. 36, p. 1136.

ITALIAN

D., A. M. Passatempi morali; ossia Scelta di novelle...da autori celebri inglesi e francesi, tradotte ad uso delle giovani... Londra, 1826. 12°.
Contains La Sposa, La Vedova e suo figlio, and La Vittima del crepacuore, translations from the *Sketch Book*.
Copy: British Museum.

RIP VAN WINKLE. Racconto di Washington Irving, con disegni di Arturo Rackham A. R. W. S. Bergamo: Istituto italiano d'arti grafiche, editore, n.d. 60 p. plates. 4°.
Copy: Circulation Department, The New York Public Library.

Translations, continued

The Sketch Book, continued

NORWEGIAN

SKISSEBOGEN. Fagerstrand. [18—?] 2 v. in 1.

Authority: Bergen, Norway. — Offentliga Bibliotek. Katalog over de aapne hylders avdeling, [part] 1, p. 421.

RUSSIAN

Безголовый мертвецъ. (Московскій Телеграфъ. Moscow, 1826. 8°. v. 9, p. 116–142, 161–187.)

The Legend of Sleepy Hollow.
Copy: The New York Public Library (* QCA).

Заколдованный домъ. (Московскій Телеграфъ. Moscow, 1827. 8°. v. 5, p. 14, 75, 125.)

The Haunted house.
Copy: The New York Public Library (* QCA).

SPANISH

For certain information relating to Spanish translations the compiler is indebted to the article by Stanley T. Williams, "The First Version of the Writings of Washington Irving in Spanish," in *Modern Philology,* v. 28, p. 185–201, cited below as Williams.

MONTGOMERY, GEORGE WASHINGTON. Tareas de un solitario, ó nueva colección de novelas. Madrid, 1829.

This book contains three works based upon Irving's writings: "El Sueño," "El Serrano de las Alpujarras," and "El Cuadro misterioso." "El Sueño" is based upon two essays in the *Sketch Book*: "The Art of Bookmaking" and "The Mutability of Literature." "El Serrano de las Alpujarras" is a version of Rip Van Winkle, also from the *Sketch Book.* "El Cuadro misterioso" is a translation of the "Story of the Young Italian" in the *Tales of a Traveller.*
Authority: Williams.

NOVELAS españolas. El serrano de las Alpujarras; y El cuadro misterioso. Brunswick [Me.]: Imprenta de Griffin, 1830. 80 p. 12°.

Contains adaptations from "Rip Van Winkle" and "The Young Italian."
Copy: Library of Congress.

El SERRANO de Las Alpujarras and El cuadro misterioso; two Spanish novels taken from Las tareas de un solitario, and adapted to be used as translating-books, by Julio Soler. New York: Printed by R. Rafael, 1842. 117 p. 12°.

Copy: Library of Congress.

El SERRANO de Las Alpujarras and El cuadro misterioso... Brunswick [Me.], 1845.

"This is a reissue of the first edition [of 1830]..."
Authority: Williams.

LEYENDAS extraordinarias. Traducción del inglés por M. Juderías Bénder. Madrid, 1882.

"El Caballero sin cabeza," a translation of The Legend of Sleepy Hollow, is printed on p. 39–79 of v. 3.
Authority: Williams.

...CUENTOS clásicos del Norte. Segunda serie. Por Washington Irving, Nathaniel Hawthorne, Edward Everett Hale... Traducción de Carmen Torres Calderón de Pinillos. Nueva York: Doubleday, Page & Company, 1920. 4 p.l., 3–307 p. 12°. (Biblioteca interamericana. [no.] 3.)

Contains Irving material as follows: p. (1), Resumé of Irving's works; p. (2), Portrait; p. 3–8, Esbozo biográfico; p. 11–42, Rip Van Winkle; p. 45–96, La leyenda del valle encantado.
Copy: The New York Public Library (NBF).

SWEDISH

Ur SKIZZBOKEN. Öfv. af Erik G. Folcker. Stockholm: Fahlcrantz & K., 1888. 107 p. 8°.

Authority: Svensk bok-katalog, 1886–1895, p. 150.

YIDDISH

ריפ וואן ווינקל. די לעגענדע פון פערשלאפענעם טאל. איבערזעצט פון ענגליש פון פ. נאוויק. ניו יארק: פארלאג ה. טויבענשלאג.
New York: H. Taubenschlag [cop. 1923]. 78 p. 24°.

Author's name, וואשינגטאן אירווינג, at head of title.

Translation of Rip Van Winkle.
Copy: The New York Public Library (* PTW p.v.6, no.7).

BRACEBRIDGE HALL

DANISH

BRACEBRIDGE-HALL, oversat af Wallich. København: Schubothe, 1829. 2 v. 8°.

Authority: Almindeligt Dansk-Norsk Forlagscatalog, Kjøbenhavn, 1841, p. 76.

DUTCH

MIJN verblijf op het kasteel Bracebridge; naar het Engelsch, door Steenbergen van Goor. Amsterdam: C. L. Schleyer, 1828. 2 v. 8°.

Authority: Alphabetische naamlijst van boeken, welke sedert het jaar 1790 tot en met het jaar 1832, in Noord-Nederland zijn uitgekomen, Supplement, p. 67.

FRENCH

Le CHÂTEAU de Bracebridge, par Geoffrey-Crayon, traduit de l'anglais par M. Jean Cohen ... Paris: Hubert, 1822. 4 v. 12°.

Copy: Bibliothèque Nationale.

Les HUMORISTES, ou le Château de Bracebridge, par Washington Irving, traduit de l'anglais par Gustave Grandpré... Paris: Corbet, 1826. 2 v. 12°.

Copy: Bibliothèque Nationale.

GERMAN

BRACEBRIDGE-HALL; übersetzt von Henriette Schubert. Zwickau: Schumann, 1826. 4 v. 16°.

Authority: C. G. Kayser, Vollständiges Bücher-Lexicon, Theil 6, Romane, p. 70.

Translations, continued

Bracebridge Hall — German, continued

BRACEBRIDGE-HALL, oder die Charaktere; aus dem Englischen übersetzt von S. H. Spiker. Berlin: Duncker und Humblot, 1826. 2 v. 2. ed. 8°.
Authority: C. G. Kayser, Vollständiges Bücher-Lexicon, Theil 6, Romane, p. 70.

BRACEBRIDGE HALL oder die Charaktere. Uebersetzt und herausgegeben von Chr. A. Fischer u. a. Frankfurt a. M., 1827. 6 v. 12°.
Authority: C. G. Kayser, Vollständiges Bücher-Lexicon, Theil 6, Romane, p. 70.

BRACEBRIDGE-HALL oder die Charaktere. Frankfurt-am-Main: Sauerländer, 1846. 2. sorgfältig verbesserte Auflage. 16°. (Ausgewählte Schriften, hrsg. von I. V. Adrian. Theil 2.)
Authority: C. G. Kayser, Vollständiges Bücher-Lexicon, Theil 9, p. 473.

RUSSIAN

Баккалавръ Саламанкскій. (Московскій Телеграфъ. Moscow, 1826. 8°. v. 12, p. 14–37, 66–83.)
The Student of Salamanca.
Copy: The New York Public Library (* QCA).

Аннета Деларбръ. (Московскій Телеграфъ. Moscow, 1828. 8°. v. 5, p. 28–49; v. 6, p. 159–171.)
Annette Delarbre.
Copy: The New York Public Library (* QCA).

SWEDISH

BRACEBRIDGE HALL eller En vår på landet i England. [Translated by J. Ekelund.] Stockholm: Hæggström, 1828. 8°.
Authority: Svensk bokhandels-katalog utgifven år 1845, p. 140.

BRACEBRIDGE HALL, eller minnen och intryck från en vår på landet in England. Översättning. Stockholm, 1865. 364 p. 8°. (Familjebibliotek. [no.] 6.)
Authority: Hjalmar Linnström, Svenskt boklexikon, åren 1830–1865, del 1, p. 751.

TALES OF A TRAVELLER

DANISH

En REISENDES Fortællinger, oversat af Wallich. Kjøbenhavn: Schubothe, 1828. 2 v. 8°.
Authority: Almindeligt Dansk-Norsk Forlagscatalog, Kjøbenhavn, 1841, p. 76.

DUTCH

VERHALEN van eener reiziger; uit het Engelsch vertaald, door Steenbergen van Goor. Amsterdam: C. L. Schleyer, 1827. 2 v. 8°.
Authority: Alphabetische naamlijst van boeken, welke sedert het jaar 1790 tot en met het jaar 1832, in Noord-Nederland zijn uitgekomen, p. 283.

FRENCH

CONTES d'un voyageur, par Geoffrey-Crayon, traduits de l'anglais de M. Washington Irving, par Mme Adèle Beaurgard [*sic!*]. Paris: Lecointe et Durey, 1825. 4 v. 12°.
Copies: Bibliothèque Nationale; British Museum.

HISTORIETTES d'un voyageur, par Geoffrey Crayon... [Traduit par Lebègue.] Paris: Carpentier-Méricourt, 1825. 4 v. 12°.
Copy: Bibliothèque Nationale.

ŒUVRES complètes de M. Washington Irving, traduites de l'anglais...par M. Lebèque d'Auteuil... Contes d'un voyageur... Paris: Boulland, 1825. 4 v. 12°.
Copy: Bibliothèque Nationale.

...Les CHERCHEURS de trésors. [Notice par H. Duclos.] Paris: Librairie illustrée [1897]. 95 p. illus. 16°. (Chefs-d'œuvre du siècle illustrés. [no.] 22.)
Part IV of the *Tales of a Traveller.*
Copy: Bibliothèque Nationale.

GERMAN

ERZÄHLUNGEN eines Reisenden; aus dem Englischen übersetzt von S. H. Spiker. Berlin: Duncker und Humblot, 1825. 2 v. 12°.
Authority: C. G. Kayser, Vollständiges Bücher-Lexicon, Theil 6, Romane, p. 70.

ERZÄHLUNGEN eines Reisenden. Frankfurt-am-Main: Sauerländer, 1847. 502 p. illus. 2. verbesserte Auflage. 12°. (Ausgewählte Schriften, hrsg. von I. V. Adrian. Theil 3.)
Authority: C. G. Kayser, Vollständiges Bücher-Lexicon, Theil 11, p. 518.

Das NOVELLENSCHATZ des Auslandes, hrsg. von Paul Heyse und Hermann Kurz. München: Oldenbourg [1872–75]. 14 v.
Bd. 3 contains "Wolfert Webber oder goldene Traüme," from the *Tales of a Traveller.*
Authority: Katalog der Berliner Stadtbibliothek, Bd. 4, p. 23.

ITALIAN

Lo STRANIERO misterioso, novella del Signor Irving. Traduzione dall' originale Inglese [the "Mysterious stranger," published in The Tales of a Traveller], di G. B. Milano, 1826. 8°.
Extracted from a periodical entitled *Il Nuovo raccoglitore.*
Copy: British Museum.

Lo STRANIERO misterioso; leggende dell' Alhambra. Milano: E. Sonzogno, 1884. 100 p. 16°. (Biblioteca universale. n. 94.)
Authority: Bibliografia italiana, anno 18, 1884, p. 139.

RUSSIAN

Вольферъ Вебберъ, или золотые сны. (Московскій Телеграфъ. Moscow, 1826. 8°. v. 7, p. 62–102, 130–150, 167–196.)
Wolfert Webber.
Copy: The New York Public Library (* QCA).

Translations, continued

Tales of a Traveller, continued

Spanish

Aventura de un estudiante alemán. (El Artista. Madrid [1835]. v. 1, p. 306 ff.)

Authority: John De Lancey Ferguson, American Literature in Spain, p. 223.

El Espectro desposado. (In: Horas de invierno. Madrid, 1836. no. 16, p. 137–168.)

Authority: Stanley T. Williams in *Modern philology*, v. 28, p. 187.

El Retrato misterioso, novela escrita en inglés por M. Whasington [*sic!*] Irving. (In: J. X. B. Saintine, Aventuras de un misántropo. Madrid and Barcelona, 1860. p. 289–335.)

Authority: Williams, p. 187.

El Misterioso extranjero. Historia del joven italiano. (In: J. X. B. Saintine, Aventuras de un misántropo. Madrid and Barcelona, 1860. p. 295–335.)

This is apparently a revision and reprinting of the previous entry.
Authority: Williams, p. 187.

...Los Buscadores de tesoros. Barcelona: J. Roura — A. del Castillo, 1893. 107 p., 2 l. illus. 16°. (Biblioteca ilustrada. Primera sección, número 3.)

Part IV of the *Tales of a Traveller.*
Copy: Columbia University Library.

Swedish

En Resandes berättelser. Öfversättning af Lars Arnell. Stockholm: Hæggström, 1829. 8°.

Authority: Svensk bokhandels-katalog utgifven år 1845, p. 140.

En Resandes berättelser. Öfversättning. Stockholm, 1865. 342 p. 8°. (Familjebibliotek. [no.] 7.)

Authority: Hjalmar Linnström, Svenskt boklexikon, åren 1830–1865, del 1, p. 752.

JONATHAN OLDSTYLE

German

Jonathan Oldstyle's Briefe. Aus dem Englischen des Washington Irving übersetzt von S. H. Spiker. Berlin: Duncker und Humblot, 1824. x, 92 p., 1 l. 16°.

Copy: The New York Public Library (NBQ).

LIFE AND VOYAGES OF CHRISTOPHER COLUMBUS

Czech

...Život a plavby Krištofa Kolumba. Z Anglického přeložil František Doucha... Prague: B. Stýbla, n. d. 3 p.l., (1)6–317(1) p., 3 l. 2. ed. illus. 12°.

Copy: Circulation Department, The New York Public Library.

Dutch

Het Leven en de reizen van Christoffel Columbus... Uit het Engelsch... Haarlem: Bij de Wed. A. Loosjes, 1828–29. 4 v. 8°.

Copies: Hispanic Society of America; Library of Congress.

French

Histoire de la vie et des voyages de Christophe Colomb, par M. Washington Irving, traduite de l'anglais par C. A. Defauconpret fils ... Paris: Charles Gosselin, 1828. 4 v. 8°.

Copies: The New York Public Library (HAM); Bibliothèque Nationale.

—— Deuxième édition, revue et corrigée. Paris: Charles Gosselin, 1836. 4 v. 8°.

Copies: The New York Public Library (HAM); Library of Congress.

Histoire abrégée de la vie et des voyages de Ch. Colomb, traduite de l'anglais par J.-A. Dufour. Genève, 1835. in-12.

Authority: J. M. Quérard, La littérature française contemporaine, tome 4, p. 358.

Voyages et aventures de Christophe Colomb. Traduit de l'anglais de Washington Irving par Paul Merruau... Paris: Lavigne, 1837. 291 p. illus. 16°. (Bibliothèque des familles.)

Copy: Bibliothèque Nationale.
The catalogue of the Bibliothèque Nationale also lists the following later editions and issues of this translation (some with varying paginations): 2. ed., 1837; 1843; 4. ed., 1851; 5. ed., 1853; 6. ed., 1857; 7. ed., 1860; 8. ed., 1863; 9. ed., 1866; 10. ed., 1869; 11. ed., 1873; 1881; 1883; 1885; 1887. All were published at Tours except the 1837 edition, published at Paris.
It is interesting to note that there were a number of editions of the English text, in abbreviated form, issued in France for the use of French students of the English language, as for instance: La Vie et le voyage de Christophe Colomb. Édition abregée, publiée avec notes en français par E. Chasles. Paris: Hachette, 1879. This went through seven reimpressions: 1881, 1884, 1887, 1896, 1898, 1901, and 1916.

Vie et voyages de Christophe Colomb. Traduction de l'anglais par G. Renson... Bruxelles et Paris: A. Lacroix, Verboeckhoven et Cie., 1864. 3 v. 8°. (Collection d'historiens contemporains.)

Copy: Hispanic Society of America.

Vie et voyages de Christophe Colomb d'après Washington Irving, par J. Girardin. Paris: Hachette, 1880. 191 p. 8°. (Bibliothèque des écoles et des familles.)

Copies: Bibliothèque Nationale; British Museum.

German

Die Geschichte des Lebens und die Reisen Christoph Columbus. Aus dem Englischen von Ph. A. G. von Meyer. Frankfurt-am-Main: Sauerländer, 1828. 4 v. 16°.

Authority: C. G. Kayser, Vollständiges Bücher-Lexicon, Theil 3, p. 274.

Des Christoph Columbus Leben und Reisen. Aus dem Englischen von F. H. Ungewitter. Frankfurt-am-Main: Wesché, 1829. 4 v. 8°.

Authority: C. G. Kayser, Vollständiges Bücher-Lexicon, Theil 3, p. 274.

Translations, continued

Life...of Columbus — German, continued

Die GESCHICHTE des Lebens und die Reisen Christoph Columbus. Im Auszug für die Jugend bearbeitet von Rud. Friedner. Neustadt: Christmann, 1829. 8°.

Authority: C. G. Kayser, Vollständiges Bücher-Lexicon, Theil 3, p. 274.

CHRISTOPH COLUMBUS Leben und Reisen. Auszug von der Verfasser. Aus dem Englischen übersetzt. Stuttgart: Cotta, 1833. 8°.

Authority: C. G. Kayser, Neues Bücher-Lexicon, Theil 1, p. 485.

GREEK

'Ο Χριστοφορος Κολομβος, ἤτοι ἱστορια της ζωης και των θαλασσοποριων αὐτου κατα τον 'Ο. 'Ιρβιγγ. 'Εκ του Γαλλικου ὑπο Γ. 'Α. 'Αριστειδου. ἐν Ἀθηναις, 1858. 8°.

Copy: British Museum.

ITALIAN

STORIA della vita e dei viaggi di Cristoforo Colombo, scritta da Washington Irving, Americano. Prima versione italiana corredata di note, adorna di carte geografiche, e ritratto... Genova: Fratelli Pagano, 1828. 4 v. in 2. 8°.

Issued in twelve parts (three parts to the volume). Though all four title-pages are dated 1828, the last four parts bear the date 1829 on the wrappers. Six wrappers (pale green) bound at the end of v. 1–2; six more (pale green) at the end of v. 3–4.
Copy: The New York Public Library (HAM).

STORIA e viaggi di Cristoforo Colombo. Milano: Bestetti, 1876. 464 p. 8°.

Authority: Bibliografia italiana, anno 11, 1877, p. 12.

SPANISH

HISTORIA de la vida y viajes de Cristóbal Colon, escrita en inglés por el caballero Washington Irving, y traducida al castellano por Don José García de Villalta. Madrid: Imprenta de D. J. Palacios, 1833–34. 4 v. 24°.

Copies: The New York Public Library (HAM); Library of Congress.

VIDA y viajes de Cristóbal Colon... Adornada con sesenta grabados. Madrid: Gaspar y Roig, 1851. 1 p.l., 251 p., 4 l. 4°. (Biblioteca ilustrada de Gaspar y Roig.)

Copy: Columbia University.
The *second edition* of the "Vida y viajes," issued under the same imprint, bears the date 1852. In all other respects the collation is that of the *first* [Gaspar y Roig] edition above. Copy: Hispanic Society of America.

VIDA y viajes de Cristóbal Colon... México: Boix, Besserer y Compañía, 1853. 2 v. 12°.

Pages [1] – 32 at the end of vol. 2 are: Elogio de Cristóbal Colon, por Eulalio Maria Ortega, presentado y premiado en el concurso del Ateneo mexicano de 20 de julio de 1845... México: Andres Boix, [1]853.
Copy: Hispanic Society of America.

VIDA y viajes de Cristóbal Colon... Tercera edición. Adornada con 60 grabados. Madrid: Gaspar y Roig, 1854. 1 p.l., 251 p., 2 l. 4°. (Biblioteca ilustrada de Gaspar y Roig.)

Copy: Hispanic Society of America.

HISTORIA de la vida y viajes de Cristóbal Colón... Reimpreso para las bibliotecas populares. Santiago [de Chile]: Imp. del Ferrocarril, 1859. 4 v. 8°.

Authority: John De Lancey Ferguson, American Literature in Spain, p. 221.

VIDA y viajes de Cristóbal Colon, escrita en ingles por Washington Irving. Edición abreviada por el mismo autor para uso de la juventud, i mandada traducir i publicar por el Ministerio de Instrucción Pública de Chile. Valparaiso: Imp. de La Patria, 1893. 2 p.l., iv, (1)6–351 p. 12°.

Translated by Alberto Berguecio.
Copies: The New York Public Library (HAM); Library of Congress.

Selections

HISTORIA del descubrimiento del Nuevo-Mundo, estractada de la Vida y viajes de Cristóbal Colon por Washington Irving. (In: Ramon de Campoamor, Colon. Poema. Valencia, 1853. 8°. p. 185–232.)

Copy: Hispanic Society of America.
Also printed in the Madrid, 1859, edition of the same work, p. 1–48. There is a copy of this edition also in the Hispanic Society.

SWEDISH

CHRISTOPHER COLUMBUS, dess lefnad och resor. Öfversättning från Engelskan [af Gustav Holmström]. Stockholm: Hjerta, 1839. 380, 4 p. 12°. (I Nytt läse-bibliothek.)

Authority: Svensk bokhandels-katalog utgifven år 1845, p. 140.

CHRISTOPHER COLUMBUS, hans lefnad och resor. Öfversättning. Stockholm, 1862. 226 p. 8°. (Böcker för folket. [no.] 4.)

Authority: Hjalmar Linnström, Svenskt boklexikon, åren 1830–1865, del 1, p. 752.

KRISTOFFER COLUMBUS, hans lefnad och resor. Stockholm: A. Bonnier, 1894. 513 p. illus. 4°.

Authority: Svensk bok-katalog for åren 1886–1895, p. 150.

KRISTOFER COLUMBUS, hans lefnad och resor, af Washington Irving. Med tvåhundraåttiofyra illustrationer. Chicago: Engberg-Holmberg Publishing Company [cop. 1893]. 513(1) p., 1 l. illus. 4°.

Copies: Columbia University; Library of Congress.

THE CONQUEST OF GRANADA

DUTCH

De VEROVERING van Granada beschreven van Washington Irving; uit het Engelsch. Haarlem: Wed. A. Loosjes, 1830. 2 v. 8°.

Copy: Columbia University.

Translations, continued

The Conquest of Granada, continued

FRENCH

HISTOIRE de la conquête de Grenade, tirée de la chronique manuscrite de Fray Antonio Agapida par Washington Irving. Traduite de l'anglais par J. Cohen... Paris: T. Dehay, 1829. 2 v. 8°.

Copy: Bibliothèque Nationale.

—— Louvain: F. Michel, 1830. 2 v. 12°.

Copies: The New York Public Library (BXI); Bibliothèque Nationale.

CONQUÊTE de Grenade, par Adrien Lemercier, d'après Washington Irving... Tours: A. Mame, 1840. 312 p. illus. 12°.

Copy: Bibliothèque Nationale.
The catalogue of the Bibliothèque Nationale also lists the following later editions and issues of this translation (some with different pagination), all published at Tours by Mame: 3. ed., 1842; 4. ed., 1845; 6. ed., 1852; 7. ed., 1856; 8. ed., 1859; 9. ed., 1862; 10. ed., 1865; 11. ed., 1868; 12. ed., 1873; 13. ed., 1877; 14. ed., 1882.

HISTOIRE de la conquête de Grenade; traduite de l'anglais, et précédée d'une étude sur les ouvrages de Washington Irving, par Xavier Eyma. Bruxelles et Paris: Lacroix, Verboeckhoven et Cie, 1864. 2 v. 8°. (Collection d'historiens contemporains.)

Reissued in 1865 in 2 v.
Authority: Otto Lorenz, Catalogue général de la librairie française, tome 3, p. 6.

GERMAN

Die EROBERUNG von Granada. Aus dem Englischen von Gustave Sellen. Leipzig: Weinbrack, 1836. 3 v. 8°.

Authority: C. G. Kayser, Neues Bücher-Lexicon, Theil 1, p. 485.

SPANISH

CRÓNICA de la conquista de Granada. Escrita en inglés por Mr. Washington Irving. Traducida al castellano por Don Jorge W. Montgomery... Madrid: I. Sancha, 1831. 2 v. 24°.

Copies: The New York Public Library (BXI); Library of Congress.

CRÓNICA de la conquista de Granada. Sacada de los manuscritos de Fr. Antonio Agapido [*sic!*] por Mr. Washington Irving, y traducida del inglés por Don Alfonso Escalante.

"This edition was advertised in *El Abencerraje*, Granada, 1844. The existence of a copy of this book in Spain or even the fact that it was actually published is unproved."
Authority: Stanley T. Williams, in *Modern Philology*, v. 28, p. 188.

BULWER, H. L. La conquista de Granada. Precedida de una Introducción por Washington Irving, traducida libremente por la Señorita Margarita López de Haro... Madrid, 1860.

"Condensed excerpts from Irving's book are prefixed to a translation of Bulwer's history."
Authority: Williams, as above.

CRÓNICA de la conquista de Granada. Estractada de la que escribío en francés Vashington [*sic!*] Irving, por Adiano Lemercier, y vertida al castellano de la 8.ª edición francesa, por J. R. Barcelona: Magrina y Subirana, 1861. iv, 282 p. 8°.

Authority: John De Lancey Ferguson, American Literature in Spain, p. 221.

SWEDISH

KRÖNIKA öfver Granadas eröfring, (utdragen) ur munken Antonio Agapidas handskrifter. Öfversättning från engelska originalet af Lars Arnell. Åbo, 1830–31. 2 v. 8°.

Authority: Hjalmar Linnström, Svenskt boklexikon, åren 1830–1865, p. 752.

VOYAGES AND DISCOVERIES OF THE COMPANIONS OF COLUMBUS

FRENCH

HISTOIRE des voyages et découvertes des compagnons de Christophe Colomb, par M. Washington Irving; suivie de l'Histoire de Fernand Cortez et de la conquête du Mexique, et de l'Histoire de Pizarre et de la conquête du Pérou. Ouvrages traduits de l'anglais par A.-J.-B. et C.-A. Defauconpret... Paris: C. Gosselin, 1833. 3 v. 8°.

Copy: Bibliothèque Nationale.

VOYAGES et découvertes des compagnons de Colomb. Traduit de l'anglais de Washington Irving, par Henri Lebrun. Tours: A. Mame, 1839. 288 p. illus. 18°. (Bibliothèque de la jeunesse chrétienne.)

Copy: Bibliothèque Nationale.
The catalogue of the Bibliothèque Nationale also lists the following later editions of this translation: 2. ed., 1841; 3. ed., 1843; 5. ed., 1851; 7. ed., 1858; 8. ed., 1861; 9. ed., 1864; 10. ed., 1867; 11. ed., 1870; 12. ed., 1873; 13. ed., 1876; 14. ed., 1879; 15. ed., 1882; 16. ed., 1885.
The Library of Congress has a copy of the 2. ed., 1841, and The New York Public Library one of the 5. ed., 1851.

VOYAGES et découvertes des compagnons de Colomb, d'après Washington Irving, récits d'exploration et de découvertes, par J. Girardin. Paris: Hachette, 1880. 207 p. illus. 8°. (Bibliothèque des écoles et des familles.)

Copy: Bibliothèque Nationale.
The catalogue of the Bibliothèque Nationale also lists a copy of the 3. ed., 1893.

GERMAN

REISEN der Gefärten des Columbus. Uebersetzt von Ph. A. G. von Meyer. Frankfurt, 1831. 3 v. in 1.

Authority: Joseph Baer & Co., Antiquariatskatalog 762, p. 109.

ITALIAN

MARMOCCHI, Francesco Constantino. Raccolta di viaggi della scoperta del nuovo continente fino a' di nostri. Compilata da F. C.

Translations, continued

Voyages and Discoveries of the Companions of Columbus — Italian, continued

Marmocchi. Prato: Fratelli Giachetti, 1840–45. 18 v. 8°.

v. 5, p. xlix–cxc, ccxv–ccxxviii contains the whole of the *Companions of Columbus*, with the exception of the life of Balboa and the appendix. The translation was made by Bartolommeo Poli.
Copy: The New York Public Library (KBD).

SPANISH

VIAJES y descubrimientos de los compañeros de Colón. Madrid: Gaspar y Roig, 1854. 79(1) p. 4°.

Copy: Columbia University.

SWEDISH

COLUMBI följeslagare, deras resor och upptäckter. Från original språket. Stockholm, 1832. 10, 388 p. 12°.

Authority: Hjalmar Linnström, Svenskt boklexikon, åren 1830–1865, del 1, p. 752.

THE ALHAMBRA

DANISH

ALHAMBRA. Af Washington Irving. Oversat af Frederik Schaldemose... Kjöbenhavn: H. G. Brill, 1833–34. 2 v. in 1. 12°.

Copy: Library of Congress.

ALHAMBRA, paa Dansk ved R. Schmidt. Kjøbenhavn, 1860. 8°.

Authority: J. Vahl, Dansk Bogfortegnelse for Aarene 1859–1868, p. 70.

FORTÆLLINGER fra Alhambra. Oversat af C. Sveistrup. Kjøbenhavn, 1888. 8°.

Authority: J. Vahl, Dansk Bogfortegnelse for Aarene 1881–1892, p. 119.

DUTCH

De ALHAMBRA, of nieuwe schetsen en portretten. Naar het Engelsch...door H. Frijlink... Amsterdam: Hendrik Frijlink, 1833. 2 v. in 1. 8°.

Copy: Columbia University.

FRENCH

Les CONTES de l'Alhambra, précédés d'un Voyage dans la province de Grenade, traduits de Washington Irving par Mlle A. Sobry... Paris: H. Fournier jeune, 1832. 2 v. 8°.

Copies: Bibliothèque Nationale; British Museum.

—— Bruxelles: Hochshausen et Fournes, 1837. 2 v. 8°.

Authority: Dr. Maurice Chazin.

L'ALHAMBRA, chroniques du pays de Grenade. Traduit par P. Christian. Paris: Lavigne, 1843. 12°.

Authority: J. M. Quérard, La littérature française contemporaine, tome 4, p. 358.

NOUVEAUX contes de l'Alhambra; traduits de l'anglais par O. Squarr [Charles Flor]. Bruxelles: Kiessling, Schnée et Ce, 1855. 167 p. 32°.

Also issued at Bruxelles by A. Cadot, 1855.
Authority: Bibliographie de la Belgique, année 18, p. 114.

L'ALHAMBRA de Grenade, souvenirs et légendes, par W. Irving. Traduit de l'anglais par M. Richard Viot. Tours: A. Mame et fils, 1886. 375 p. illus. 16°.

Copy: Bibliothèque Nationale.

...CONTES de l'Alhambra. Traduit de l'anglais, par Émile Godefroy. Paris: G. Crès, 1921. 327 p. 16°.

Copy: Bibliothèque Nationale.

Selection

Le SOUTERRAIN de l'Alhambra, conte par Washington Irving. Limoges: M. Barbou, 1890. 70 p. illus. 18°.

Copy: Bibliothèque Nationale.

GERMAN

Die ALHAMBRA; aus den Englischen übertragen von Theodor Hell. Berlin: Duncker und Humblot, 1832. 2 v. 12°.

Authority: C. G. Kayser, Vollständiges Bücher-Lexicon, Theil 6, Romane, p. 70.

Die ALHAMBRA; aus den Englischen von Johann Sporschil. Braunschweig: Vieweg, 1832. 2 v. 8°.

Authority: C. G. Kayser, Vollständiges Bücher-Lexicon, Theil 6, Romane, p. 70.

ALHAMBRA, oder das neue Skizzenbuch. Abbotsford und Newstead-Abtei. Eine Reise auf den Prairien. Frankfurt am Main: Sauerländer, 1847. 692 p. 2. sorgfältig verb. Auflage. 16°. (Ausgewählte Schriften. Theil 4.)

Authority: C. G. Kayser, Vollständiges Bücher-Lexicon, Theil 11, p. 518.

Die ALHAMBRA oder das neue Skizzenbuch von Washington Irving. Mit einer Einleitung von L. Pröscholdt. Stuttgart: W. Spemann [1881?]. 2 p.l., (1)6–240 p. 12°. (Collection Spemann. Bd. 19.)

Copy: Circulation Department, The New York Public Library.

Die ALHAMBRA oder das neue Skizzenbuch. Gesamt-Ausgabe. Halle an der Saale: Hendel [1887]. vi, 229 p. 8°. (Bibliothek der Gesamt-Litteratur des In- und Auslandes. Nr. 198–200.)

Authority: C. G. Kayser, Vollständiges Bücher-Lexicon, Bd. 25, p. 135.

Die ALHAMBRA oder das neue Skizzenbuch. Wortgetreu nach H. R. Mecklenburg's Grundsätzen aus dem Englischen übersetzt von G. R. Berlin: H. R. Mecklenburg, 1890. 256 p. 32°.

Authority: C. G. Kayser, Vollständiges Bücher-Lexicon, Bd. 25, p. 674.

Translations, continued

The Alhambra — German, continued

Selections

SAGEN von der Alhambra. Übersetzt von Adolf Strodtmann. Leipzig: Meyer, 1887. 52 p. (Meyer's Volksbücher. Nr. 180.)

Authority: C. G. Kayser, Vollständiges Bücher-Lexicon, Bd. 26, p. 126.

Das VERMÄCHTNIS des Mauren. Aus dem Englischen. Donauwörth: Buchhandlung L. Auer, 1915. 20 p. 8°. (Deutsche Jugendhefte. Nr. 19.)

Authority: Deutsches Bücherverzeichnis, Bd. 4, p. 1348.

ICELANDIC

PÍLAGRÍMUR Ástarinnar, eða Sagan af Ahmed al Kamel. Kampmannahöfn, 1860. 12°.

Copy: British Museum.

ITALIAN

NUOVI racconti dell' Alhambra. Milano: Società editoriale milanese, 1911. 16°. (Biblioteca per tutti.)

Authority: Giornale della libreria, anno 24, p. 184.

SPANISH

CUENTOS de la Alhambra... Traducidos por D. L. L[amarca]. [Valencia: Librería de Mallén y Berard, frente á San Martin, 1833.] 4 p.l., 248 p. 32°.

Note: There are apparently variant issues of this edition. In the Hispanic Society copy the verso of the half-title reads: Con Licencia Impr. de J. Ferrer de Orga. Valencia: 1833. The engraved t.-p. reads: Valencia: Librería de Mallen y Berard, 1833. The BM copy has Paris on the t.-p.; Valencia on the engraved t.-p., as well as on the half-title.

Copies: Hispanic Society of America; British Museum.

CUENTOS de la Alhambra... Madrid: Casa de la Unión comercial, 1844.

Translated by D. Manuel M. de Santa Ana from the French of Mlle. Sobry.

Authority: John De Lancey Ferguson, American Literature in Spain, p. 222.

Las CINCO perlas de la Alhambra: cuentos originales... Escritos en inglés por Washington Irving, y traducidos del francés por D. Manuel M. de Santa Ana. Madrid, 1844.

"Apparently another and revised edition of the preceding."

Authority: Stanley T. Williams, in *Modern Philology*, v. 28, p. 189.

CUENTOS de la Alhambra de Washinglon [*sic!*] Irving. Granada: Zamora, 1859. 327 p. 24°.

On the board cover: ...Washington Irwing [*sic!*] ... Granada, 1861.

Copy: Hispanic Society of America.

CUENTOS de la Alhambra... Madrid: Manuel Tello, 1882.

Advertised on the cover of Hawthorne's *El tesoro escondido*, as in preparation.

Authority: Ferguson, p. 222.

LEYENDAS extraordinarias por N. Hawthorne, E. Poe y Washington Irving. Madrid: Manuel Tello, 1882. 16°.

Authority: Ferguson, p. 222.

CUENTOS de la Alhambra... Versión directa del inglés por el doctor José Ventura Traveset ...precedida de una nota biográfica del autor por D. A. González Garbín... Granada: P. V. Sabatel, 1888. xxii, 432 p. illus. 16°.

Authority: Ferguson, p. 222.

—— Segunda edición, corregida y augmentada, é ilustrada con retratos, vistas, apuntes á la pluma y planos de la Alhambra. Granada: Viuda é hijos de P. V. Sabatel, 1893. 432 p., 4 l. 24°.

Copy: Hispanic Society of America.

LEYENDAS de la Alhambra. Barcelona: Olegario Salvatella [1906?].

Advertised to appear "dentro de breves días" in Poe's *Narraciones extraordinares,* Barcelona [1906?].

Authority: Ferguson, p. 222.

CUENTOS de la Alhambra. Versión española con una nota biográfica sobre el autor y sus obras por Pedro Umbert. Con aprobación de la autoridad eclesiástica. Barcelona: Henrich y Comp. [1910.] 2 p.l., (1)8–109 p., 1 l. illus. 8°.

Copy: Hispanic Society of America.

CUENTOS de la Alhambra. Valencia [1926?]. (Nueva biblioteca de literatura.)

Authority: Williams, p. 190.

LEYENDAS de el Alhambra, by Carlota Matienzo and Laura B. Crandon... Illustrated by Willis S. Levis... Boston, New York: Ginn and Company [cop. 1927]. viii, 270 p. illus. 12°. (International modern language series.)

Largely translations from *The Alhambra.*

Copy: Library of Congress.

LEYENDAS de la Alhambra. Barcelona, n. d. (La novela breve.)

Authority: Williams, p. 190.

CUENTOS de la Alhambra. Escritos en inglés por el caballero norte-americano Washington Irving, traducción española de Don Domingo Sicilia y San Juan. Barcelona, n. d.

Authority: Williams, p. 190.

CUENTOS de la Alhambra, por el caballero Wáshington Irving. Versión completa del inglés por J[osé] Ventura Traveset y noticia biográfica por A. G[onzález] Garbín. Valencia: Prometeo, n.d. 2 p.l., (i)vi–x, (1)12–234 p., 3 l. 12°.

Copy: Circulation Department, The New York Public Library.

Selections

CUENTO de la Alhambra. El Comandante Manco y el soldado. (Semanario pintoresco español. Madrid, 1840. Oct. 18, p. 333; Oct. 25, p. 341.)

Authority: Ferguson, p. 223.

Translations, continued

The Alhambra — Spanish, continued

Las TRES bellas infantas: leyenda de la Alhambra. Por Washington Irving; versión castellana de Natalia Cossío de Jímenez. Madrid, n. d.

Authority: Williams, p. 190.

El LEGADO del Moro: leyenda de la Alhambra. Por Washington Irving; versión castellana de Natalia Cossío de Jímenez. n. p., n. d.

Authority: Williams, p. 190.

LEYENDAS maravillosas. (In: Biblioteca de la juventud. n. p., n. d. p. 35–75.)

Authority: Williams, p. 190.

El LEGADO del Moro. Leyenda de la Alhambra por Washington Irving. Versión castellana de Natalia Cossío de Jiménez. Madrid: Jiménez Fraud, editor, n. d. 43 p. illus. 12°.

Copy: Circulation Department, The New York Public Library.

SWEDISH

ALHAMBRA eller nya utkast af Geoffrey Crayon... Stockholm: Hjerta, 1833. 1. ed. 12°. (Läsebibliothek af den nyaste utländska litteraturen i svensk öfversättning. [no.] 1.)

Translated by Mattias Ziedner.
Authority: Hjalmar Linnström, Svenskt boklexikon, åren 1830–1865, del 1, p. 751.

—— Stockholm: Hjerta, 1834. 306 p. 2. ed. 12°. (Läsebibliothek af den nyaste utländska litteraturen i svensk öfversättning. [no.] 1.)

Translated by Mattias Ziedner.
Authority: Same as previous entry.

ALHAMBRA. Öfversättning [af Mattias Ziedner]. Stockholm, 1863. 282 p. 3. ed. 8°.

Authority: Same as the two previous entries.

ALHAMBRA. Öfversättning af O. V. Ålund. Stockholm: Aktiebolaget Hiertas bokförlag, 1881. 224 p. 8°. (Vitterlek. Tidskrift för skönliteratur. [no.] 2.)

Authority: Svensk bok-katalog för åren 1876–1885.

THE CRAYON MISCELLANY

GERMAN

NEUESTE Crayon-Skizzen. Skizzenbuch und Novellen von 1839. Nach dem Nordamerikanische Originale von Carlo Brunetti. Hamburg: Herold, 1840. 8°.

Authority: C. G. Kayser, Neues Bücher-Lexicon, 1833–1840, Theil 1, p. 485.

1

A Tour on the Prairies

DUTCH

TOGT door de prairiën van Noord-Amerika. Naar het Engelsch van W. Irving. Amsterdam: H. Frijlink, 1835. xii, 260 p., 1 port. 8°.

Copy: Library of Congress.

FRENCH

VOYAGE dans les prairies à l'ouest des États-Unis, par Washington Irving. Traduit par Mademoiselle A. Sobry, traducteur des Contes de l'Alhambra. Paris: Fournier jeune, 1835. 2 p.l., 306 p., 1 l. 8°.

Copy: Collection of the compiler.

Un TOUR dans les prairies, à l'ouest des États-Unis. Traduit de l'anglais de Washington Irwing [*sic!*] par Ernest W***. Tours: R. Pornin et Cie., 1845. 2 p.l., 296 p., 2 pl. 12°. (Gymnase moral d'éducation.)

Copies: Library of Congress; Bibliothèque Nationale.

Un TOUR dans les prairies, à l'ouest des États-Unis. Traduit de l'anglais de Washington Irving par Ernest W***. Tours: A. Mame, 1850. 235 p. illus. 16°.

Copy: Bibliothèque Nationale.
According to the catalogue of the Bibliothèque Nationale this edition was reissued in 1851, 1854, 1858, 1862, and 1866.

—— Tours: A. Mame et fils, 1872. 239 p. new ed. illus. 16°. (Bibliothèque de la jeunesse chrétienne... série 3.)

Copies: Library of Congress; Bibliothèque Nationale.

GERMAN

Eine WANDERUNG in die Prairien. Aus dem Englischen von H. Roberts. Braunschweig: Vieweg, 1835. 16°. (Miscellaneen. Bd. 1.)

Authority: C. G. Kayser, Neues Bücher-Lexicon, Theil 1, p. 485.

AUSFLUG auf die Prairien zwischen den Arkansas und Red-River, von Washington Irving. Stuttgart und Tübingen: J. G. Cotta, 1835. 2 p.l., 136 p. 8°. (Reisen und Länderbeschreibungen der älteren und neuesten Zeit. Lieferung 4.)

Copies: Library of Congress; British Museum.

Eine REISE auf den Prairien (Arkansas)... Aus dem Englischen... Frankfurt am Main: Sauerländer, 1835. 256 p.

Authority: Katalog der Berliner Stadtbibliothek, Bd. 3, p. 295.

2

Abbotsford and Newstead Abbey

FRENCH

WALTER SCOTT et Lord Byron, ou Voyages à Abbotsford et à Newstead, par Washington Irving. Traduit par Mlle A. Sobry... Paris: Fournier jeune, 1835. iv, 294 p. 8°.

Copy: Bibliothèque Nationale.

GERMAN

ABBOTSFORD und Newstead-Abtei. Aus dem Englischen von H. Roberts. Braunschweig: Vieweg, 1835. 16°.

Authority: C. G. Kayser, Neues Bücher-Lexicon, Theil 1, p. 485.

Translations, continued

The Crayon Miscellany, continued

3

Legends of the Conquest of Spain

GERMAN

SAGEN von der Eroberung und Unterjochung Spaniens. Aus dem Englischen übersetzt von Lenardo. Aachen: Hensen und Comp., 1839. 12°.

Authority: C. G. Kayser, Neues Bücher-Lexicon, Theil 1, p. 485.

SPANISH

LEYENDAS españoles, por Wáshington Irving ...versión castellana por José F. Godoy... Nueva York y Londres: D. Appleton y Cia, 1919. xvi p., 1 l., 402 p. 8°.

Copy: Library of Congress.

ASTORIA

DUTCH

ASTORIA; of, Avontuurlyke reize naar en over het Klipgebergte van Noord-Amerika, ondernomen in het belang der door den Heer J. J. Astor opgerigte peltery compagnie, en beschreven door Washington Irving... Naar het Engelsch. Haarlem: Wed. A. Loosjes, pz., 1837. 2 v. 8°.

Copies: The New York Public Library (IW); Library of Congress.

FRENCH

VOYAGES dans les contrées désertes de l'Amérique du Nord, entrepris pour la fondation du Comptoir d'Astoria sur la côte nord-ouest. Par Washington Irving... Traduit de l'anglais par P. N. Grolier... Paris: P. Dufart, 1839. 2 v. in 1. 8°.

Copies: The New York Public Library (IW); Library of Congress.

ASTORIA, voyages au delà des Montagnes Rocheuses, par Washington Irving. Traduit de l'anglais par P.-N. Grolier. Paris: A. Allouard, 1843. 2 v. in 1. 2. ed. 8°.

Copy: Bibliothèque Nationale.

GERMAN

ASTORIA, oder die Unternehmung jenseit des Felsengebirges. Von Washington Irving... Aus dem Englischen von A. von Treskow... Quedlinburg und Leipzig: Gottfr. Basse, 1837. 2 v. in 1. 12°.

Copy: The New York Public Library (IW).

ASTORIA, oder Abenteuer in den Gebirgen und Wäldern von Canada. Aus dem Englischen von Dr. E. Brinckmeier. Braunschweig: G. C. E. Meyersen, 1837. 3 v. 12°.

Authority: C. G. Kayser, Neues Bücher-Lexicon, Theil 1, p. 485.

ASTORIA. Von Washington Irving. Aus dem Englischen... Frankfurt am Main: J. D. Sauerländer, 1837. 3 v. 24°.

Copy: The New York Public Library (IW).

ASTORIA; oder, Geschichte einer Handelsexpedition jenseits der Rocky Mountains. Aus dem Englischen des Washington Irving. Stuttgart und Tübingen: J. G. Cotta, 1838. 1 p.l., (i)vi–xviii, 390 p. 8°. (Reisen und Länderbeschreibungen der älteren und neuesten Zeit. Lieferung 14.)

Copies: The New York Public Library (IW); British Museum.

ASTORIA. Frei aus dem Englischen übertragen von E. von Kraatz. Braunschweig: G. Westermann, 1910. iv, 200 p. illus. 8°. (Lebensbücher der Jugend. Bd. 10.)

Authority: C. G. Kayser, Vollständiges Bücher-Lexicon, Bd. 36, p. 33.

SWEDISH

ASTORIA; eller kolonien bortom Klippbergen ... Af...författare till "Alhambra"... Öfversättning. Stockholm: Hjerta, 1837. 2 v. 8°. (I Nytt läse-bibliotheket.)

Authority: Hjalmar Linnström, Svenskt boklexikon, åren 1830–1865, del 1, p. 751.

THE ROCKY MOUNTAINS (THE ADVENTURES OF CAPTAIN BONNEVILLE)

DUTCH

LOTGEVALLEN en ontmoetingen van Kapitein Bonneville, op zijne avontuurlijke togten aan gene zijde van het Klipgebergte van Noord-Amerika; beschreven door Washington Irving ... Naar het Engelsch. Haarlem: Wed. A. Loosjes, pz., 1838. 2 v. in 1. 8°.

Copy: The New York Public Library (IW).

FRENCH

VOYAGES et aventures du capitaine Bonneville, à l'ouest des États-Unis d'Amérique, audelà des Montagnes Rocheuses, par Washington Irving... Traduits de l'anglais par Benjamin Laroche... Paris: Charpentier, 1837. 2 v. in 1. 8°.

Copy: Bibliothèque Nationale.

GERMAN

ABENTEUER des Capitain Bonneville, übertragen von Dr. Ed. Freisleben. Leipzig: B. Tauchnitz, Jr., 1837. 3 v. 8°.

Authority: C. G. Kayser, Neues Bücher-Lexicon, Theil 1, p. 485.

Translations, continued

The Rocky Mountains — German, continued

ABENTEUER des Capitain Bonneville. Aus dem Englischen von A. von Treskow. Quedlinburg: Basse, 1837. 2 v. 8°.

Authority: C. G. Kayser, Neues Bücher-Lexicon, Theil 1, p. 485.

OLIVER GOLDSMITH

GERMAN

OLIVER GOLDSMITH. Eine Lebensbeschreibung. Aus dem Englischen. Berlin: Mertens, 1858. 1 p.l., x, 365 p. 8°.

Authority: C. G. Kayser, Vollständiges Bücher-Lexicon, Theil 13, p. 496.

WELSH

HANES y ddaear a'r creadwriaid byw, gan O. G.: gyda Golygiad arweiniol o'r deyrnas anifeilaidd, gan y Baron Cuvier...a bywgraffiad yr awdwr [i. e. of O. G.] gan W. Irving. Wedi ei gyfieithu a'i olygu gan R. E. Williams. 2 Cyf. Edinburgh [printed], a Llundain [1868]. 4°.

Translation: History of the earth and animated nature, by O. G.: together with...by Baron Cuvier... with biography of the author (O. G.) by W. Irving. After his translation by R. E. Williams.
Copy: British Museum.

BIOGRAPHY OF MARGARET DAVIDSON

GERMAN

BIOGRAPHIE der jungen amerikan. Dichterin Margarethe M. Davidson. Aus dem Englischen. Leipzig: Brockhaus, 1843. 12°.

Authority: C. G. Kayser, Vollständiges Bücher-Lexicon, Theil 9, p. 473.

LIFE OF MAHOMET

FRENCH

...VIE de Mahomet. Traduit de l'anglais par Henry Georges. Paris: A. Lacroix, Verboeckhoven et Cie, 1865. 359 p. 8°.

Copy: Bibliothèque Nationale.

GERMAN

Das LEBEN Mohammed's, von Washington Irving... Leipzig: G. B. Lorck, 1850. 254 p., 1 port. 8°. (Historische Hausbibliothek. Bd. 16.)

Reprinted in 1865.
Copy: Bibliothèque Nationale.

GESCHICHTE der Kalifen. Vom Tode Mohamed's bis zum Einfall in Spanien. Von Washington Irving. Leipzig: G. B. Lorck, 1854. viii, 333 p. 8°. (Historische Hausbibliothek. Bd. 33.)

Reprinted in 1865 and 1874.
Copy: Bibliothèque Nationale.

GREEK

Βίος τοῦ Μωάμεδ [The Life of Mahomet] Μετὰ παραρτήματος Περὶ ισλαμικῆς θρησκείας. ῾Υηὸ Οὐασιγτῶνος ῎Ιρβινγγος. Μετάφρασις ἐκ τοῦ αγγλικοῦ ᾿Ανδρέου Σ. Φαραοῦ [Pharaos]. ᾿Εν Σακύνδῳ: ῾Ραφτάνης, 1866. 351 p. 8°.

Authority: Berliner Titeldrucke, 1929, Nr. 67601.

ITALIAN

VITA di Maometto. Versione di Giuseppe de Tivoli. Milano: Guglielmini, 1854. 312 p. 16°.

Authority: Attilio Pagliaini, Catalogo generale della libreria italiana dall' anno 1847 a tutto il 1899.

POLISH

KORAN (Al-Koran) z Arabskiego przekład Polski J. Murzy Tarak Buczackiego... Wzbogacony objaśnieniami W. Kościuszki. Poprzedzony zyciorysem Mahometa z W. Irving... Warszawa, 1858. 2 v. 8°.

The Irving 'Life' is in v. 1.
Copy: British Museum.

SPANISH

HISTORIA de Mahoma. Escrita en inglés por Washington Irving; traducida al español por J. S. Facio. México, 1857.

Authority: Stanley T. Williams, in *Modern Philology*, v. 28, p. 190.

LIFE OF WASHINGTON

GERMAN

Das LEBEN George Washingtons. Leipzig: Lorck, 1855–60. 5 v. 8°.

Bd. 1–3 issued as Bd. 5–7 of the series, Moderne Geschichtschreiber.

Bd. 1–3, "aus dem Englischen von W. C. Drugulin"; Bd. 4–5, "hrsg. von Fr. Bülau."

Authority: Katalog der Berliner Stadtbibliothek, Bd. 2, p. 247.

LEBENSGESCHICHTE Georg Washington's. Von Washington Irving. Aus dem Englischen von dem Uebersetzer der Werke Prescott's... Leipzig: F. A. Brockhaus, 1856–59. 5 v. 12°.

According to the catalogue of the library of the German Reichstag published in 1882, Bd. 1 was translated by Julius Hermann Eberty; Bd. 2–5, by Franz Moritz Kirbach.
Copy: Library of Congress.

SWEDISH

GEORGE WASHINGTONS lefnad. Öfversättning [af O. V. Ålund]. del 1. Stockholm, 1857–59. 8°.

Issued in parts.
Authority: Hjalmar Linnström, Svenskt boklexikon, åren 1830–1865, del 1, p. 752.

Translations, continued

WOLFERT'S ROOST

German

WOLFERT'S Rust. Transatlantische Skizzen von Washington Irving. Aus dem Englischen von W. E. Drugulin. Leipzig: Lorck [1855–56?]. vii, 130 p. 8°. (Conversations- und Reisebibliothek. Bd. 11.)
Authority: C. G. Kayser, Vollständiges Bücher-Lexicon, Theil 13, p. 192.

Russian

Похожденія Ралфа Рингвуда... Американская быль. С. Петербургъ, 1856. 96 p. 16°.
The Early Experiences of Ralph Ringwood.
Copy: British Museum.

Spanish

MEMORIAS de un gobernador... Traducción del inglés por M. Juderías Bénder. Madrid: Manuel Tello, 1882. 92 p., 2 l. 2. ed. 16°.
Copy: Hispanic Society of America.

SELECTIONS

French

...L'HÉRITAGE du More. [Le gouverneur Manco. La légende de l'astrologue arabe. Le fiancé fantôme.] Avec étude littéraire sur la vie et l'œuvre d'Irving. Paris: H. Gautier [1887]. 32 p. 16°. (Nouvelle bibliothèque populaire à 10 centimes. n°. 36.)
Copy: Bibliothèque Nationale.

...L'HÉRITAGE du More... Paris: Lecène, Oudin et Cie, 1895. 71 p. illus. 12°. (Nouvelle bibliothèque illustrée de vulgarisation.)
Copy: Bibliothèque Nationale.

...RIP. Le fiancé-fantôme. La légende du Vallon-Endormi. Le legs du Maure. Traduction de George Elwall... Paris: C. Delagrave, 1898. 125 p. illus. 8°.
Copy: Bibliothèque Nationale.

German

ERZÄHLUNGEN; aus dem Englischen von W. A. Lindau. Dresden: Arnold, 1822. 8°.
Authority: C. G. Kayser, Vollständiges Bücher-Lexicon, Theil 6, Romane, p. 70.

AUSWAHL aus seinen Schriften. Illustrirt von Henry Ritter und W. Camphausen... Leipzig: Brockhaus, 1856. xv, 291 p. illus. 4°.
Authority: C. G. Kayser, Vollständiges Bücher-Lexicon, Theil 13, p. 496.

Die LEGENDE von der Schlafhöhle. Dolph Heyliger. Nach Washington Irving. Aus dem Englischen von Adolf Strodtmann. Leipzig: Meyer, 1889? 108 p. 16°. (Meyer's Volksbücher. Nr. 651–652.)
Authority: C. G. Kayser, Vollständiges Bücher-Lexicon, Theil 26, p. 126.

Italian

NEL regno fatato: racconti di fate, geni e folletti. Versione italiana di F. Verdinois. Napoli: Società editrice Partenopea, 1909. 113 p. 16°.
Authority: Bollettino delle pubblicazioni italiane, 1909, p. 144.

Spanish

El ALBUM de Waterloo. (El Museo de familias. Barcelona [1840]. v. 4, p. 168 ff.)
Authority: John De Lancey Ferguson, American Literature in Spain, p. 223.

El ALBUM de Waterloo. (El Nuevo siglo ilustrado. Madrid, 1869. May 2, p. 72; May 9, p. 79.)
Authority: Ferguson, p. 223.

Colomb. Colomb á Barcelona. La vida rural á Anglaterra. (In: Prosadors nord-americans. Barcelona, 1909.)
Authority: Ferguson, p. 223.

UNIDENTIFIED

KERKERGENOSSEN. Roman. Nach dem Englischen von Geo. Lotz. Berlin: Jonas Verlagsbuchhandlung, 1841. 2 v. 8°.
Authority: C. G. Kayser, Vollständiges Bücher-Lexicon, Theil 9, p. 473.

COLLECTED WORKS

German

SÄMMTLICHE Werke. Uebersetzt von Mehreren und hrsg. von Chr. Aug. Fischer. Bandchen 1–74. Frankfurt am Main: Sauerländer, 1826–37. 12°.

Contents: Bd. 1–6. Gottfried Crayons Skizzenbuch. 1826. Bd. 7–12. Erzählungen eines Reisenden. 1827. Bd. 13–18. Bracebridge-Hall. 1827. Bd. 19. Eingemachtes. 1827. Bd. 20–31. Die Geschichte des Lebens und die Reisen Christoph Columbus. 1828–30. Bd. 32–37. Die Eroberung von Granada. 1829. Bd. 38–40. Humoristische Geschichte von New-York. 1829. Bd. 41–43. Reisen der Gefährten des Columbus. 1831. Bd. 44–47. Die Alhambra oder das neue Skizzenbuch. 1832. Bd. 48–50. Eine Reise auf den Prairien. 1835. Bd. 51–53. Abbotsford und Newstead-Abtei. 1835. Bd. 54–56. Erzählungen von der Eroberung Spaniens. 1836. Bd. 57–65. Astoria. 1836. Bd. 66–74. Abentheuer des Capitäns Bonneville, oder Scenen jenseits der Felsgebirge des fernen Westens. 1837.
Authority: C. G. Kayser, Vollständiges Bücher-Lexicon, Theil 6, Romane, p. 70, and Neues Bücher-Lexicon, Theil 1, p. 485.

EDITIONS IN SHORTHAND

Certain of Irving's stories, popular for teaching purposes in our schools, have proven equally useful for students of shorthand. The following list of translations into shorthand is compiled from the holdings of The New York Public Library.

DEMOTIC shorthand reader. Irving's Rip Van Winkle written in demotic shorthand with fonetic print key by Godfrey Dewey... Lake Placid Club, N. Y.: Forest Press, 1923. iv, 60 p. 16°.

The LEGEND of Sleepy Hollow... In the reporting style of phonography. London: F. Pitman, 1883. 62 p., 1 l. 16°.

—— London: [Isaac Pitman & Sons,] 1889. 62 p., 1 l. 16°.

—— London: Sir Isaac Pitman & Sons, 1895. 62 p. 16°.

The LEGEND of Sleepy Hollow... In the advanced corresponding style of Graham's standard phonography. New York: Andrew J. Graham & Co. [cop. 1899.] 39 p. 16°.

—— New York: Andrew J. Graham & Co. [cop. 1899.] 39(1) p., 3 l. 12°.

The LEGEND of Sleepy Hollow... Printed in the easy reporting style of phonography, in accordance with the "Manual of phonography," by Benn Pitman and Jerome B. Howard. Cincinnati: The Phonographic Institute Company, 1902. 31 p., 1 l. 16°.

—— Cincinnati: The Phonographic Institute Company, 1903. 31 p. 16°.

Probably the same as the 1902 edition by the same publishers. This copy has the date 1902 altered to 1903, and the change initialled by Mr. Howard.

—— Cincinnati: The Phonographic Institute Company, 1904. 31 p., 1 l. 16°.

—— Cincinnati: The Phonographic Institute Company, 1908. 31 p., 1 l. 16°.

The LEGEND of Sleepy Hollow... Advanced style of Pitman's shorthand... London: Sir Isaac Pitman & Sons [191-?]. 68 p. 16°.

Centenary edition.

The LEGEND of Sleepy Hollow... In the reporting style of Pitman's shorthand... London: Sir Isaac Pitman & Sons [191-?]. 63(1) p. 16°.

Twentieth century edition.

—— London: Sir Isaac Pitman & Sons [191-?]. 62 p., 1 l. 16°.

Twentieth century edition.
This is not the same edition as the other Pitman [191-?].

The LEGEND of Sleepy Hollow... Printed in Gregg shorthand. New York [1916]. 58 p. 16°.

The LEGEND of Sleepy Hollow... In Graham shorthand. [New York: Andrew J. Graham & Co., 1918.] 39 p. 16°.

Title from cover.

The LEGEND of Sleepy Hollow... Printed in the advanced stage of Pitman's shorthand... London: Sir Isaac Pitman & Sons [192-?]. 68 p. 16°.

New era edition.

The LEGEND of Sleepy Hollow. Revised. Printed in Gregg shorthand... New York: Gregg Publishing Company [192-?]. 76 p., 1 l., 1 port. 16°.

On cover: English classics in Gregg shorthand.

RIP VAN WINKLE... Printed in the advanced stage of Pitman's shorthand. Illustrated ... London: Sir Isaac Pitman & Sons [19—?]. 30 p., 1 l. 16°.

New era edition.

RIP VAN WINKLE... In the reporting style of Pitman's shorthand. Illustrated... New York: Isaac Pitman & Sons [190-?]. 30 p. 16°.

Twentieth century edition.

RIP VAN WINKLE... In Graham standard phonography, written by Edwin M. Williams... New York: E. N. Miner, 1900. 47 p., 8 l. 12°.

RIP VAN WINKLE... Printed in the easy reporting style of phonography, in accordance with the "Manual of phonography," by Benn Pitman and Jerome B. Howard. Cincinnati: The Phonographic Institute Company, 1902. 22, 8 p. 16°.

—— Cincinnati: The Phonographic Institute Company, 1908. 22, 8 p. 16°.

RIP VAN WINKLE... Printed in Gregg shorthand. New York: Gregg Publishing Company [1914]. 18 p. 8°.

RIP VAN WINKLE. Revised. Printed in Gregg shorthand... New York: Gregg Publishing Company [192-?]. 51(1) p., 1 port. 16°.

On cover: English classics in Gregg shorthand.

RIP VAN WINKLE and the Creole village... Printed in the easy reporting style in accordance with the Manual of phonography by Benn Pitman and Jerome B. Howard. Cincinnati: Phonographic Institute, 1886. 30 p., 2 l. 16°.

—— Cincinnati: Phonographic Institute, 1889. 30, 8 p. 16°.

This was reprinted in 1892.

RIP VAN WINKLE and The legend of Sleepy Hollow... In the amanuensis style of phonography by Jerome B. Howard. Cincinnati: The Phonographic Institute Company, 1919. 51 p. 16°.

At head of title: The American system of shorthand.

Editions in Shorthand, continued

The SKETCH-BOOK... (A selection.) Transcribed into Gabelsberger-Richter phonography by Richard Preuss. Dresden: Wilhelm Reuter's Stenographie-Verlag, 1900. 30 p. 16°.

At head of title: Reuter's Bibliothek für Gabelsberger-Stenographen. Band 105.

TALES of the Alhambra... (A selection.) Transcribed into Gabelsberger-Richter phonography by Richard Preuss. Dresden: Wilhelm Reuter's Stenographie-Verlag, 1900. 22 p. 16°.

At head of title: Reuter's Bibliothek für Gabelsberger-Stenographen. Band 104.

TALES and sketches... In the corresponding style of phonography. London: Isaac Pitman & Sons, 1884. 96 p. 16°.

—— London: Isaac Pitman & Sons, 1890. 96 p., 4 l., 8 p. 16°.

TALES and sketches... In the corresponding style of Pitman's shorthand... London: Sir Isaac Pitman & Sons, Ltd. [191–?] 96, 8 p. 16°.

Twentieth century edition.

ILLUSTRATED EDITIONS

The standard by which an "illustrated edition" is measured must be wholly arbitrary, since conceptions are as numerous as owners. For the purposes of this bibliography, an *illustrated edition* is thus defined: Any edition containing illustrative matter, other than an ornamental title-page and frontispiece, not included in the first edition, is an illustrated edition. This eliminates those editions boasting merely one or two illustrations, and all those which are ornamented with abstract designs, curlicues about the text, and other devices of a purely decorative nature. The purpose of this section of the bibliography is to call attention to those editions which were obviously brought out as illustrated, and not those which were merely ornamented or embellished.

SALMAGUNDI

SALMAGUNDI... A new and improved edition, with tables of contents and a copious index... New-York: Published by David Longworth, at the Shakspeare-Gallery, 1814. 2 v. 24°.

Illustrated partly by Alexander Anderson.
Reissued in 1820 by Thomas Longworth & Co.; copy in the collection of the compiler.
Copies: The New York Public Library (* KL); Library of Congress; collection of the compiler.

SALMAGUNDI... New edition, corrected and revised by the author. London: Printed for Thomas Tegg [etc.], 1839. 1 p.l., (i) vi–x, 378 p. 16°.

A few line drawings by George Cruikshank.
Copies: The New York Public Library (NBX); collection of the compiler.

SALMAGUNDI... London: C. Daly, 1841. xii, 363 p. 32°.

Has a few plates by unidentified artists.
Copies: The New York Public Library (8–NBX); Library of Congress.

...SALMAGUNDI... New York & London: G. P. Putnam's Sons, 1897. 2 v. 8°.

Author's autograph edition. 500 sets printed.
Illustrations include steel engravings, etchings, and lithographs. These are reproduced from photographs, old prints and other pictures, also from illustrations in old books of travel. There is an average of about twelve illustrations to the volume.
Copy: Library of Congress.

KNICKERBOCKER'S HISTORY OF NEW YORK

A HISTORY of New-York... London: Printed for Thomas Tegg and Son, 1836. xxvi, 397 p. 16°.

Four Cruikshank plates.
This was re-issued by Thomas Tegg in 1839, with an additional illustration by Cruikshank on the title-page.
Copies: The New York Public Library (MEM); collection of the compiler.

A HISTORY of New-York... With illustrations by Felix O. C. Darley, engraved by eminent artists. New-York: George P. Putnam, 1850. xvi, (1) 14–454 p. 8°.

With large folding plate by Heath of Stuyvesant's army entering New Amsterdam.
Copies: The New York Public Library (NBX); Library of Congress; collection of the compiler (2 copies in different bindings).

A HISTORY of New York... The author's revised edition. New York: George P. Putnam and Son, 1867. 459 p. 4°.

Plates and sketches by Darley, Cruikshank, and others.
Large paper edition. 110 copies printed.
Copy: The New York Public Library (NBX).

KNICKERBOCKER sketches from "A history of New York"... Illustrated by F. O. C. Darley. Philadelphia: J. B. Lippincott Company, 1886. 87 p. 8°.

Copy: Library of Congress.

A HISTORY of New-York... A new edition, containing unpublished corrections of the author, with illustrations by Geo. H. Boughton, Will H. Drake, and Howard Pyle, and etchings by Henry C. Eno and F. Raubicheck... New York: Printed for the Grolier Club, 1886. 2 v. 8°.

Copies: The New York Public Library (* KP – Grolier); Library of Congress.

A HISTORY of New York... The author's revised edition... New York: G. P. Putnam's Sons, 1889. xii, 525 p. 8°.

At head of title: Hudson edition.
Plates and headpieces by various artists.
Copy: The New York Public Library (NBX).

KNICKERBOCKER'S History of New York... With illustrations by E. W. Kemble. New

Illustrated Editions, continued

Knickerbocker's History of New York, cont'd

York: G. P. Putnam's Sons, 1894 [1893]. 2 v. 8°.

Van Twiller edition.
Also issued as a limited edition, 281 copies, and called Peter Stuyvesant edition.
Copies: Leon C. Sunstein, Elkins Park, Pa.; British Museum; collection of the compiler.

A HISTORY of New York... Embellished by eight pictures from the hand of Maxfield Parrish, Esqre. New York: R. H. Russell, 1900. xxxi p., 1 l., 298 p., 1 l. illus. f°.

Also issued in London the same year by John Lane, copy in the collection of the compiler, and republished by Dodd, Mead & Co., in 1915.
Copy: Library of Congress.

KNICKERBOCKER'S History of New York... Edited by Anne Carroll Moore; with pictorial pleasantries by James Daugherty. Garden City, New York: Doubleday, Doran & Company, Inc., 1928. xi p., 1 l., 427 p. 8°.

Copies: The New York Public Library (NBX); Library of Congress; collection of the compiler.

THE SKETCH BOOK

The SKETCH BOOK... London: John Murray, 1822. 2 v. new ed. 8°.

Engravings by Heath and Rolls after C. R. Leslie. Another copy has been seen with engravings by Heath and Mitchell after R. Westall; collection of the compiler.
Copy: The New York Public Library (NBQ).

The SKETCH BOOK... Author's revised edition, with original designs by F. O. C. Darley, engraved by Childs, Herrick, etc. New-York: George P. Putnam, 1848. xii, (1)10–465 p. 8°.

Copy: The New York Public Library (MEM and NBQ).

The SKETCH BOOK... Illustrated with original designs. London: John Murray, 1849. xii, (1)10–465 p. 8°.

The illustrations are by Darley.
Copy: Collection of the compiler.

SKETCH BOOK... Artist's edition. Illustrated with one hundred engravings on wood, from original designs. New York: G. P. Putnam, 1864. 504 p. 8°.

Plates engraved by Richardson and Cox, after various artists.
Reissued in 1865, with the addition of the name of Hurd & Houghton in the imprint, and a new publisher's note. Copy in The New York Public Library (NBQ).
Copies: The New York Public Library (NBQ); Library of Congress.

The SKETCH BOOK... Illustrated with one hundred and twenty engravings on wood... London: Bell and Daldy, 1865. 1 p.l., 504 p. 8°.

Illustrations by many different artists.
Copy: Collection of the compiler.

...The SKETCH-BOOK... Author's revised edition. New York: G. P. Putnam's Sons [cop. 1880]. 4 p.l., 532 p. 8°.

In addition to the frontispiece, there are eight plates illustrative of the text.
Copy: Library of Congress.

SKETCH BOOK... Philadelphia: J. B. Lippincott & Co., 1882. 437 p. 4°.

Illustrations by many different artists, engraved on wood by Richardson.
Edition de luxe, 500 copies.
Copies: The New York Public Library (NBQ); Library of Congress; collection of the compiler.

SKETCH BOOK... Illustrated... London: J. M. Dent & Co., 1894. 2 v. 8°.

The illustrations are by many artists.
Copy: Collection of the compiler.

...The SKETCH-BOOK... New York [etc.]: G. P. Putnam's Sons, 1895. 2 v. illus. 8°.

Van Tassel edition.
The thirty-two plates include photographs and drawings by F. O. C. Darley, Arthur Rackham, and Allan Barraud.
Copies: Library of Congress; collection of the compiler.

The SKETCH BOOK by Washington Irving with illustrations by Edmund J. Sullivan. London: George Newnes, Limited, 1902. 2 v. 16°.

Copy: Collection of the compiler.

The SKETCH-BOOK...together with Abbotsford and other selections from the writings of Washington Irving... Edited with comments, notes, bibliography, and topics for study, by H. A. Davidson, M. A. Boston: D. C. Heath & Co., 1910 [cop. 1907]. xx, 419 p. 16°.

Has line drawings, half-tones, etc., by various artists.
Copy: The New York Public Library (NBQ). Copy in collection of the compiler has imprint 1908.

...The SKETCH-BOOK, edited by Elmer E. Wentworth. Boston, New York [etc.]: Allyn and Bacon [cop. 1928]. viii, 582 p. 16°. (The academy classics.)

The plates and other illustrations, both photographs and drawings (a total of forty-four) illustrate more or less specifically the adjacent text.
Copy: Library of Congress.

The SKETCH BOOK...revised by H. Y. Moffett. Illustrated by Curtiss Sprague. [New York:] The Macmillan Company [cop. 1929]. xxxii, 487 p. 16°. (New pocket classics.)

Copy: Library of Congress.

The SKETCH BOOK... With an introduction by Talcott Williamson... New York: The Macmillan Company, 1929. xxxiv, 463 p., 2 l. 12°. (Modern reader's series.)

Illustrations are black and white sketches by Sprague.
Copies: Library of Congress; collection of the compiler.

The SKETCH BOOK. New York: Thomas Y. Crowell & Co., n.d. 406 p. illus. 12°.

Copy: Dr. Roderick Terry.

Rip Van Winkle

ILLUSTRATIONS of Rip Van Winkle; designed and etched by Felix O. C. Darley, for the members of the American Art-Union, 1848. [New York: The American Art-Union, 1849.] 10 p., 1 l., 6 plates (2 in text). obl. f°.

Copies: The New York Public Library († MEM – Darley); Library of Congress; collection of the compiler.

Illustrated Editions, continued

The Sketch Book, continued

RIP VAN WINKLE... Illustrated with six etchings on steel, by Charles Simms, from drawings by Felix Darley (New York). London: Joseph Cundall, 1850. 31 p. 8°.

Colored etchings.
Copy: The New York Public Library (MEM).

RIP. A legend of the Kaatskill Mountains. Illustrated with original designs by eminent artists. New York: G. P. Putnam and Sons, 1870. 32 p. illus. 4°.

Cover-title: Irving's Rip Van Winkle. The Jefferson Booth's Theatre edition, illustrated. Henry L. Hinton, publisher. Two leaves of advertising matter precede title-page.
Also issued with a different wrapper and with no advertising leaves.
Line drawings by Darley, Hart, and others.
Copy: The New York Public Library (* KL).

RIP VAN WINKLE: a legend of the Hudson ... Illustrated by Gordon Browne. London [etc.]: Blackie & Son, 1887. 127(1) p. 8°.

Copy: Collection of the compiler.

RIP VAN WINKLE... Illustrated by Frank T. Merrill. Boston: S. E. Cassino, 1888. 49 p. f°.

Republished in Boston in 1894 by J. Knight; copy in the collection of the compiler.
Copies: Library of Congress; collection of the compiler.

RIP VAN WINKLE... Illustrated with original designs by eminent artists. Philadelphia, London: J. B. Lippincott Company, 1888.

Copy: Collection of the compiler.

RIP VAN WINKLE, as played by Joseph Jefferson. Now for the first time published. New York: Dodd, Mead and Company, 1895. 199 p. 8°.

Illustrated by photographs of the play.
Copies: Library of Congress; collection of the compiler (1899).

RIP VAN WINKLE... New York and London: G. P. Putnam's Sons, 1899. v, 115 p. 8°.

Photogravures from designs by Frederick Simpson Coburn. Borders and cover by Margaret Armstrong.
Copy: Library of Congress.

RIP VAN WINKLE... With forty-six illustrations. Philadelphia: Henry Altemus Company, 1900. 1 p.l., 7–230 p. 16°. (Altemus' young people's library.)

"The legend of Sleepy Hollow": p. 129–230.
Copy: Library of Congress.

RIP VAN WINKLE... With drawings by Arthur Rackham, A.R.W.S. London: William Heinemann; New York: Doubleday, Page, & Co., 1905. viii, 57 p. 4°.

Also issued in an edition de luxe, limited to 250 copies; copy in the collection of the compiler.
Republished in 1910; copies in The New York Public Library (MEM – Rackham) and Library of Congress.
Copy: Collection of the compiler.

RIP VAN WINKLE. Illustriert durch 50 Aquarelle von Arthur Rackham. Leipzig: E. A. Seemann, 1905. 47 p. 4°.

RIP VAN WINKLE... Illustré par Arthur Rackham. Paris: Hachette et Cie., 1906. x, 69(1) p., 1 l. 4°.

Large paper edition of 200 copies.
Copy: Collection of the compiler.

RIP VAN WINKLE. Racconto di Washington Irving, con disegni di Arturo Rackham, A.R.W.S. Bergamo: Istituto italiano d'arti grafiche [19—?]. 60 p. 4°.

The CHILD'S Rip Van Winkle, adapted from Washington Irving; with twelve illustrations in colours by M. L. Kirk. New York: F. A. Stokes Company [1908]. 4 p.l., 39 p. 8°.

Copy: Library of Congress.

RIP VAN WINKLE... Philadelphia: H. Altemus Company [cop. 1908]. 48 p. 16°.

Contains nineteen full-page sketches, some of a humorous character.
Copy: Library of Congress.

RIP VAN WINKLE... Decorations by R. W. Sawyer. Boston [etc.]: J. W. Luce & Company [cop. 1909]. [34] p. 8°.

Copy: Library of Congress.

RIP VAN WINKLE... Illustrated by Charles Robinson. London: T. C. & E. C. Jack; New York: Frederick A. Stokes Co. [1915?] 63(1) p. 8°. (Stories we love.)

Copy: Library of Congress.

RIP VAN WINKLE... Pictures & decorations by N. C. Wyeth. Philadelphia: David McKay Company [cop. 1921]. 5 p.l., 86 p. 4°.

Copies: Library of Congress; collection of the compiler.

RIP VAN WINKLE... With illustrations in color by Edna Cooke, and in line by Felix O. C. Darley. Philadelphia & London: J. B. Lippincott Company [cop. 1923]. 69(1) p. 12°. (The children's classics.)

Copies: Library of Congress; collection of the compiler.

RIP VAN WINKLE; a tale of the Hudson... Illustrated by Frances Brundage. Akron, O., New York: The Saalfield Publishing Company [cop. 1927]. 3 p.l., 11–92 p. 8°.

Copy: Library of Congress.

...RIP VAN WINKLE... With an introduction by Mark Van Doren. New York: The Limited Editions Club, 1930. 2 p.l., 3–57(1) p. 4°.

Reproductions of the Darley plates.
Copies: The New York Public Library (* KP – Limited); Library of Congress.

Rip Van Winkle and The Legend of Sleepy Hollow

The HUDSON legends. Rip Van Winkle. Sleepy Hollow... New York: G. P. Putnam; Hurd and Houghton, 1867. 50 p. 8°.

Illustrations by Hoppin, Parsons, Darley, and Hart.
Copy: Collection of the compiler.

Illustrated Editions, continued

The Sketch Book, continued

The KAATERSKILL region. Rip Van Winkle and Sleepy Hollow... [New York:] Published by The Kaaterskill Publishing Company, 1884. 46, 16 p., 3 l. obl. 12°.

Illustrations by Darley. This volume was apparently issued as an advertisement for one of the hotels in the region.
Copies: The New York Public Library (NBO); Library of Congress; collection of the compiler.

RIP VAN WINKLE and The legend of Sleepy Hollow... With fifty-three illustrations by George H. Boughton, A.R.A. London and New York: Macmillan and Co., 1893. xi, 218 p. 12°.

Also issued in a large-paper edition of 250 copies; copy in the collection of the compiler.
Reprinted by Macmillan and Co., London, in 1908; copy in the Library of Congress.
Copy: Collection of the compiler.

RIP VAN WINKLE and The legend of Sleepy Hollow...with illustrations in color by Edna Cooke and in line by Felix O. C. Darley. Philadelphia: J. B. Lippincott Company [cop. 1924]. 148 p. 8°.

Copies: Library of Congress; collection of the compiler.

RIP VAN WINKLE and The legend of Sleepy Hollow... Illustrated by Eric Pape. New York: The Macmillan Company, 1925. xi(i) p., 1 l., 183(1) p. 12°.

Copies: Library of Congress; collection of the compiler.

RIP VAN WINKLE and The legend of Sleepy Hollow... Introduction and notes by Blanche E. Weekes. Illustrated by John Fitz, Jr. Philadelphia [etc.]: The John C. Winston Company [cop. 1928]. x, 106 p. 8°.

Copy: Collection of the compiler.

The Legend of Sleepy Hollow

ILLUSTRATIONS of The legend of Sleepy Hollow, designed and etched by Felix O. C. Darley for the members of the American Art-Union. [New York: The American Art-Union,] 1849. 16 p., 6 pl. obl. f°.

Copies: The New York Public Library († MEM – Darley); collection of the compiler.

LEGEND of Sleepy Hollow... Illustrated with original designs by Huntington, Kensett, Darley [etc.]. New York: G. P. Putnam, 1864. 50 p. 8°.

Copy: Library of Congress.

LEGEND of Sleepy Hollow... Illustrated with original designs by Huntington, Kensett, Darley, Hoppin, Leutze, Richards, Wm. Hart, Oertell, F. A. Chapman. New York: G. P. Putnam; Hurd and Houghton, 1867. 50 p. 8°.

Copy: The New York Public Library (Irving Case).

The LEGEND of Sleepy Hollow... New York and London: G. P. Putnam's Sons, 1899. v p., 1 l., 191 p. 12°.

"The photogravures in this volume are from designs by Frederick Simpson Coburn. The borders and cover are by Miss Margaret Armstrong."
Copies: The New York Public Library (NBO); Library of Congress; collection of the compiler.

The LEGEND of Sleepy Hollow... Boston: D. Estes & Co. [1900.] 63 p. 12°.

Has six plates illustrative of the text.
Copy: Library of Congress.

...The LEGEND of Sleepy Hollow; designed and hand colored by Lolita Perine. New York: Dodge Publishing Company, 1903. 1 p.l., 59 p. 8°.

Copy: Library of Congress.

The LEGEND of Sleepy Hollow... Drawings by Arthur I. Keller. Indianapolis: The Bobbs-Merrill Company [cop. 1906]. 91(1) p. 8°.

Copies: Library of Congress; collection of the compiler.

The LEGEND of Sleepy Hollow...with illustrations in color by Edna Cooke. Philadelphia & London: J. B. Lippincott Company [cop. 1924]. 82 p. 12°.

Copy: Library of Congress.

The LEGEND of Sleepy Hollow... Illustrated by Arthur Rackham. London: George G. Harrap & Co., Ltd. [1928.] 102 p., 1 l. 4°.

Also issued in a large-paper edition of 375 copies.
Also issued by David McKay Co., Philadelphia, in 1928; copies in The New York Public Library and the Library of Congress.
Copy: Collection of the compiler.

The LEGEND of Sleepy Hollow... Illustrated with original etchings by Bernhardt Wall. New York: Published by Cheshire House, 1931. 4 p.l., 3–63(1) p., 6 pl. 4°.

Edition limited to 1200 copies.
Copies: The New York Public Library (†* KP – Cheshire); Library of Congress; collection of the compiler.

The Legend of Sleepy Hollow, and Other Essays

The LEGEND of Sleepy Hollow, and The spectre bridegroom... Illustrated with original designs by eminent artists. Philadelphia, London: J. B. Lippincott & Co. [cop. 1875.] 2 p.l., (1)8–78 p. 8°.

Plates by Oddie, Darley, Richardson, Cox, etc.
Copies: Library of Congress; collection of the compiler.

The LEGEND of Sleepy Hollow...with other fanciful tales. Illustrated by Frances Brundage and Lillian Sturges. Akron, Ohio, and New York: The Saalfield Publishing Company [cop. 1926]. [170] p. 8°. (Old trail series.)

Copies: Library of Congress; collection of the compiler.

LITTLE BRITAIN together with The Spectre bridegroom & A Legend of Sleepy Hollow... Illustrated by Chas. O. Murray. London: Sampson Low, Marston, Searle, & Rivington, n.d. xi(i), 176 p. 12°.

Copy: Collection of the compiler.

Smaller Selections

The ANGLER... With etched illustrations by Louis K. Harlow. Boston: S. E. Cassino, 1892. 1 p.l., 21 numb. l. 12°.

Copy: Library of Congress.

Illustrated Editions, continued

The Sketch Book, continued

CHRISTMAS at Bracebridge Hall... Illustrated by Arthur A. Dixon. London: Ernest Nister; New York: E. P. Dutton & Co., n.d. 120 p. 16°.

Copy: Circulation Department, The New York Public Library.

The CHRISTMAS dinner, from The Sketch Book... Illustrations by Gordon Ross. New York: William Edwin Rudge, 1929. 3 p.l., 3–22 p., 1 l. 8°.

Copies: The New York Public Library (* KP – Rudge); Library of Congress; collection of the compiler.

CHRISTMAS in England. Papers from the "Sketch-book"... New York: G. P. Putnam; Hurd and Houghton, 1867. 94 p. 8°.

Cuts by various artists.
Copy: Collection of the compiler.

ENGLISH sketches, from "The sketch book" ... Philadelphia, London: J. B. Lippincott Company [1886]. 80 p. 8°.

"Illustrated with original designs by eminent artists." Twenty-three small engravings, generally illustrative of the text.
Copy: Library of Congress.

The KEEPING of Christmas at Bracebridge Hall...with twenty-four illustrations by C. E. Brock. London: J. M. Dent & Co.; New York: E. P. Dutton & Co., 1906. xvi, 267(1) p. 12°.

Copy: Collection of the compiler.

OLD CHRISTMAS: from the Sketch Book... Illustrated by R. Caldecott. London: Macmillan & Co., 1876. xiv p., 1 l., 165(1) p. 12°.

Plates engraved by J. D. Cooper.
Frequently re-issued. A large-paper edition limited to 250 copies was published in 1892; copy in collection of the compiler.
Copies: The New York Public Library (MEM); collection of the compiler.

OLD CHRISTMAS... Pictured by Cecil Aldin. London: Hodder & Stoughton [1908]. 175(1) p. 8°.

Also issued in New York by Dodd, Mead & Co. [1908]; copies in The New York Public Library (NBQ) and the Library of Congress.
Copy: Collection of the compiler.

OLD CHRISTMAS... Illustrated by Frank Dadd. New York and London: G. P. Putnam's Sons [cop. 1916]. vii, 115 p. 8°.

Copy: Library of Congress.

OLD CHRISTMAS... With upward of one hundred illustrations from original designs by Randolph Caldecott. New York: Pollard & Moss, publishers, 47 John Street, n.d. 47(1) p. 4°.

Copy: The New York Public Library († NAC p.v. 155, no.3).

OLD CHRISTMAS and Bracebridge Hall... with illustrations by Lewis Baumer. London: Constable and Company, Limited, 1918. xi, 284 p., 1 l. 8°.

Copy: Collection of the compiler.

The PRIDE of the village, and other tales. From "The sketch book"... Illustrated with original designs by eminent artists. Philadelphia, London: J. B. Lippincott Company [cop. 1886]. 80 p. 8°.

Copy: Library of Congress.

RIP VAN WINKLE, and other sketches... Edited...by Francis Kingsley Ball; illustrated by Sears Gallagher. Boston [etc.]: Ginn and Company [cop. 1923]. xii, 242 p. 12°.

Copies: Library of Congress; collection of the compiler.

RURAL LIFE in England... Illustrated by Alan Wright and Vernon Stokes. London: G. Routledge & Sons; New York: E. P. Dutton & Co., n.d. 2 p.l., vii–viii, 104 p. 8°. (The photogravure and colour series.)

Copy: Library of Congress.

...SELECTIONS from the Sketch-book...with biographical sketch, explanatory notes, critical opinions and directions to teachers, by A. J. Demarest... Philadelphia: Christopher Sower Company [cop. 1912]. 154 p. 16°. (Classics in the grades.)

In addition to the frontispiece, there are five plates of scenes in the Sleepy Hollow country.
Copy: Library of Congress.

STRATFORD-UPON-AVON, from "The sketch book"... Edited by Richard Savage and William Salt Brassington, F.S.A. Stratford-upon-Avon: Printed by Edward Fox, at the Shakespeare Quiney Press, 1900. 2 p.l., 144 p. 8°.

Issued in an edition of 75 copies.
Reproductions of relics and historic sketches.
Copy: Collection of the compiler.

BRACEBRIDGE HALL

BRACEBRIDGE HALL... Illustrated with fourteen original designs by Schmolze, engraved on steel by Greatbach and others. New York: G. P. Putnam, 1858. vi, (1)10–465 p. 8°.

Copy: The New York Public Library (NBO).

BRACEBRIDGE HALL, or The humorists... Author's revised edition. New York: G. P. Putnam, 1860. vi p., 1 l., (1)10–465 p. 8°.

Plates by Schmolze; vignettes by Richardson after Herrick. This edition reproduces only five of the Schmolze plates prepared for the 1858 edition.
Copy: The New York Public Library (NBO).

BRACEBRIDGE HALL, or The humorists... By Geoffrey Crayon, Gent... The author's revised edition. New York: G. P. Putnam and Son, 1867. vi, (1)8–543 p. 12°.

This edition reproduces only eight of the Schmolze plates prepared for the 1858 edition.
Copy: The New York Public Library (NBO).

BRACEBRIDGE HALL... Illustrated by R. Caldecott. London: Macmillan & Co., 1877. xiv, 284, 4 p. 12°.

Plates engraved by J. D. Cooper.
Copies: The New York Public Library (MEM); Library of Congress; collection of the compiler.

...BRACEBRIDGE HALL... Author's revised edition. New York: G. P. Putnam's Sons [cop. 1880]. 561 p. 8°.

Has a few engravings by unidentified artists.
Copies: Circulation Department, The New York Public Library; Library of Congress.

Illustrated Editions, continued

Bracebridge Hall, continued

BRACEBRIDGE HALL or The Humourists... New York & London: G. P. Putnam's Sons, 1896. 2 v. 8°.

Surrey edition.
Plates by Reinhart, Schmolze, Rackham, Rix, Hyde, Sandham, and Miller; designs for page borders and initials by Armstrong and Christy.
Copy: Collection of the compiler.

BRACEBRIDGE HALL... Chicago: W. B. Conkey Company [cop. 1900]. 201 p. 16°.

Three drawings and frontispiece portrait of Irving.
Copy: Library of Congress.

Bachelors

A Bachelor's Confessions

BACHELORS and A Bachelor's confessions. Illustrated partly in color by Cecil Aldin. London and New York: William Heinemann, 1909. 32 p. 16°.

Copy: Collection of the compiler.

Dolph Heyliger

ILLUSTRATIONS of Washington Irving's Dolph Heyliger, designed and etched by John W. Ehninger. New-York: George P. Putnam, 1851. 32 p., 10 l. obl. 4°.

Copy: The New York Public Library († NBO).

DOLPH HEYLIGER...with forty-two illustrations and maps. Boston: D. C. Heath & Co., 1904. 113 p. 12°.

Illustrations unsigned; a few are reproductions of portraits.
Copy: The New York Public Library.

TALES OF A TRAVELLER

TALES of a traveller. London: John Murray, 1825. 2 v. 12°.

Engravings by Charles Heath after drawings by T. Stothard.
Copy: Collection of the compiler.

TALES of a traveller... With illustrations by Felix O. C. Darley, engraved by eminent artists. New-York: George P. Putnam, 1850. 3 p.l., (i) vi–xi p., 1 l., (1) 16–456 p. 8°.

Seventeen drawings by Darley, engraved by various artists.
Copies: The New York Public Library (NBO); Library of Congress; collection of the compiler.

TALES of a traveller... Author's revised edition... New York: Geo. P. Putnam, 1860. 477 p. 8°.

Vignettes by Darley and Herrick, and two of the Darley plates prepared for the 1850 edition, reduced in size.
Copy: The New York Public Library (NBO).

TALES of a traveller... The author's revised edition. New York: G. P. Putnam and Son, 1868. vi, (1) 8–530 p. 12°.

Knickerbocker edition.
Drawings by Darley, engraved by various artists.
Copy: The New York Public Library (NBO).

...TALES of a traveller... The author's revised edition... New York: G. P. Putnam's Sons, 1889. 1 p.l., 7–546 p. 8°.

At head of title: Hudson edition.
Has a few drawings by Darley.
Copy: The New York Public Library (NBO).

TALES of a traveller... New York & London: G. P. Putnam's Sons, 1895. 2 v. 8°.

Buckthorne edition.
Illustrations by Dielman, Rackham, Wilson, Church, Barraud, Willmore, Sandham, and Burt. Borders and title-page design by George Wharton Edwards; initials by Walter C. Greenough.
Copies: The New York Public Library (NBO, v. 2 only); Library of Congress; collection of the compiler.

TALES from Washington Irving's Traveller. With illustrations by George Hood... Philadelphia & London: J. B. Lippincott Company, 1913. 235 p. 8°.

Copies: Circulation Department, The New York Public Library; Library of Congress.

TALES of a traveller... New York: Thomas Y. Crowell & Company, n.d. 307 p. 12°.

Plates by Frank E. Merrill.
Copy: Circulation Department, The New York Public Library.

LIFE AND VOYAGES OF CHRISTOPHER COLUMBUS

The LIFE and voyages of Christopher Columbus... Boston: Marsh, Capen, Lyon, and Webb, 1839. xi (i), (1) 10–325 p. 12°.

Copies: The New York Public Library (HAM); Library of Congress.

The LIFE and voyages of Christopher Columbus... (Condensed by the author from his larger work)... New York: G. P. Putnam's Sons [cop. 1870]. x p., 2 l., (1) 10–325 p. 12°.

A few cuts by Richardson.
Copy: The New York Public Library (HAM).

The LIFE and voyages of Christopher Columbus... Philadelphia: J. B. Lippincott & Co., 1873. 3 v. 16°.

Reproductions of woodcuts, etc.
Copy: Circulation Department, The New York Public Library.

...The LIFE and voyages of Christopher Columbus and the voyages and discoveries of the companions of Columbus... Author's revised edition. New York [etc.]: G. P. Putnam's Sons [cop. 1892]. 3 v. 4°.

Isabella edition. 1100 copies printed.
Finely illustrated, including colored pictures and steel engravings. Reproductions of paintings and "old prints," many "redrawn" from early works on discovery, geography and travel. Volume 1 has fifty-seven; v. 2, thirty-eight illustrations; v. 3, thirty-five illustrations and a chart.
Copies: Library of Congress; collection of the compiler.

The LIFE and voyages of Christopher Columbus... (Condensed by the author from his larger work)... New York [etc.]: G. P. Putnam's Sons [cop. 1893]. 1 p.l., xiv p., 1 l., 412 p. 12°. (Heroes of the nations, edited by A. E. Abbott.)

Has fifty-eight illustrations from the preceding title.
Copy: Library of Congress.

Illustrated Editions, continued

CONQUEST OF GRANADA

CHRONICLE of the conquest of Granada... Author's revised edition... Philadelphia: David McKay, 1894. 528 p. 8°.

Photographs.
Copy: Collection of the compiler.

THE ALHAMBRA

The ALHAMBRA... Author's revised edition. With illustrations by Felix O. C. Darley, engraved by the most eminent artists. New-York: George P. Putnam, 1851. 1 p.l., (1)10–425 p. 8°.

Copies: The New York Public Library (BXVN); collection of the compiler.

...The ALHAMBRA... Author's revised edition. New York & London: G. P. Putnam's Sons, 1889. 1 p.l., 5–8, 13–511 p. 8°.

At head of title: Hudson edition.
Has a few drawings by various artists.
Copies: The New York Public Library (BXVN); Library of Congress.

The ALHAMBRA. New York: G. P. Putnam's Sons, 1892. 2 v. 8°.

Varro edition.
Illustrated with full-page engravings from photographs taken by R. H. Lawrence and others.
Reprinted in 1897.
Copy: Collection of the compiler.

The ALHAMBRA... With an introduction by Elizabeth Robins Pennell. Illustrated with drawings of the places mentioned; by Joseph Pennell. London: Macmillan and Co., Ltd.; New York: The Macmillan Company, 1896. xx, 436 p. 12°.

Republished by Macmillan and Co., London, 1906 and 1925.
Copies: The New York Public Library (BXVN); collection of the compiler.

The ALHAMBRA. The author's revised text edited by Arthur Marvin... New York, London: G. P. Putnam's Sons, 1905. 525 p. Fourth impression. 12°.

Illustrations by various artists.
Copy: Circulation Department, The New York Public Library.

LEGENDS of the Alhambra... With illustrations and decorations by George Hood and an introduction by Hamilton Wright Mabie. Philadelphia & London: J. B. Lippincott Company, 1909. xvi p., 1 l., 229(1) p. 8°.

Copies: Library of Congress; collection of the compiler.

TALES from the Alhambra...adapted by Josephine Brower; with illustrations in colour by C. E. Brock. Boston and New York: Houghton Mifflin Company, 1910. xxi(i), 213(1) p., 1 l. 8°.

Copy: Library of Congress.

The ALHAMBRA... Edited by Edward K. Robinson; illustrated by Norman Irving Black. Boston, New York [etc.]: Ginn and Company [cop. 1915]. viii, 370 p. 12°.

Copy: Library of Congress.

...The ALHAMBRA, edited by Frederick Houk Law... Boston, New York [etc.]: Allyn and Bacon [cop. 1926]. xi, 401 p. 16°.

Has twenty-six illustrations, all but three being plates.
Copy: Library of Congress.

The ALHAMBRA, palace of mystery and splendor... Tales selected and rearranged by Mabel Williams, illustrated by Warwick Goble. New York: The Macmillan Company, 1926. ix, 295 p. 12°.

Copies: Circulation Department, The New York Public Library; Library of Congress.

THE CRAYON MISCELLANY

ABBOTSFORD, and Newstead Abbey. By the author of "The Sketch-book." London: John Murray, n.d. iv, 290 p. 12°.

With numerous engravings from paintings by various artists.
Copy: Collection of the compiler.

ASTORIA

ASTORIA... New York and London: G. P. Putnam's Sons, 1897. 2 v. 8°.

Tacoma edition.
Illustrations by Zogbaum, Catlin, Church, Eaton, Davis, Held, Clement; photographs and sketches.
Copy: Collection of the compiler.

Waldorf edition. Text within gilt borders. Limited to 100 copies, printed on linen paper with proofs on Japan paper of the full-page illustrations. Probably a finer issue of the Tacoma edition. No copy has been examined by the compiler.

The FUR traders of the Columbia River and the Rocky Mountains as described by Washington Irving in his account of "Astoria," and the record of "The adventures of Captain Bonneville," with some additions by the editor. New York and London: G. P. Putnam's Sons, 1903. xvii, 222 p. 12°.

Edited by Frank Lincoln Olmsted.
Has nine plates, including the frontispiece; reproductions of drawings, photographs, prints, and engravings.
Copy: Library of Congress.

THE ROCKY MOUNTAINS (THE ADVENTURES OF CAPTAIN BONNEVILLE)

The ADVENTURES of Captain Bonneville... New York: G. P. Putnam's Sons [cop. 1868]. 1 p.l., (1)8–524 p. 12°.

Hudson edition.
A few plates by different artists.
Copy: Collection of the compiler.

The ADVENTVRES of Captain Bonneville, V.S.A., in the Rocky Movntains and the Far West. Digested from his jovrnal and illvstrated from variovs other sovrces... New York & London: G. P. Pvtnam's Sons, 1898. 2 v. 8°.

Pawnee edition.
Probably also issued as a limited edition, 100 copies, and called Colorado edition.
Copies: The New York Public Library (IW); Library of Congress.

Illustrated Editions, continued

LIFE OF OLIVER GOLDSMITH

OLIVER GOLDSMITH: a biography... With illustrations. New-York: George P. Putnam, 1861. 1 p.l., 382 p. 12°.

Illustrations by various artists.
Copy: Collection of the compiler.

...OLIVER GOLDSMITH... The author's revised edition... New York: G. P. Putnam's Sons [1902]. 1 p.l., 7–448 p. 8°.

At head of title: Hudson edition.
Has a number of drawings by W. Roberts.
Copies: The New York Public Library (AN); Library of Congress.

...OLIVER GOLDSMITH... Edited, with introduction, notes, and questions, by H. E. Coblentz... Boston: D. C. Heath & Co., 1904. xxx, 298 p. 12°. (Heath's English classics.)

Has eight illustrations, including portraits of Irving, Goldsmith, and Johnson.
Copy: Library of Congress.

THE BOOK OF THE HUDSON

STORIES of the Hudson...with illustrations by Clifton Johnson. New York: Dodge Publishing Company [cop. 1912]. xvi, 289 p. 8°.

Copy: Library of Congress.

LIFE OF MAHOMET

...MAHOMET and his successors... New York & London: G. P. Putnam's Sons, 1896–97. 3 v. 8°.

Author's autograph edition.
500 sets printed.
Illustrations include steel engravings, etchings, and lithographs. These are reproduced from photographs, old prints and other pictures, also from illustrations in old books of travel. There is an average of about twelve illustrations to the volume.
Copy: Library of Congress.

LIFE OF WASHINGTON

ILLUSTRATIONS to Irving's Washington. Quarto edition. Proofs on India paper. New York: G. P. Putnam, 1857–59. 5 portfolios. 4°.

Copies: The New York Public Library († AN); collection of the compiler.

...LIFE of George Washington... New York and London: G. P. Putnam's Sons, 1855–59. 5 v. 4°.

One hundred and ten copies printed.
One hundred and twenty engravings on steel and forty on wood.
Copies: The New York Public Library; Library of Congress; collection of the compiler.

...The LIFE and times of Washington... Illustrated ed., with fine engravings on steel, from drawings by Darley, Trumbull and others ... New York: G. P. Putnam & Sons [etc.], 1872. 4 p.l., x, (1)6–790, 31 p. 4°.

Copy: Library of Congress.

...LIFE of George Washington... New York: G. P. Putnam's Sons [1902]. 5 v. 8°.

At head of title: Hudson edition.
Has a few drawings by various artists.
Copies: The New York Public Library (AN); Library of Congress.

The LIFE of George Washington... Revised edition. New York: Thomas Y. Crowell Company [1916?]. 4 v. in 2. 8°.

Has eighteen portraits of eminent men of the period, reproduced from paintings.
Copy: Library of Congress.

WOLFERT'S ROOST

WOLFERT'S ROOST, and other papers, now first collected... New York: G. P. Putnam and Son, 1868. 3 p.l., iv, (1)6–431 p. 12°.

In addition to the frontispiece and the two added half-titles (one illustrated and one engraved), there are six plates.
Also issued by J. B. Lippincott & Co., Philadelphia, in 1871.
Copy: Library of Congress.

...WOLFERT'S ROOST and other papers; now first collected... Author's revised edition. New York: G. P. Putnam's Sons [1902]. 2 p.l., 7–453 p. 8°.

At head of title: Hudson edition.
Has a few drawings from various sources.
Copies: The New York Public Library (NBO); Library of Congress.

ILLUSTRATED BOOKS OF SELECTIONS

The BEAUTIES of Washington Irving, Esq... Illustrated with six etchings, by William Heath, Esq. London: Printed for J. Bumpus, 1825. vii, 316 p. 16°.

Copies: The New York Public Library (NBQ); Library of Congress.

The BEAUTIES of Washington Irving, Esq... Illustrated with six etchings, by William Heath, Esq. Glasgow: Printed for Richard Griffin & Co., 1825. vii, 316 p. 16°.

A new edition was issued in 1830.
Copy: Collection of the compiler.

The BEAUTIES of Washington Irving... Illustrated with wood cuts, engraved by Thompson; from drawings by George Cruikshank, Esq. London: Printed for Thomas Tegg and Son [etc.], 1835. viii, 291 p. 4. ed. 16°.

Copies: The New York Public Library (MEM); Library of Congress; collection of the compiler.

The BOLD dragoon and other ghostly tales... selected and edited by Anne Carroll Moore with decorative diversions by James Daugherty. New Amsterdam [i. e. New York]: Alfred A. Knopf, 1930. 4 p.l., xi–xiii, 240 p. 8°.

Copies: The New York Public Library (NBO); Library of Congress; collection of the compiler.

The GENTLEMAN in black, and Tales of other days. With illustrations by George Cruikshank and others. London: C. Daly, 1840. 1 p.l., v, 392 p., 18 pl. 12°.

"The same as *Beauties of Irving.*" Sabin 35148.
Copy: Library of Congress.

Illustrated Editions, continued

Illustrated Books of Selections, continued

ILLUSTRATED beauties of Irving. Vignette illustrations of the writings of Washington Irving... Philadelphia: Childs & Peterson, 1858. 3 p.l., (1)10–287 p. 8°.

Illustrations by many different artists.
Copy: Collection of the compiler.

The IRVING gift: being choice gems from the writings of Washington Irving. Illustrated. Buffalo: Phinney & Co., 1853. 270 p. 16°.

A few plates, by Darley, Wade, and Herrick.
This was republished in 1857, with some of the illustrations changed, all in black and white; copy in the collection of the compiler.
Copy: Collection of the compiler.

IRVING vignettes. Vignette illustrations of the writings of Washington Irving, engraved on steel by Smillie, Hall, and others... New York: G. P. Putnam, 1858. 3 p.l., (1)10–287 p. 12°.

Illustrations by many artists.
Copies: The New York Public Library (NBQ); Library of Congress; collection of the compiler.

SELECTIONS from the works of Washington Irving. Illustrated by Henry Ritter and William Camphausen... Leipzig: F. A. Brockhaus, 1856. xiv p., 2 l., (1)4–276 p. 4°.

Copies: The New York Public Library (NBO); collection of the compiler.

STORIES and legends from Washington Irving. Illustrated. New York & London: G. P. Putnam's Sons [cop. 1896]. 2 p.l., iii–viii p., 1 l., 312 p. 8°.

Has several plates by various artists.
Copies: The New York Public Library (NBO); Library of Congress.

BOOKS DEDICATED TO IRVING

COLTON, George Hooker. Tecumseh; or, The West thirty years since. A poem. New-York: Wiley and Putnam, 1842. vii, (1)10–312 p. 12°.

Copies: The New York Public Library (NBHD); Library of Congress; collection of the compiler.

DAVIDSON, Lucretia Maria. Poetical remains of the late Lucretia Maria Davidson, collected and arranged by her mother: with a biography, by Miss Sedgwick. Philadelphia: Lea and Blanchard, 1841. xv, (1)34–312 p. 12°.

Revised edition published in 1843.
Copies: The New York Public Library (NBHD); Library of Congress; collection of the compiler (1849).

GRATTAN, Thomas Colley. High-ways and by-ways. London: G. and W. B. Whittaker, 1824. 2 v. 12°.

Copy: Collection of the compiler (3. ed., 1824).

IRVING, Theodore. The conquest of Florida, by Hernando de Soto. Philadelphia: Carey, Lea & Blanchard, 1835. 2 v. 8°.

Copies: The New York Public Library (ITL); Library of Congress; collection of the compiler (London, 1824).

LATROBE, Charles Joseph. The rambler in North America. London: R. B. Seeley and W. Burnside [etc.], 1835. 2 v. 12°.

Second edition was published in 1836.
Copies: The New York Public Library (IID); Library of Congress; collection of the compiler.

MITCHELL, Donald Grant. Dream life; a fable of the seasons. By Ik Marvell [pseud.]. New York: C. Scribner, 1851. 1 p.l., vii, (1)12–286 p., 1 pl. 12°.

Copies: The New York Public Library (NBO); Library of Congress; collection of the compiler.

MYERS, Peter Hamilton. The first of the Knickerbockers: a tale of 1673. New-York: G. P. Putnam [etc.], 1848. vi, (1)10–221 p. 8°.

Published anonymously. The second edition, 1849, was published under the author's name.
Copies: Library of Congress; collection of the compiler (2. ed., 1849).

TAYLOR, Bayard. The lands of the Saracen; or, Pictures of Palestine, Asia Minor, Sicily, and Spain. New York: G. P. Putnam & Co., 1855. 451 p., 1 map, 2 pl. 12°.

Copies: The New York Public Library (* OFV); collection of the compiler.

BIOGRAPHIES OF IRVING

No attempt has been made to include a representative list of critical articles on, or references to, Irving, nor all the short biographical sketches published separately or as parts of other books. The *Cambridge History of American Literature* contains a lengthy list of such items. The following list includes, it is believed, all the full-length biographies:

IRVING, Pierre Munroe. The life and letters of Washington Irving. By his nephew, Pierre M. Irving. New York: G. P. Putnam, 1862–64. 4 v. 12°.

Also issued in a large-paper edition of 50 copies.
This is the most complete and comprehensive biography of Irving. Written by his nephew and published soon after his death, it is natural that the book should be colored by the atmosphere in which it was composed. There are certain phases of Irving's life on which it is silent, or possibly misleading.
The library of the Rev. Dr. Roderick Terry contains a copy of the three-volume edition, published later, which is extra-illustrated and expanded to seven volumes. The New York Public Library contains an extra-illustrated copy extended to nine volumes.
Copies: The New York Public Library (AN); Library of Congress; collection of the compiler (both the 4 v. and the 3 v. editions).

Based largely upon the foregoing work, but adding more or less critical material, are the following shorter biographies:

ADAMS, Charles. Memoir of Washington Irving. With selections from his works, and criticisms. New York: Carlton & Lanahan;

Biographies of Irving, continued

San Francisco: E. Thomas [etc., 1870]. 299 p. 12°.

Copies: The New York Public Library (AN); Library of Congress; collection of the compiler.

BOYNTON, Henry Walcott. Washington Irving. Boston: Houghton and Mifflin, 1901. 3 p.l., 116 p., 1 l., 1 port. 16°. (Riverside biographical series. no. 11.)

Copies: The New York Public Library (AN); collection of the compiler.

HELLMAN, George Sidney. Washington Irving, Esq., ambassador from the new world to the old... New York: A. A. Knopf, 1925. xi, 355(1) p. illus. 8°.

While not a biography in the strict sense of the word, this work throws light on many phases of Irving's life and character not covered in any of the more strictly biographical works. Most of the material is from sources untouched by and, in many cases, unknown to previous writers.

Copies: The New York Public Library (AN); Library of Congress; collection of the compiler (inscribed copy).

HILL, David Jayne. Washington Irving. New York: Sheldon and Company, 1879. 2 p.l., 5–234 p., 1 pl., 1 port. 12°. (American authors. [v. 1.])

Copies: Library of Congress; collection of the compiler (inscribed copy).

WALDRON, William Watson. Washington Irving and contemporaries in thirty life sketches, edited by William Watson Waldron, A. B. New York: W. H. Kelley & Co., n.d. xviii, (17) – 247 p. 16°.

Pages (17)–54 contain a short life of Irving. There are also the letters mentioned on page 55.

Copies: The New York Public Library (AB); collection of the compiler.

WARNER, Charles Dudley. Washington Irving. Boston: Houghton, Mifflin and Company, 1881. vi, 304 p., 1 port. 12°. (American men of letters.)

Copies: The New York Public Library (* R – AN); Library of Congress; collection of the compiler (1882).

The following list includes some of the more important booklets, pamphlets or short monographs written exclusively or largely on Irving:

CURTIS, George William. Washington Irving. A sketch. New York: The Grolier Club, 1891. 4 p.l., 115 p., 1 l. illus. 8°. (Grolier Club. [Publications.])

Issued in an edition of 347 copies.

Copies: The New York Public Library (* KP – Grolier); Library of Congress; collection of the compiler.

FETTEROLF, Adam H. Washington Irving. Philadelphia: J. B. Lippincott Co., 1897. 48 p.

Copy: Collection of the compiler.

HAWEIS, Hugh Reginald. American humorists. New York: Funk and Wagnalls [pref. 1882]. iv p., 1 l., (1)8–179 p. 12°. (Standard library. no. 82.)

Pages 1–34 contain a short biography of Irving.

Copies: The New York Public Library (NBW); Library of Congress; collection of the compiler (dated 1885; 192 p.).

HOMES of American authors; comprising anecdotical, personal, and descriptive sketches, by various writers. New York: G. P. Putnam & Co., 1853. 1 p.l., viii, 366 p., 16 facsims., 15 pl., 4 ports. 8°.

This contains an article on Irving by H. T. Tuckerman, p. 33–61. This article was reprinted in *Little journeys to the homes of American authors,* New York: G. P. Putnam's Sons, 1896, p. 267–296.

Copies: The New York Public Library; collection of the compiler.

MABIE, Hamilton Wright. The writers of Knickerbocker New York... [New York:] The Grolier Club of the City of New York, 1912. viii, 121 p. illus. 12°.

Issued in an edition of 303 copies.

Copies: The New York Public Library (IRGC); Library of Congress; collection of the compiler.

MITCHELL, Donald Grant. American lands and letters. The Mayflower to Rip-Van-Winkle. New York: C. Scribner's Sons, 1897. xxii p., 1 l., 402 p. illus. 8°.

This contains a sketch of Irving on p. 300–330.

The preface of the 1863 edition of the same author's *Dream life* is devoted to reminiscences of Irving; collection of the compiler.

Copies: The New York Public Library (* R – NBB); Library of Congress; collection of the compiler.

PAYNE, William Morton. Leading American essayists... New York: H. Holt and Company, 1910. xi, 401 p., 4 ports. 8°. (Biographies of leading Americans, edited by W. P. Trent.)

Copies: The New York Public Library (* R – AGZ); Library of Congress.

PUTNAM, George Haven. Washington Irving; his life and work. [By G. H. P.] [New York: G. P. Putnam's Sons, 1903.] 56 p., 1 facsim., 1 port. illus. 12°.

Contains a short sketch of 41 pages and a brief bibliography of the main works of Irving, with a price list of G. P. Putnam & Co. The pamphlet is in the nature of a semi-advertisement.

Copies: The New York Public Library (AGZ p.v.34, no.6); collection of the compiler.

SAUNDERS, Frederick. Character studies, with some personal recollections. [By Frederick Saunders.] New York: T. Whittaker, 1894. viii p., 2 l., 177 p. 12°.

Copy: The New York Public Library (NBY).

STODDARD, Richard Henry. The life of Washington Irving. New York: John B. Alden, 1883. (1)10–70 p. 24°. (The Elzevir library. v. 1, no. 4.)

Copies: The New York Public Library (AN p.v.66, no.13); collection of the compiler.

VINCENT, Leon Henry. American literary masters. Boston: Houghton, Mifflin and Company, 1906. xiv, 517(1) p., 1 l. 8°.

Copies: The New York Public Library (NBQ); Library of Congress.

REPRINTED WITH ADDITIONS AND
REVISIONS FROM THE BULLETIN OF
THE NEW YORK PUBLIC LIBRARY
OF JUNE – DECEMBER 1932
IN AN EDITION OF
FOUR HUNDRED AND FIFTY COPIES
THE NEW YORK PUBLIC LIBRARY
SEPTEMBER 1933